Perspectives on Rescuing Urban Literacy Education:

Spies, Saboteurs, and Saints

Perspectives on Rescuing Urban Literacy Education:

Spies, Saboteurs, and Saints

Edited by

Robert B. Cooter, Jr.
University of Texas at Arlington
The University of Memphis

LEA LAWRENCE ERLBAUM ASSOCIATES, PUBLISHERS
2004   Mahwah, New Jersey   London

Lawrence Erlbaum Associates, Inc., Publishers
10 Industrial Avenue
Mahwah, New Jersey 07430

Library of Congress Cataloging-in-Publication Data

Perspectives on rescuing urban literacy education : spies, saboteurs, saints / edited by
  Robert B. Cooter, Jr.
    p. cm.
  Includes bibliographical references and index.
  ISBN 0-8058-4289-6 (cloth : alk. paper) — ISBN 0-8058-4290-X (pbk. : alk. paper)
    1. Education, Urban—Texas—Dallas—Case studies. 2. Language
arts—Texas—Dallas—Case studies. I. Cooter, Robert B.

LC5128.P47   2003
372.4'09764'2812—dc21   2002192826
                                                             CIP

Books published by Lawrence Erlbaum Associates are printed on acid-free paper,
and their bindings are chosen for strength and durability.

Printed in the United States of America
10 9 8 7 6 5 4 3 2 1

For the children and teachers of Dallas

Contents

Foreword

In the 1950s, beginning with the historic *Brown v. Board of Education* Supreme Court decision, the United States embarked on a much needed reformation in public schooling. The central goal was equal educational opportunities for all children regardless of race, heritage, or socioeconomic status (SES). Later in the 1970s, when the National Assessment of Educational Progress (NAEP) began to chronicle academic progress (or lack thereof) by racial and socioeconomic groups, reading, writing, and mathematics education logically became focal points for research. It was soon apparent that children living in urban and greater metropolitan areas were at increased risk of failure in the "Three Rs."

At the turn of the 21st century, we still have many more questions than answers about why urban children fail in such alarming numbers in learning to read proficiently. Scientific research data published in the International Reading Association (IRA) journals regularly note that reading problems are continuing for urban students. Low-achievement indicators for ninth-grade readers, for example, virtually match dropout rates in the major cities. However, we are learning a great deal through research about some of the critical factors that tend to inhibit reading acquisition and, conversely, what helps make a difference in young learners' achievement.

Several key research summaries (e.g., *Reading Researchers in Search of Common Ground* [Flippo, 2001], *Report of the National Reading Panel* [2000], *Preventing Reading Difficulties in Young Children* [Snow, Burns, & Griffin, 1998]) offer insights and important avenues for investigation.

Some of these areas for further study include alphabetics (phonological awareness, alphabetic principle, phonics), reading comprehension, vocabulary acquisition, reading fluency, meeting the needs of second language learners and other special populations (e.g., slow learners, children with attention deficit hyperactivity disorder [ADHD] and/or other learning differences), and ways to involve families in their children's learning.

This important book represents a major contribution to the emerging field of *urban literacy education*. It addresses yet another critical area for reading research and practice—meeting the particular needs of children living in metropolitan areas. Individual chapters open the door to inner-city classrooms and their educational realities and challenges. The contributors move us beyond stale stereotypes about the teachers who work there and the children whom they faithfully serve.

We also get a closer look at the systemic level of urban literacy education: central office leaders and their decision making. The Dallas, Texas, school district from 1996 through 2001 serves as the context for most of the chapters. This was a period in which Dallas area business leaders and philanthropists teamed with the school district to create the Dallas Reading Plan. Its goal was to help at least 90% of all children read on grade level by the end of third grade. This was a formidable challenge because only about 25% of the children in third grade were reading on level in 1996. The Dallas initiative, which began with a great deal of political fanfare and press attention, soon faced some daunting challenges. During this time frame, the school district had a veritable parade of superintendents come and go—five in 5 years! This dynamic initiative, although certainly challenging, allowed the contributors of this book to learn a great deal about the systemic reform of urban literacy education.

Perspectives on Rescuing Urban Literacy Education: Spies, Saboteurs, and Saints offers an inside look at the machinations of a large urban school district as it attempted to grapple with a severe crisis in reading education during stressful times. It is a collection of eyewitness accounts of the crucial roles played by dedicated principals and teachers, the involvement of key community stakeholders locking arms to support their schools, and the efforts of a *reading czar* and his staff in trying to serve teachers' needs. It is also an account of the challenges associated with systemic change in a large organization, the different roles people play during the change process, and the misunderstandings that can breed conflict.

You will not have trouble discerning why the authors chose the rather *apropos* subtitle for this book—*Spies, Saboteurs, and Saints*. Included are the accounts of outsiders who committed their careers to the Dallas Reading Plan and reports on what they have learned (the spies). You will read about those whose thirst for power and/or financial rewards sometimes caused them to place children's needs in a subordinate role (the sabo-teurs) to their own motivations. Finally, efforts of reading teachers, princi-pals, and their colleagues who tirelessly serve the literacy rescue effort are chronicled.

Although many of the chapters are scholarly in nature, this is not a book of pure research. Instead, you will discover what might be termed a *hybrid* academic text containing numerous research studies wrapped com-fortably around chapters written by classroom practitioners. It is the research that gives the book its backbone and credibility within the aca-demic community. Nevertheless, it is the chapters that add reality, charac-ter, and depth of understanding.

There are several potential problems in investigating urban literacy ed-ucation that are overcome in this book. Researchers from outside the sys-tem (e.g., university professors) often conduct studies of urban education. Although this paradigm can bring a degree of objectivity to the enterprise, it can also be problematic due to researcher bias, insufficient or unreliable data, false fronts, and so on. Similarly, those few accounts extant written by insiders with a school district can be subject to their own related foi-bles. In *Perspectives on Rescuing Urban Literacy Education: Spies, Sabo-teurs, and Saints,* the reader has the advantage of looking at the Dallas initiative as a kind of case study told from multiple perspectives. The trian-gulation is made complete with the reporting of data in many of the re-ports enabling the reader to draw his or her own conclusions.

Beyond the academic insights available in this book, I believe the reader may find that the moral messages are powerful. Some of the ques-tions raised in my mind are these:

Which urban school districts have a sustained effort aimed at improving reading instruction for the poorest among us?

Is high-stakes testing a fair yardstick for the learning of urban students or does it tend to favor the more economically advantaged?

Do urban children have adequate materials with which to learn?

How well are colleges and universities preparing reading teachers for urban classrooms? Is there a one-size-fits-all mentality that only benefits more affluent students?

Why is there such an ongoing exodus of quality teachers from inner-city schools? How can this reality be reversed?

There is a multidimensional need for this type of resource. Urban school administrators, curriculum directors, teachers, urban literacy re-searchers, and community stakeholders may all find helpful information within the covers of this book. The reader will come away with a better un-

derstanding of at least one school district's struggle to help children become better readers. Facts and data abound in this volume, but it is the
personal accounts of the teachers working *in the trenches* that you will
find inspiring and passionate. In the end, we walk away with renewed
faith and a sense of pride for reading teachers everywhere.

—Jerry L. Johns, President (2002–2003),
International Reading Association
Distinguished Teaching Professor Emeritus,
Northern Illinois University

Preface and Introduction

Perspectives on Rescuing Urban Literacy Education: Spies, Saboteurs, and Saints is an exploration of the variables that contribute to the improvement of literacy instruction in large urban school districts. This book grew out of a 5-year initiative known as the Dallas Reading Plan—a $50 million collaborative effort among area business and corporate interests, philanthropists, and the Dallas Independent School District (DISD).

The DISD (Texas) is the 10th largest school district in the United States. Demographics of its 163,000 students are quite diverse: 53% Latino, 38% African American, 7% White, and 3% Asian and other groups. About 75% of the students are from poverty and qualify for free breakfast and lunch programs under federal guidelines. When the Dallas Reading plan began in 1996, only one in four Dallas students was able to read by the end of Grade 3. By the end of Grade 9, some 70% of students read 3 or more years below level, contributing to the district's 50% dropout rate. Unfortunately, these statistics are not uncommon among the nation's large urban school districts. In 2001, the Dallas Reading Plan succeeded in removing all involved schools ($n = 146$) from the state's low-performing list and, more important, helped improve student reading performance dramatically. This was largely accomplished through massive teacher education involving 3,000 teachers from Grades K to 3. The Dallas Reading Plan serves as the central context of this book—a case study, if you will, for discussing systemic reform of urban literacy programs in *Spies, Saboteurs, and Saints*.

OUTSTANDING FEATURES

Following are some of the unique features of *Perspectives on Rescuing Urban Literacy Education: Spies, Saboteurs, and Saints*:

- Analyses of systemic reform factors from the varied viewpoints of key stakeholders involved (e.g., change management experts, university scholars, school leaders, teachers, and educational researchers) in the improvement of urban literacy education in a major school district.
- Clear and concise reporting on the effects of long-term teacher development programs built on scientific research.
- Quantitative and qualitative research data on the improvement of teacher performance in literacy instruction gathered over a 5-year period.
- A candid analysis of behaviors that can enhance, restrain, and/or destroy systemic reform efforts in urban settings.
- Insights into the benefits of principal training as part of creating effective schoolwide literacy programs.
- Compelling data showing that previously ineffective teachers can become effective literacy educators through deep and sustained professional development.

Urban education is a rapidly emerging field of investigation. Harvard University, for example, recently announced that their teacher education programs would be overhauled so as to better serve urban populations. Columbia University and New York University have a long-standing commitment to the needs of urban children.

This text is of great interest to higher education faculty involved with urban education. It is particularly well suited to graduate-level studies associated with reading/literacy education, special education, urban studies, change management theory, and educational leadership. Teachers and administrators who plan to practice their profession in urban settings (or already are) may find the information presented to be invaluable.

Many corporate-based foundations and philanthropic organizations are involved with the rescue of public-funded urban schools. This book can help inform their future decisions regarding grants and other forms of aid.

A BRIEF TOUR OF *PERSPECTIVES ON RESCUING URBAN LITERACY EDUCATION: SPIES, SABOTEURS, AND SAINTS*

The contributors to this book are from varied professions and perspectives. As with most academic texts, many of the chapters are quite *scholarly* in the traditional sense of the term. Webster's (chap. 5) analysis of high-stakes testing, *Accountability in Texas: Fair or Foul?*, Baskin's (chap. 3) *Change Management Concepts and Models: Sponsorship, Early Adopters, and the Development of Urban Teachers*, and Denson's (chap. 9) *Minimizing the Effects of Student Mobility Through Teacher and Administrator Training* are three such examples.

Some chapters are theory into practice in nature, as is the case for most of the chapters in the final section entitled "Saints and Their Rescue Efforts." Here you find longitudinal examinations of literacy programs and practices that have found a degree of success with urban students. Thompson's (chap. 11) *Logistics of Systemic Change: The Reading Academy* and Zimny's (chap. 15) *Creating a Balanced Literacy Curriculum: One Elementary School Principal's Perspective* both offer fascinating insights.

A unique aspect of this book is what I think of as *the practitioner's voice*. Fullinwider's (chap. 1) *De Scholarum Natura*, K. Cooter's (chap. 16) *Marry Well . . . Divorce Less: Helping Principals Choose Effective Literacy Programs*, and Walker's (chap. 14) *Teaching the Teacher: Reflections of a Reading Academy Laureate* serve to put us *in the skin* of urban teachers and principals and their realities.

Perspectives on Rescuing Urban Literacy Education: Spies, Saboteurs, and Saints is divided into three parts, with a brief introduction for each. Although an examination of urban literacy education rescue efforts seldom falls into distinct realms, we have nevertheless attempted to apply some logic to the three groupings. In "Part One: Perspectives From the Spies," the reader finds essential foundation research on bringing about systemic change in literacy education in an urban school district. "Part Two: Overcoming the Effects of Saboteurs" examines more closely some of the chief impediments to positive change in urban literacy education from both within a school district and without. "Part Three: Saints and Their Rescue Efforts" primarily focuses on the many lessons learned from the Dallas Reading Plan initiative from 1997 through 2001. Along with final reflections and suggestions for future research provided in the concluding section by the editor, the reader also discovers a short, but constructive, glossary of selected terms.

SPIES, SABOTEURS, AND SAINTS: WHO ARE THESE PEOPLE, AND HOW DO THEY AFFECT URBAN LITERACY RESCUE EFFORTS?

In 1997, after some 25 years as a teacher and college administrator, I was offered an incredible learning experience in urban education. A search committee representative contacted me regarding an opening in Texas for an assistant superintendent over reading and language arts education for some 163,000 students in the Dallas Independent School District (DISD). The chief responsibility was to steer the development of a major campaign known as the Dallas Reading Plan, which already had strong support from Metroplex corporations, philanthropy, area universities, and the Dallas Chamber of Commerce. In fact, $5 million had already been pledged by business leaders to begin innovative comprehensive reading instruction for the 3,000 teachers serving kindergarten through Grade 3, the salary of the new *reading czar* (the media's name for this new assistant superintendent), and other start-up expenses.

The challenge was daunting. Only about one fourth of third-grade children could read on grade level, and the problem seemed to cascade downhill after that. About 43% of ninth-grade students were reading 3 or more years below level (i.e., below the 25th percentile)—a figure almost identical to the dropout rate for the district if you compared ninth-grade enrollments to graduation figures. Writing performance was at least as substandard. Indeed, the more I peeled back information layers to better understand why the district was failing so miserably in meeting the basic literacy needs of its children, the more complex and disheartening the picture became.

I feel that I must, in good conscience, interject something at this juncture. As I look back on my two tours of service with DISD—first as assistant superintendent for 2 years and later when I was asked to return to the district for another year as an associate superintendent—my memories are rather bittersweet. I recall with great fondness the legions of dedicated and talented professionals diligently pursuing the great work of helping urban children become literate. They pursued with intelligence and energy their noble task despite extremely difficult circumstances. I drew strength from these intelligent and heroic people daily and learned more about teaching city kids how to read and write in those few years than I had in the two decades before. Indeed it was a postgraduate experience beyond compare taught by these humble *saints*. I must admit, however, that I also harbor some not so pleasant feelings from the Dallas experience. *Saboteurs* within the urban education establishment (i.e., some, certainly not all school district leaders, publishers of commercial reading programs, politicians, education consultants)—those who put self-interest, financial rewards, and power thirsts above the needs of the children—left me cold and often angry. I trust that readers can understand this perspective as I continue to describe the Dallas context as a tool for defining some of the issues in urban literacy education urgently requiring our attention.

As noted earlier, children in the DISD typically come from poverty. The school population is also quite diverse, and, with nearly 50,000 students coming to school with a native language other than English, there are obviously language issues that complicate the equation further. Because so many native English speakers have poorly developed oral language skills—a prerequisite to success in reading and writing—language development issues are considered pervasive. Mobility is another confounding literacy variable in that a high percentage of students, perhaps 40% in many of the elementary schools, move one or more times during the school year.

DISD has also experienced personnel problems that are noteworthy even among other large urban districts. From 1996 through 2001, DISD had five superintendents, one of whom was fired after only 10 months and another who was sentenced to a penitentiary for embezzling federal funds. Needless to say, turnover in the superintendency, often for infamous reasons, and the accompanying media circus resulted in a serious loss of morale for the district's employees. Teacher turnover has also been incredibly high in DISD. From 1997 through 2001, there were typically about 1,200 teacher vacancies each fall, and in 2002 it was announced that 2,000 teachers were needed (this amounts to one fourth of the district's teaching force). This sort of professional hemorrhaging, I soon learned, makes it nearly impossible to build capacity through teacher development programs.

Of course there are many success stories in urban education. School districts in California, Texas, North Carolina, Maryland, Illinois, Kansas, Florida, and New York, just to name a few, are bringing together committed teachers, teacher leaders, researchers, and business and political stakeholders to assist urban children. As with most complicated endeavors, progress has been slow and fragmentary, but meaningful. What is needed now is for success stories to be shared to speed the urban literacy rescue effort. This small book is a collection of such success stories (as well as a few disaster stories because we learn as much or more from our failures as our successes).

During my tenure in Dallas, I got to know some gifted professionals from Dallas and other school districts with an abiding sense of mission in serving city kids. My wife, Kathleen, a teacher and researcher who has served the needs of city kids for more than two decades, summed up a philosophy commonly held by inner-city school folk when she said, "Urban teachers know that literacy is the gateway to social justice." In discussions with my counterparts from other metropolitan school districts and universities, I soon learned that we had many challenges, questions, successes, and frustrations in common.

DEFINING *URBAN LITERACY EDUCATION*

For one thing, educators involved with city schools seem to have a common view of what *urban literacy education* is and how it differs from, say, literacy education in a suburban or rural school. Urban literacy education is an emerging field of research and teaching expertise focusing on the diverse needs of children living in metropolitan areas. These populations generally have one or more of the following characteristics: high student mobility, poverty levels well in excess of the national average, majority minority populations, large concentrations of English language learners (ELL), unstable and ineffective school leadership (e.g., principals, superintendents), many inadequately trained educators (i.e., teachers, principals, central office supervisors), and excessive teacher turnover.

IDENTIFYING ISSUES AND QUESTIONS

Urban literacy educators and related professionals appear to be focused on several issues that affect systemic improvement or, perhaps better labeled, *rescue* efforts. Here are just a few issues and questions discussed in *Perspectives on Rescuing Urban Literacy Education: Spies, Saboteurs, and Saints*:

- Standards Versus Academic Freedom

Because so many of our children reside in highly mobile families, many feel the time has come for national standards in reading and other literacy areas so that we can all have common developmental targets at each grade level. Some argue that setting national or even state performance standards in reading and writing is an abridgement of a teacher's academic freedom. Do the educational needs of highly mobile children supersede the discretion of teachers to decide their own curricula?

- The Teacher Pipeline

Teachers' colleges tend to train future teachers using a kind of one-size-fits-all framework (i.e., undergraduates get the same teacher education program regardless of whether they plan to teach inner-city, suburban, or rural children, although their learning needs can be quite different). To what extent should teachers' colleges serving urban areas be restructured to meet the literacy needs of urban students? Would such restructuring leading, presumably, to designated urban education programs curtail the teacher turnover problem that is so debilitating to urban school districts? What kinds of incentives are needed to keep teachers in urban classrooms?

- Student Mobility

Student mobility fragments learning, leads to gaps in instruction (due to receiving teachers conducting preliminary assessments), and creates a sense of disenfranchisement between the mobile child and the new school. All of these factors and more are devastating to literacy learning. How can we better meet the literacy needs of urban children who are highly mobile?

- High-Stakes Testing and Accountability

Many states are adopting high-stakes testing in reading and writing. Frequently these states punish or reward individual schools and school districts based on how children perform on this single measure. Are high-stakes tests fair for urban kids?

- School Leadership

Recruitment of highly skilled professionals to lead our urban schools and school districts is extremely problematic. Superintendents have an average tenure of little more than 2 years, and principals likewise change frequently. As with the teacher education question, is it time for a radical restructuring of the way school leaders are trained and credentialed?

- Central Office Wars

There appears to be a mammoth and dysfunctional power struggle in many school district central offices that, in the end, is bad for schools and children. What are the roots of these power struggles, and what must be done to establish literacy education systems that work for kids?

- K–16 Partnerships

Many university schools of education and school districts are coming together to improve literacy education for children. To what extent are these efforts bearing fruit?

- The Role of Vendors

Urban school districts spend billions of dollars each year purchasing learning materials that claim to be research based. These companies have persuasive salespersons who sometimes find their way into closed-door sessions where district, state, and national policy and purchasing decisions are made. To what extent are such practices legal and/or in the best interest of children?

- Use of Data for Decision Making

Although most would agree that important decisions about literacy curricula and policy should be based on local empirical data, most funds in urban districts are spent purchasing reading and writing programs that only pass *the cardiac test* (It feels right in my heart, sooooo . . .). To what extent are data useful in decision making that results in improved literacy instruction?

- Change Variables

Attempting to change the literacy education bureaucracy can be slow and painful at best. What does the research on change and change management teach us that might be helpful in urban schools?

SPIES, SABOTEURS, AND SAINTS: ARCHETYPES OF PLAYERS WHO AFFECT URBAN LITERACY RESCUE EFFORTS

In *Perspectives on Rescuing Urban Literacy Education: Spies, Saboteurs, and Saints*, we were particularly interested in identifying the special literacy needs of urban students, examining requisite teacher and administrator competencies for meeting those needs, looking at systemic change factors that help urban literacy programs move forward, and assessing impediments to change. Obviously all of these factors involve people serving urban schools in myriad professional assignments.

As the classroom stories, data analyses, and research summaries began to come together for this book, it became clear that there are several archetypes, if you will, describing the people involved in urban literacy rescue efforts. To be honest, none of the archetypes is pure nor does any one player in this unfolding drama fit exclusively into one of the archetypal molds. Nevertheless, the interplay between perception of student needs, personal and professional goals, resources, and political motivations represented in the archetypes seem to have an effect on how well we are able to help city kids develop in reading and writing and may prove helpful in analyzing the chapters presented in this book. Here is how I defined each of the archetypes:

- *Spies*—Although not always so, *spies* is really another name for professionals who are directly involved in urban literacy education, but who are often considered *outsiders* by others in the school district. For example, although I am a former elementary teacher and Title I reading specialist who served several urban schools in Tennessee and Ohio, I was always considered an outsider by many in the Dallas schools—not in a negative way per se, just never one of the insiders who had spent 20 or more years in Dallas. Several of the contributors to this book are this sort of *spy*.

Spies are necessarily participant observers—they are researchers deeply involved in finding systemic solutions to the literacy crisis in urban schools and committed to rescue efforts, a different motivation than *saboteurs* (although, like *sin*, none of us is immune from inadvertent or even intentional sabotage).

Some spies are stakeholders from outside the school system entirely, but who contribute much to the urban literacy rescue effort and have a great deal of power. This may include corporate leaders, concerned parents, university faculty and deans, classroom teachers, private foundation personnel, chamber of commerce officials, and politicos of different stripes.

• *Saboteurs*—These are folks who, either by design or incompetence, derail rescue efforts in urban literacy education. In my view, for example, some central office leaders in urban public school districts do more to harm literacy education reform than any other subgroup, although usually attributable to ignorance about literacy instruction and/or change dynamics. Central office saboteurs kill innovation almost daily by failing to provide teachers with proper training, teaching materials that are research proved with urban populations over time, or adequate amounts of time to implement and sustain new approaches (some implementations can easily take 3 to 5 years to see results). In the most calamitous cases, we have seen central office leaders driven by an insatiable thirst for power (i.e., larger turf and authority over bigger budgets) or succumbing to *payola* from unscrupulous outside vendors and consultants selling poorly researched, oversold, and all too often impotent instructional solutions.

Because the stakes are so high—we are, after all, talking about the lives and future of children—some saboteurs rather innocently contribute to the literacy collapse. As a case in point, principals sometimes become saboteurs by changing literacy programs regularly, often yearly, before determining whether the old one is succeeding. This is what many teachers refer to as the *program-of-the-month* scenario. Many elementary principals have sole authority over large Title I budgets from federal sources and purchase reading and writing programs that are incongruous with district-adopted curricula. Thus, it is not too surprising that so many children are having a literacy crisis.

Hopefully this gives the reader an inkling of what we mean by *saboteurs*. To be sure, the prior description only scratches the surface of confounding variables injected into urban literacy rescue efforts by saboteurs.

• *Saints*—Saints are the folks working in the trenches daily—those who never give up on the dream of universal literacy. This includes, but is not limited to, teachers, activist parents, principals, business and community leaders, and, yes, even central office personnel who have weathered many a season with saboteurs. Saints are hard-working, persistent, intelligent people who have the spirit of freedom fighters. They know that "literacy is the gateway to social justice" and clutch tightly to the *Churchillesque* motto—to never, never, never give up on a child. Intuitively, one knows that the central trait of the saint archetype is their genuine love of children and a devotion to their future potential. I regard all of the contributors of this book to be both *spies* and *saints* of the highest order.

On behalf of all the contributors to *Perspectives on Rescuing Urban Literacy Education: Spies, Saboteurs, and Saints*, thank you for your interest in this topic, for choosing to read our book, and especially for your commitment to city kids.

My most sincere thanks go out to the reviewers of our book proposal and their insightful comments: Timothy Rasinski, Kent State University; and Kouider Mokhtari, Oklahoma State University. We also wish to thank our taskmasters and friends at Lawrence Erlbaum Associates, Naomi Silverman and her able colleagues, Erica Kica and Art Lizza.

Special thanks go out to professors selecting our book for their classes, professional development providers likewise using this book as a training guide, and all who are committed to meeting urban children's literacy needs. Please send me your comments and observations about *Perspectives on Rescuing Urban Literacy Education: Spies, Saboteurs, and Saints* so that we might find ways to improve our next edition. Here's wishing you every success as you labor to help all children succeed as readers and writers!

—Robert B. Cooter, Jr.
University of Texas at Arlington
cooter@uta.edu

PERSPECTIVES FROM THE SPIES

CHAPTER ONE

De Scholarum Natura

John Fullinwider
Dallas Independent School District

CAST

ISAAC RAINWATER, middle-aged Anglo teacher

JAMISHA, 18, African-American, hip, outgoing, take-no-nonsense kind of girl

RUBEN, 17, Latino, popular, energetic, joker, party animal

RUSSELL, 17, African-American, intellectual, politicized, fearless

CASSANDRA, 17, Latina, sensitive, thoughtful, well read, unsure of herself

MARIO, 18, Latino, ex-gangbanger, low-rider style

I.
ETYMOLOGY

(Classroom. ISAAC and four students: CASSANDRA, JAMISHA, RUSSELL, and RUBEN. JAMISHA standing at a flip chart holding a dictionary and a marker.)

ISAAC:	Okay, Jamisha, remind us what the assignment is.
JAMISHA:	We are supposed to choose any two pages in this dictionary and identify the percentage of the words that come from Latin.
ISAAC:	And why are we doing this?

RUBEN: Finally, an interesting question.

RUSSELL: To bore ourselves sick so that we'll be ready for our dead-end jobs after graduation?

ISAAC: You know what they say, Russell, "If you like school, you'll love work."

CASSANDRA: A lot more English words than you might think come out of Latin. And Spanish has even more.

ISAAC: That's the idea. Once you begin to notice it, you'll see traces of it everywhere.

MARIO: *(Entering)* In the church, they still use it for mass sometimes. *(Then to Cassandra)* But I don't go to mass anymore because I don't believe it's true.

CASSANDRA: *Mi abuela* says her prayers in Latin.

RUBEN: Forgive me, Father, for I have sinned!

ISAAC: Not mortally, I hope.

RUBEN: *No lo se*, Mr. Rain. It all happened in Latin!

RUSSELL: *Exit* is Latin, isn't it? That's a word I wouldn't mind studying right now.

JAMISHA: Ahem, can I finish? There are 76 words on the pages I picked, and 47 of them started out being Latin. Some were Latin at first, then went to French, then came into English.

ISAAC: What's the percentage?

JAMISHA: One sixty one?

ISAAC: Divide it the other way.

JAMISHA: I knew that. *(She does it quickly, then triumphantly announces.)* Yo, all you Latin Lovers—and Haters, Russell—on pages 248 and 249 of the *Oxford Concise Dictionary*—drum roll, please—61.8% of the words are ultimately derived from Latin. Thank you, thank you, thank you.

ISAAC: Thank you, Jamisha. Now write out the most interesting word you found.

JAMISHA: My pages ran from *cubeb* to *cup*, and this is by far the most interesting word. *(Speaking the letters as she writes)* C-U-N-N-I-L-I-N-G-U-S. What's it mean, Mr. Rain?

ISAAC: Well . . . *lingus* comes from the Latin word meaning "to lick" . . . *(pauses)*

RUSSELL: Go ahead and talk that talk, Mr. Rain.

JAMISHA: What? What is it?

(Bell rings.)

ISAAC: *(as they start to leave)* It is still illegal in most Southern states, Jammie, that's what it is.

RUSSELL: "The glory that was Rome"—the original freaky town!

(Lights down.)

II.
THE WESTERN CANON

(Classroom.)

ISAAC: *(standing at the flip chart writing: "Lacrimae rerum et mentem mortalia tangunt.")* The *Aeneid* is an epic poem about the founding of an empire, but it begins with history's greatest losers, the Trojans.

RUBEN: Trojans go hard, man!

ISAAC: Not that kind of Trojan, Ruben, though I'm glad to see you have learned at least one lesson in here.

RUBEN: Doing my homework, too.

ISAAC: But the name stands for endurance—

RUBEN: And let's not forget comfort.

ISAAC: —because of the mythical Trojan warriors.

RUSSELL: This the story about that horse?

ISAAC: It's the losers' version. The Greeks told it as a triumph, but for Virgil it was a catastrophe.

RUSSELL: That's a kid's story.

ISAAC: It's got everything kids like—battles, big monsters, gods and goddesses. And for older kids—doomed love!

RUSSELL: Here we go, man.

ISAAC: But Virgil found something else in the story. He saw the cost of all that glory, and he called it, "the tears of things." *Lacrimae rerum.*

CASSANDRA: *(taking notes)* The tears of things?

ISAAC: The poet's hero is Aeneas. In this part, Aeneas and another warrior are looking at a mural that depicts scenes from the destruction of their hometown, Troy. All the battles they lost, all their friends that got killed. They are in Carthage. They're refugees. They have lost everything.

	And he says, "The tears of things and mortality touch the heart." He understood the real cost of the Roman empire.
RUSSELL:	Empire's built on the tears of slaves—not to mention blood.
ISAAC:	You're right. The tears of slaves, and the blood of fallen warriors, the heartache of women in mourning—like Hecuba for her dead son.
JAMISHA:	Don't forget the passion of the queen, Dido.
CASSANDRA:	Who's that?
RUBEN:	Dildo?
JAMISHA:	Dido. *(To ISAAC)* I read ahead. And *(to CASSANDRA)*, girl, you should see how Aeneas played that woman! Queen of Carthage. She did everything for that baller, and he left her colder than breakfast with a man who don't really love you.
RUSSELL:	You lost me now. Who don't love you?
JAMISHA:	It's all in book four—hopeless love for a heartless man.
RUBEN:	This story's kinda' old, though, isn't it? Give me something closer to now, Mr. Rain.
RUSSELL:	Yeah, for real, why we got to study this?
ISAAC:	The simple answer is, you don't. Most of you are taking Latin because you hate the Spanish teacher.
RUSSELL:	You got me there.
MARIO:	Ya entiendo Espanol.
ISAAC:	Or you already understand Spanish. But can I answer your question with some more questions? Ruben, get that light projector, will you? And two chairs. Over here. Russell, you sit here. Face the screen. Jamisha, cover his eyes *(hands her a blindfold)*. Cassandra, you sit here. Mario, blindfold her. *(To JAMISHA and MARIO)* You two stand behind their chairs.
	Ruben, cut the lights and turn on the projector. *(Lights lowered.)*
	Russell and Cassandra, you have to picture yourselves locked in a cave. It's very dark. You have been there your whole life. You don't know anything else. Take off their blindfolds, but hold their heads still so they can't look side to side or backwards.
RUSSELL:	Are we prisoners?
ISAAC:	In a sense. All you can do is look at the screen.

RUSSELL:	I'm a political prisoner.
RUBEN:	You wish. You got busted in an Internet pornography scandal. *(Beat.)* But what about Cassandra?
JAMISHA:	She's a woman. What else could it be but selling the wrong thing?
CASSANDRA:	Hey!
JAMISHA:	*(a la Lauryn Hill)* "That thing, that thing / She was sellin' that thing / that thing."
MARIO:	No way. She is in here for being too honest. *(To ISAAC)* Some kind of strange prisoners.
ISAAC:	We'll see how strange. Now suppose people are walking behind you, out of your sight, and you can only see their shadows. *(Walks between light and screen, casting a shadow.)*
RUSSELL:	Okay.
ISAAC:	Having never seen anything but shadows, isn't it possible that you and Cassie might think those shadows are the real thing?
CASSANDRA:	I guess if we can't turn our heads.
MARIO:	*(Straightens her head, gently.)* In this prison you can't.
ISAAC:	And if you and Russell get to talking and describing the shadows of the people and objects moving by giving names to each one, wouldn't you come to believe eventually that you are naming the actual person or things instead of just a shadow?
RUSSELL:	Where are you taking this?
JAMISHA:	*(Southern drawl, as if his West Texas warden)* Just answer the question, boy, and you won't have any more trouble.
RUSSELL:	We probably would, then, since we don't know any better.
ISAAC:	To you guys, the truth would literally be nothing but shadows. *(JAMISHA and MARIO put the blindfolds back on.)* You would be blindfolded in a way.
CASSANDRA:	*(quietly, almost to herself)* Have you ever felt like you were dreaming when you're awake? Like your whole life's just a dream?
RUBEN:	All the time. Except when I'm asleep. Then I feel like I'm at school.
MARIO:	Better wake up, fool!

JAMISHA: Worst dream I ever had was my nightmare of a stepfather, unh-huh.

RUSSELL: Me? I don't care what kind of prison you build, I'm gonna' be bustin' out. *(Takes off blindfold, stands up.)*

ISAAC: Let's suppose you do. You get out of the cave. But as you stand and walk and turn your head for the first time, all you feel are sharp pains. The first time your eyes are hit by real sunlight, the glare blinds you. For awhile, you can't really see people and things for real. You're accustomed to seeing shadows in a half light.

RUSSELL: I'd still be trying to see.

ISAAC: Suppose Mario comes over and says that what you are used to seeing isn't really there. It is just an illusion that you thought was real.

MARIO: Yeah. Hey, dog, you were just looking at shadows. Out here, we can see the real deal.

ISAAC: But you can't, Russ, because your eyes haven't adjusted. Your arms and legs still hurt, your step is unsure, and you start wondering if you can make it out here.

RUSSELL: You're stacking the deck so I can't.

ISAAC: Not me. But that's my point. Isn't it possible, if this were the situation, that you might remember those shadows fondly and start thinking they were more real than the actual world?

RUSSELL: People get satisfied with what they are used to.

ISAAC: You might want to go back to what you thought was real.

JAMISHA: Or they get stuck in a bad situation and can't get themselves out.

CASSANDRA: Hel—lo! I'm still here in the prison of shadows.

MARIO: Prisoner's getting restless, Captain Rain.

ISAAC: No, she's not. While you're forcing Russell to see another world, Cassandra and all the other prisoners are analyzing the shadows, naming them, putting them in classifications, charting their various qualities.

RUBEN: Oh, no! Now they have to study shadows in their schools. They give out shadow diplomas.

CASSANDRA: And we have all kinds of awards for who can paint the best shadow or write the best song about a shadow.

ISAAC: Or perhaps make up social theories to demonstrate the necessity of shadows?

RUSSELL: Or use shadow power to enslave others.

MARIO: Yeah, put shadow chains on everybody. Tie us all up in shadows.

ISAAC: Okay. Let's say that Mario keeps walking Russell around until his eyes adjust and his arms and legs get stronger, until he finally sees another world, one that's solid and real. Do you think Russell would care about all the honors and rewards of the shadow world?

RUSSELL: I'd think they were for fools.

ISAAC: Would you go back down there?

RUSSELL: Not on your life. *(To JAMISHA)* Except maybe to pull my sister out.

JAMISHA: *(softly)* You probably wouldn't want no shadow girl.

CASSANDRA: If Jammie tried to leave, we would put her down and try to stop her, all of us. We'd say she was trying to be all that, to be better than everyone else.

MARIO: We would say that Russell was a punk, too scared to face the shadows. That he was in a fantasy world, scared of the dark.

ISAAC: Tell me, how strange is this prison?

RUBEN: It's weirder than juvenile lockup.

ISAAC: When Plato wrote about a prison like this, in the "allegory of the cave," the ancient city of Athens was at the height of its power and glory. It was like Washington, DC, or New York, Tokyo, London—but he saw it differently. Plato thought his countrymen were locked in an illusion.

RUBEN: I got locked in an illusion once.

MARIO: That was no illusion, *pendejo*—it was the big freezer at work!

RUBEN: It was colder than a *pinche* cave—but when I got out, Mr. Rain, I was disillusioned for real.

ISAAC: The Latin language you're struggling to learn was the language of the Roman Empire. It was a worldwide language, the language of conquest. Like English today, the language of the old British Empire—and its successor, the American Empire.

RUBEN: *(saluting)* "Oh, say can you see by the bomb's early light . . ." *(whistles the rest)*

MARIO: You're saying it's an illusion?

ISAAC: Maybe. But not the power.

CASSANDRA:	We don't want to know what it's built on. That's the illusion.
RUSSELL:	Like what?
CASSANDRA:	Like when I go buy a blouse. It's always made in Indonesia or Bangladesh. You think the people sewing our clothes have good paying jobs?
RUSSELL:	Yeah, like that Nike shit. I can't wear any of that shit. I don't even want to think that some kid in a sweatshop is making the shoes I'm hooping in.
JAMISHA:	What about all these fights over "he say / she say"—if that ain't fighting over a shadow, I don't know what is.
MARIO:	I'll tell you about an illusion. I used to run with the Wayne Street Warriors. We would stomp on anybody who came in our turf that didn't belong there. We even used to steal from the Mexican guys, hard working guys, roofers, you know, concrete men. We jumped on them when they got drunk. They didn't go to the cops because they were illegal themselves. Yeah, we were representing East Side. It was our area. Trouble is we didn't own one blade of grass on our turf, not one house, not one *tienda*, not one apartment. The landlords owned our area—the investors. They may as well have owned us. Half our familias had to move in one year, when the yuppies started to buy in. *(Bitterly)* "Our" area . . . we couldn't control any of it. Hell, we couldn't even control ourselves.
RUSSELL:	Turn on your TV. Now there's a shadow prison. People think it's real, watching 6, 7 hours a day. They laugh at the fools on Jerry Springer, not knowing the joke is the audience. Don't know the difference between the news and the ads.
RUBEN:	There's a difference? *(Flips on a computer monitor to Netscape homepage.)* What about this? w-w-w-dot-illusion-dot-com!
CASSANDRA:	So how do we know what's real, Mr. Rain?
ISAAC:	That's the best question that I won't try to answer today.
JAMISHA:	Just like a man, won't answer a serious question.
ISAAC:	Russell, what do you think?
RUSSELL:	Hm. *Allegory* means you lay out one scene and it stands for another, right?
ISAAC:	Right.

RUSSELL: Okay. Cassie and I were prisoners in two ways. First, we were bound by force, kept from any natural way of moving and living. Then we were trapped by our false, uh, impressions—no, perceptions, false perceptions. We thought the shadows were real.

ISAAC: Is it possible that false perceptions make the other forces stronger? Or even unnecessary?

CASSANDRA: This might not be right, or what you mean, but nobody forces girls to, well, you know, try to be "tall and blonde"? But we get the message. It's all around us.

JAMISHA: Hello! I get so tired of these skinny bright girls with that straight hair!

CASSANDRA: That would be a false perception controlling us, wouldn't it?

ISAAC: It's certainly a false image that affects real women.

MARIO: Hey, you two prove it's a lie every day.

JAMISHA: Gentlemen—and the rest of you—it's official. Feast your eyes. This is the beauty of the future.

RUBEN: Low-rider babes of the 21st century!

MARIO: *(to CASSANDRA)* You're beautiful, too, Cass.

RUSSELL: What I'm thinking about is Nelson Mandela under apartheid. They had to lock him up because he wouldn't stay in the shadows. He wouldn't buy into the lie that Black people were inferior. He wouldn't buy into a false perception no matter how powerful it was. *(Beat.)* But they didn't have to lock everybody up.

ISAAC: Some people suffered in silence, waiting for a better time.

RUSSELL: I can't be silent. That's not for me.

CASSANDRA: It's like a woman getting beaten. Sometimes she might think she deserves it. She might think she only deserves a life in shadows.

JAMISHA: *(as if her mother)* "Now, honeychile, we can't let no man define our reality." That's one lesson my pig of a stepfather taught me but good.

RUBEN: Yeah? What'd you teach him?

(Lights up.)

JAMISHA: I taught him I'd kill him if he ever opened my door again.

(Bell rings.)

ISAAC: On that liberating note, I will see you all tomorrow.

(Goodbyes all around.)

ISAAC: Hey, Russell *(as he is leaving)*, they broke out of both kinds of prisons.

RUSSELL: Better watch yourself, Mr. Rain. America's next up.

ISAAC: Not a moment too soon.

RUBEN: Mr. Rain, I'm going to tell my probation officer that we're studying Plateau and Immanuel Couldn't and Virgil's Anus, and all those philosophers. You back me up, now? She thinks I'm just playing around over here.

ISAAC: Ruben, she will know it's true by your discourse.

(Lights down. Curtain.)

Glossary

de scholarum natura: concerning the nature of schools

mi abuela: my grandmother

no lo se: I don't know

pendejo: a fool, stupid person

pinche: damned

tienda: store

Resources

Educating for Justice. (2002). *Nike corporate accountability campaign*. Internet: www.nikewages.org. Accessed: 12/23/02.

FairTest. (2002). *The national center for fair & open testing*. Internet: http://www.fairtest.org/index.htm. Accessed: 12/23/02.

Howatson, M. C. (Ed.). (1993). *The Oxford companion to classical literature*. Oxford: Oxford University Press.

Knox, B. (1993). *The Norton book of classical literature*. New York: W.W. Norton & Company.

Smithsonian Institution. (2002). *Between a rock and a hard place: A history of American sweatshops 1820–present*. Internet: http://americanhistory.si.edu/sweatshops/. Accessed: 12/23/02.

For a pretty good, ready-to-use lesson plan for the *Aeneid, Book II*: Contact fullinwider@hotmail.com.

CHAPTER TWO

The Pillars of Urban Literacy Instruction: Prerequisites for Change

Robert B. Cooter, Jr.
University of Texas at Arlington

A LITERACY CRISIS IN URBAN SCHOOLS

Large urban school districts face mounting literacy problems. High truancy, spiraling dropout rates, and increasing teenage crime all seem to have a common denominator—illiteracy. In the Dallas Independent School District (DISD), an inner-city school district of about 165,000 students, recent data revealed that nearly half of all students read significantly below grade level at the end of third grade, and by the end of ninth grade some 70% read below grade level (~40% read below the 25th percentile on standardized measures—3 or more years below grade-level expectancy). Data like these have an amazing correlation with the dropout rate; nearly 50% in Dallas when comparing average enrollment figures in ninth grade compared with yearly graduation figures. Unfortunately, this scenario has become commonplace in many urban school districts around the nation.

As the literacy crisis spirals out of control, many school districts are feeling political and community pressure to respond. State legislators now see education as a front burner issue and are pushing for change. California, Texas, New York, and Florida are prime examples of states with activist legislatures on the education front. Locally, school boards are demanding that superintendents react to poor reading and writing test scores—so much so that the tenure of the average urban superintendent is less than 2.5 years.

A National Emphasis on Reading

President George W. Bush has made education his number one domestic priority (U.S. Department of Education, 2002, p. 1). On January 23, 2001, he sent his *No Child Left Behind* plan for comprehensive education reform to Congress. The president emphasized his deep belief in the power of our public schools, but expressed concern that "too many of our neediest children are being left behind" despite nearly $200 billion being spent since the passage of the Elementary and Secondary Education Act of 1965 (ESEA).

Following the events of September 11, 2001, President Bush and a bipartisan coalition in Congress succeeded in the passage of the *No Child Left Behind Act of 2001* (NCLB Act), also known as H.R. 1. Intended to close the achievement gap between disadvantaged and minority students and their peers, H.R. 1 has four key provisions: stronger accountability for positive results, expanded flexibility and local control, expanded options for parents, and an emphasis on teaching methods that have been proved to work. It is the fourth element—focusing on teaching methods that have been proved to work—that I address in this chapter.

HOW SCHOOL DISTRICTS COMMONLY RESPOND TO A LITERACY CRISIS

There is no question at all that the statistics in urban settings (i.e., those school districts having diverse populations, high teacher turnover, high student mobility, and a high percentage of low-income families) are dreadful and require proactive thinking. The two most common methods of attack for addressing poor reading performance have been (a) *scripted program interventions*—adoption of highly scripted reading programs having primary emphasis on decoding; and/or (b) *teacher development*—aggressive professional development programs focusing on developing teacher capacity, typically using comprehensive reading instruction methods. Let us briefly examine the pros and cons of each.

Scripted Program Interventions

The common response to a literacy crisis for many urban superintendents is to adopt and rigidly enforce the use of a so-called *scripted* reading program that focuses heavily on phonemic awareness, phonics, and decoding. These are commercial reading programs having teacher's editions with prepared scripts that literally tell the teacher exactly what to say to students. A superintendent in Louisiana once told me he liked scripted

reading programs because they were *teacherproof*. The assumption in this
instance was that most teachers are not teachable in more effective reading instruction approaches, at least not in a short time frame (say, the typical tenure of a superintendent of just 2 years). Such programs as SRA/
McGraw-Hill's *Reading Mastery, Corrective Reading,* and *Open Court* are,
at least for the moment, the apparent front-runners in the scripted reading program arena.

Pros of Scripted Reading Programs.   Some urban school systems
have gained a measure of relief using this scripted program interventions
for several reasons.

• *Stabilization of Instruction With Undertrained Teachers.*   Scripted
approaches can be helpful in quickly stabilizing instruction across an urban school district, especially where a sizable percentage of the workforce
is undertrained (e.g., those teaching on emergency certificates with little
or no training, graduates of alternative certification programs that involve
minimal training laced with copious amounts of unsupervised on-the-job
training). Many urban school districts suffer from a great deal of teacher
turnover—as much as 50% in the first 3 years of employment. The growing teacher shortage has forced many urban districts to employ new teachers who have come through the aforementioned alternative certification
programs or on emergency certificates. In the DISD, for example, a majority of new teachers hired come through these alternative channels armed
with precious few arrows in their teaching strategies quiver.
    A scripted program, at least in a teacher shortage, offers school officials
a degree of certitude that reading instruction occurs in most classrooms in
a coherent and consistent way. In the case of the Fort Worth, Texas,
schools, where scripted reading instruction was instituted in the mid-
1990s, one school official reported that on any given day every kindergarten and first-grade teacher in the district was assigned to teach the same
lesson in the basal reader and practice the same skills. This intervention
helped Fort Worth schools improve their dismal reading test scores to
near-average levels. So effective was this tactic in Fort Worth that former
Texas education commissioner, Mike Moses, on assuming the superintendent's office in the Dallas school district in 2001, immediately directed his
underlings to duplicate Fort Worth's example and stabilize instruction
through scripted programming in reading.
    It seems worth mentioning that an important advantage of scripted
programs to many superintendents is that training is relatively quick and
inexpensive, with the added bonus that this level of stability usually results in a gain in reading scores on standardized tests, albeit limited (a
"glass ceiling effect") and temporary.

• *Districtwide Implementation of Scripted Programs Addresses the Mobility Issue.* A second advantage of scripted program interventions is that they partly address the student mobility issue. (For a full examination of the student mobility issue, see Denson, chap. 9, this volume.) In many urban school districts, children move around a good deal. In Dallas, the student mobility rate hovers around 35%. In many elementary schools, the mobility rate can be 45% or more, with many students moving three or more times per year. The root cause is usually poverty: The primary caregiver is unable to pay the rent when it comes due, so she and the children move to another apartment nearby offering a move-in special. The scenario repeats itself, and the mother is forced to move again and again—a process that utterly fragments a child's learning. The one encouraging statistic is that most students stay within the school district boundaries during the year. Scripted reading programs rigidly enforced with a monthly *implementation calendar* for each grade level (as was tried in the Fort Worth schools) can create a kind of safety net ensuring at least basic coverage of fundamental reading skills.

• *Scripted Programs Mainly Benefit Special Populations.* One of the most curious developments in urban literacy education is the notion that scripted reading programs, such as *Success for All* or *Reading Mastery*, are a research-based solution for *all* children, although there is no convincing evidence.

Do scripted program interventions work? Yes, to an extent. For the reasons cited previously, there can be a nice gain in standardized reading test scores for Grades K through 3, especially if (a) the test is heavily oriented toward decoding because that is the *forte* of most scripted program interventions, and (b) the school district's reading scores on norm-referenced tests at the median (i.e., Iowa Test of Basic Skills, Stanford 9 Achievement Test, etc.) hover near or below the 35th percentile. As educational assessment specialists know, a small amount of gain with low students can yield a substantial improvement in test scores, percentiles, and the like. So in this case, implementation of a scripted program can enable a district to virtually scream toward the average range.

Careers and fortunes have been made in urban school districts by raising reading scores at the third grade level to near-average levels or, in the case of Texas, have a greater percentage of children passing the state's minimum competency TAAS test even if a majority of youngsters still cannot read on grade level.

Cons of Scripted Programs. There are several drawbacks to scripted program interventions when used as the only path of attack in urban literacy instruction.

• *Glass Ceiling Effect.* First and foremost is the *glass ceiling effect* mentioned earlier. Scripted program interventions typically do a poor job of building receptive and productive vocabularies (particularly listening and speaking vocabularies). The same is true for developing higher order reading comprehension (i.e., children with limited vocabularies may become pretty good decoders, but poor comprehenders, which seems to be a growing consensus nationally; Bowie, 2002). There may be a nice spike in reading scores through Grade 3, where the emphasis on standardized tests is largely on decoding, but students often crack their heads on a veritable glass ceiling in the upper elementary grades when they are expected to perform higher cognitive tasks and demonstrate their understanding of nonfiction materials.

• *Poor Teacher Capacity Building.* Veteran teachers often observe that no one reading program, no matter how well designed, can meet the needs of all children. Thus, when implementing a scripted program as described before, some children fail to make adequate progress in their reading development (e.g., Greenlee & Bruner, 2001; Jones, Gottfredson, & Gottfredson, 1997; Pogrow, 2002). Teachers armed only with the knowledge of how to implement a scripted program adopted by the district, and whose daily use is mandated, are hamstrung in adapting instruction to meet the needs of struggling readers. Teachers in this situation are forced to simply do more of the same, rather than take another instructional tack, because they have not developed requisite knowledge and skills with alternative teaching strategies. Without teacher capacity building that goes beyond scripted programming, 5% to 20% of urban children can be relegated to certain failure in reading. Dropout rates of nearly 50% in urban centers is not uncommon, and poor reading ability is a correlate.

The reverse scenario is equally problematic: Average and above average readers can actually have their growth in reading inhibited by scripted programs. For example, the much debated *Success for All* (SFA) reading program has been shown through independent research studies to be less beneficial for learners in Title I schools than those in non-SFA classrooms or even result in poorer test scores (e.g., Claxton, 2003; Pogrow, 2000, 2002).

• *Spurious claims that they are appropriate stand-alone programs.* Related to the prior limitations of scripted programs is the notion that they are appropriate for all students. For example, one Fort Worth school official and a SRA/McGraw-Hill representative remarked that they had seen reading test scores improve quicker with African-American students using the *Reading Mastery* program and the same company's *Corrective Reading* with Hispanic students. The notion that one size fits all for an entire ethnic or racial group seems egregious at best and certainly is not supported with any credible independent research evidence.

This brings up another related point: Publishers are increasingly fond of sponsoring so-called *research studies* to validate claims that their reading programs are scientifically based and appropriate for all urban populations. Two of the more prominent programs whose sales force reportedly makes such claims are *Success for All* and the SRA/McGraw Hill *Open Court* reading programs. In the case of *Success for All*, research on its benefits seems limited to some kindergarten and first-grade populations who are significantly behind in reading development, yet some major school districts (e.g., San Antonio, Houston Independent School District) adopted the program wholesale for dozens of campuses and experienced limited improvement or even negative results (Pogrow, 2002). A careful review of the extant research literature reveals no evidence of SFA's claimed benefits beyond those published by those on the company's payroll. In the case of SRA/McGraw Hill's *Open Court* reading program, no evidence was found in the independent extant educational research databases as to the current program's benefits to any school population urban or otherwise.

The shortcomings of scripted program interventions have caused many of their most staunch proponents to look in another direction for rescuing urban literacy instruction: teacher development.

TEACHER DEVELOPMENT AS AN INTERVENTION

Some urban districts (e.g., Kansas City, St. Louis, Chicago, Dallas, Los Angeles) have responded in recent years to the literacy crisis with aggressive teacher development programs—sometimes operating as public school/university partnerships, but more often taking the form of internal staff development initiatives. Please note that I do not refer here to teacher inservice sessions that most districts have offered for many decades—usually a series of brief (1- to 2-day) workshops on a popular topic heralded in the teaching journals (e.g., phonemic awareness, left brain/right brain research). Inservice sessions like these have wasted literally hundreds of millions of taxpayer dollars in past decades and yielded no real improvement in reading performance in children—in fact, quite the reverse (see National Assessment of Educational Progress, 2000). The aggressive teacher development programs of which I speak are research based, both distributive and longitudinal in nature (i.e., they involve training over time, lasting 1 or more years), and are in-depth (i.e., these capacity-building efforts usually last 80 or more hours spread over the course of 1 year). The goal of these programs is to improve student performance in reading by improving the quality of instruction. It is the notion that teachers, not programs, are the ultimate driving force for improving instruction.

In constructing effective capacity-building programs for teachers of reading, this important question has arisen: What should be the key areas of focus in urban literacy education that will help teachers and children succeed? The answer to this question must be founded on rigorous research, rather than simply passing what Reutzel (2001) termed the "cardiac test" (i.e., if it *feels* right in my heart, then it must be good for children . . .). In the balance of this chapter, I briefly summarize the results of an extensive study commissioned by a major grant as part of the *Dallas Reading Plan* initiative to learn the answer to this critical question.

A Failure Analysis of Urban Reading Instruction

One of the great advantages of the Dallas Reading Plan project was having numerous corporate and philanthropic partners who contributed their resources for our effort. It was recommended early on that a failure analysis of reading instruction in Dallas be conducted to find out what was going wrong and where energies should be focused in creating effective professional development programs for kindergarten through third-grade teachers (May & Rizzardi, 2002). Following is a brief history and findings from what appears to be the first failure analysis conducted in a large urban school district.

Evolution of the Failure Analysis Model

When John F. Kennedy announced to the world in the early 1960s that the United States would send a man to the moon and back before the end of the decade, folks at NASA were both ecstatic and apprehensive. Ecstatic because they would doubtless get a much-needed infusion of resources, and apprehensive because they were not quite sure how they would pull off such a feat.

The NASA brain trust invented a concept called *failure analysis* that literally got them to the moon. The concept was this: To fully succeed in any great human endeavor, you usually have to do hundreds of things well. However, there are typically only three or four things you *must* do well or the project will definitely fail; hence, failure analysis. It is much like erecting an office building. If you want to end up with a beautiful edifice, you have to do hundreds of things well to create a first-class workspace—superlative glass, imported marble floors, spectacular wall treatments, artwork, and so on. These things may help create the aesthetics of the structure, but, according to failure analysis thinking, they are not essential to the mission of the building—providing a safe and weather-free environment for workers. However, if the load-bearing supports or pillars are not put in place correctly, then the entire building will be in danger of collapse. Identifying these essential pillars in any complicated operation is the stuff of failure analysis.

Failure Analysis: Focus on Urban Reading Instruction

The failure analysis of Dallas' reading instruction programs was conducted under a major grant by national consultants/reading researchers, master teachers from Dallas, and change management experts from an international consulting firm. Dallas leaders wanted to know, of course, why three fourths of the children were failing to learn how to read by the end of third grade and, thus, what could be done to better support classroom teachers in the way of professional development. The failure analysis—costing more than a half-million dollars donated by an area foundation—identified five key areas related to reading instruction. Like the load-bearing pillars of a great building, these five instructional supports must be in place for *all* children in Dallas to learn to read. It is up to teachers and principals to ensure that the pillars are put into place, and it is the responsibility of district-level administrators in charge of reading instruction to ensure that teachers and principals have the ongoing training, support, and instructional materials needed to implement them. Following is a description of the five areas identified in the failure analysis (see also Fig. 2.1).

Teachers Must Know the Basic Reading Skills to Be Taught. Educational research over recent decades has verified the basic skills of reading. We also understand the approximate order in which they should be taught. Effective teachers know this sequence of skills and structure their teaching accordingly.

Teachers Must Know How to Assess Each Student's Knowledge of the Basic Reading Skills. Teachers must know which reading skills each child already knows and does not know. Master teachers are able to quickly test each student's knowledge, create a kind of reading roadmap of what is known, and then teach students according to their needs. It is the only way to make sure every student receives appropriate instruction and verify that learning takes place.

Teachers Must Know the Best Ways to Teach Each Reading Skill. There is a veritable mountain of research on the best ways to teach reading. For example, Perkins (2001), an educational researcher at Southern Methodist University, identified research-proved methods for helping urban African-American children become excellent readers. Her study is re-

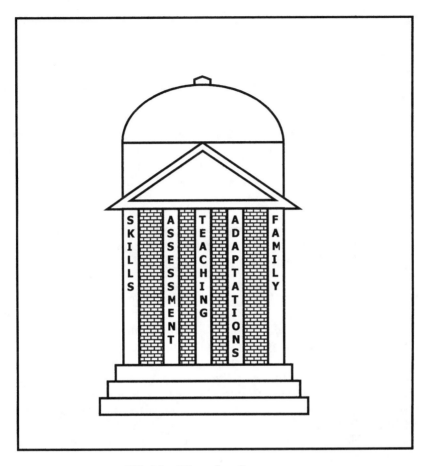

FIG. 2.1. Pillars of reading success.

ported, in part, later in this book. Escamilla and her colleagues (Galindo & Escamilla, 1995; Medina & Escamilla, 1994) also provided compelling ideas for teaching children who speak Spanish as their first language. Great teachers must have a plethora of tools in their educational toolbox if every child is to be helped to reach his or her full potential.

Families Must Be Included in Their Children's Education. It has been said that 80% of what students learn happens outside of school. We know from research, for instance, that children who have been read to a great deal before entering kindergarten have a much stronger language base and are far more likely to succeed in reading (Snow, Burns, & Griffin, 1998). Research also shows (National Assessment of Educational Progress, 2000) that the more TV children watch, the poorer their reading ability.

Most parents help their children at home if they know what to do; thus, teachers must be supported in their efforts to educate families in ways they can help their children succeed in the home.

Learners With Special Needs Require an Appropriate Education. It has been estimated that up to 20% of urban students come to school with special learning needs. This includes such conditions as attention deficit disorder (ADD), dyslexia, language deficiencies, and emotional problems. Our goal must be to help *all* urban students succeed and leave no one behind. Therefore, teachers must receive ongoing training and building-level support to assist special populations.

COMBINING SCRIPTED PROGRAM AND TEACHER DEVELOPMENT INTERVENTIONS TO ADDRESS URBAN LITERACY NEEDS

In the United States, we often search for quick and simple solutions to complex problems, although this dream is rarely, if ever, realized. Complicated problems require complex solutions implemented over time (Delisle, 2001). Improving literacy levels in urban schools is certainly a formidable problem complicated by numerous factors (e.g., poverty, high student mobility, inadequate teacher capacity) and requires complicated solutions implemented over a period of years, not months. We know this is so because no short-term solution of 1 to 3 years using simplistic methods (neither commercial reading programs—scripted or otherwise—nor teacher education alone) has succeeded in helping a majority of urban children attain and sustain acceptable reading proficiency.

A Simple Equation With Complicated Implications

The answer lies, at least in part, in combining both scripted reading programs *and* ongoing teacher development/capacity building, using each to their best advantage.

• *Use scripted programs to stabilize instruction.* Scripted programs, as already noted, can be used to stabilize instruction across a school district. They provide an instructional scope and sequence of minimum reading skills at each grade level and help even the most novice teacher deliver satisfactory instruction. If the scope and sequence of skills are correlated with state-required skills, as with the *Texas Essential Knowledge and Skills* (TEKS) curriculum document, for example, then a comprehensive curriculum roadmap can be created for each grade level. However, there is a cautionary note: Scripted programs should be used with flexibility, and teachers should be encouraged to go beyond the script as their expertise allows to assist learners with special needs and those reading above grade level. Where so many school districts lose the literacy battle is by implementing scripted programs only. It is an approach that essentially calculates that a substantial number of students will fail from the outset because no program has ever been capable of meeting all students' needs. That is why teacher development is the critical tandem partner in this equation for success.

- *Implement an aggressive teacher development program.* There is no substitute for having a competent teacher in every classroom. Teacher development programs should begin within 1 year of installing a scripted reading program as outlined earlier. Teacher development programs should (a) be deep (80+ clock hours per year, every year); (b) focus initially on the five pillars of reading success identified in the failure analysis presented earlier, (c) be followed each year thereafter with professional development opportunities focused on each teacher's specific needs, and (d) include peer coaching to ensure implementation of best teaching practices. Teachers should also be provided with materials to support their instruction. As new scientifically proved methods are learned by independent research teams, teachers should be encouraged to replace elements of the commercial scripted reading program as they deem appropriate to meet the needs of all their children.

Later in this book (chap. 6), this model for teacher capacity building is further described.

CONCLUSION

Great teachers are the critical factor in building great school systems. The Reading Academy in DISD was based on the five pillars of great teaching, and the results were in evidence by 2001—children whose teachers (kindergarten through third grade) graduated from the Reading Academy were doing significantly better in reading as measured by the state's high-stakes test (TAAS) and national tests than their counterparts in other Dallas classrooms. Over 2,000 DISD teachers voluntarily took the year-long Reading Academy class before it was dismantled in 2002, and the positive results have continued to swell.

There was great strength discovered in these five pillars as we constructed the Dallas Reading Academy—strength that helped teachers succeed as they labored to help every child become a successful reader.

REFERENCES

Bowie, L. (2002, February 24). *Phonics text for reading questioned: Balanced literacy curriculum gains favor in city schools; State may question goal; Multiple approaches for different needs.* Baltimore Sun. Accessed online at sunspot.net.

Claxton, D. J. (2003, August 14). News release: Superintendent close to making recommendation to Board about Edison. *Dallas Independent School District Home Page/News Releases.* Available online at www.dallasisd.org

Delisle, P. (2001, October 4). *The change process.* Information presented at The DISD Principals' Fellowship, Dallas, TX.

Galindo, R., & Escamilla, K. (1995). A biographical perspective on Chicano educational success. *Urban Review, 27*(1), 1–25.

Greenlee, B. J., & Bruner, D. (2001). Effects of *Success for All* reading programs on reading achievement in Title I schools. *Education, 122*(1), 177–189.

Jones, E. M., Gottfredson, G. D., & Gottfredson, D. C. (1997). Success for some: An evaluation of a *Success for All* program. *Evaluation Review, 21*(6), 643–670.

May, F. B., & Rizzardi, L. (2002). *Reading as communication* (6th ed.). Upper Saddle River, NJ: Merrill/Prentice-Hall.

Medina, M., & Escamilla, K. (1994). Language acquisition and gender for limited-language-proficient Mexican Americans in a maintenance bilingual program. *Hispanic Journal of Behavioral Sciences, 16*(4), 422–437.

National Assessment of Educational Progress. (2000). *The Reading Report Card.* Washington, DC: U.S. Department of Education.

Perkins, J. H. (2001). Listen to their teachers' voices: Effective reading instruction for fourth grade African American students. *Reading Horizons, 41*(4).

Pogrow, S. (2000). The unsubstantiated "success" for *Success for All. Phi Delta Kappan, 81*(8), 596–600.

Pogrow, S. (2002). *Success for All* is a failure. *Phi Delta Kappan, 83*(6), 463–469.

Reutzel, D. R. (2001). *Using research-proven strategies to improve reading development in urban schools.* Information presented at the DISD Reading Academy Fall Conference, Dallas, TX.

Snow, C. E., Burns, M. S., & Griffin, P. (Eds.). (1998). *Preventing reading difficulties in young children.* Washington, DC: National Academy Press.

U.S. Department of Education. (2002). *The No Child Left Behind act.* Accessed online at www.nochildleftbehind.gov/

Change Management Concepts and Models: Sponsorship, Early Adopters, and the Development of Urban Teachers

E. F. Baskin
Baskin & Associates

Change is tough. Although change impacts most of us much of the time, we do not have ways to communicate about change. Yet most of us know a lot about change because we have our experiences. The purpose of this chapter is to help us understand the change process by examining models that have been used in both profit and nonprofit situations. Also we begin to develop a vocabulary that can enable us to continue our change education, educate others, and enhance communication. With these concepts, tools, and techniques, our ability to understand, implement, and deal with change should be enhanced.

CASE STUDY FACTS

The approach utilized in this chapter is a case study. Use of a case study that mirrors the environment of a large, urban school system gives us a common, friendly framework to use our own experiences.

School System X is a large, urban system in the state of Texas. Initially headed by Superintendent A, it contains 215 schools (K–12) in nine geographic areas. These geographic areas are headed by a like number of district superintendents. There are 8,000 teachers and 160,000 students of White (6%), African American (38%), Hispanic (53%), and other minority backgrounds (3%). The English language is not necessarily predominant in many of the schools. Students classified as economically disadvantaged

25

are about 70%. The system has the normal staff functions of any large organization (treasury, etc.), but we are only concerned with the curriculum and instruction staff functions, which include a well-respected research and evaluation group.

System X has always had emphasis on reading and writing literacy, but events in the last few years have seen an increased need to focus on these areas. The state legislature and recent governors have emphasized testing students utilizing the Texas Assessment of Academic Skills (TAAS), which is designed and administered by the Texas Education Agency (TEA). TEA also administered literacy grants to school districts and appeared to favor those school districts that focused across all grade levels using specific off-the-shelf commercial materials presumably because this would reduce the time to bring programs online. Immediately prior to an increased statewide push on high-stakes testing, System X, driven by a contingent of local business-men (some with national and international orientations), established a Reading and Writing Literacy Initiative (Reading Literacy [RL]). This unit was independently housed (not in curriculum and instruction) and headed by a newly hired academic with a national reputation in the literacy area. The System X Literacy Head's (LH) salary was substantially supplemented through a foundation funded and established by business leaders.

The overall objective of the RL initiative was to have 90% of the K–3 students—some 60,000 in all—reading at grade level in 5 years from the start point. In the first year, the LH began to attack this objective by creating a positive image internally and externally and developing an organization that included Lead Reading Teachers (LRTs). LRTs were used to coach teachers and develop innovative reading and writing materials and modules inclusive of selected textbooks (as opposed to off-the-shelf materials or *basals* as they are called). These LRTs received a five-figure annual salary supplement.

Materials developed by the LH and LRTs formed the basis of a literacy curriculum including a unique assessment regime and other teaching tools. The curriculum was offered through local universities 4 nights a week at various sites around the city. The objective of this curriculum was to increase the competency of the system's K–3 teachers in dealing with student needs in reading and writing literacy. The sessions were initially jointly taught by university professors and selected LRTs in what came to be known as the Reading Academy (RA). Subsequently, the sessions were offered through only one university and taught exclusively by LRTs. System X school teachers were to attend a special class 1 night per week (3 hours) for two semesters and received graduate credit toward a master's degree from the university.

Principals in all nine geographic districts were given criteria to select teacher attendees to the RA. The selections were not monitored, so the attendees ranged from those who were forced (a few) to primarily volunteers who were interested in the goal and methods within the curriculum to achieve the goal. The RA began with 600 participants from a target audience of 3,000 K–3 teachers in Year 2 of the initiative. In the second semester, an additional 100 teachers started the training. Years 3 and 4 saw an additional 700 and 800 participants, respectively.

Image building done by the LH also got off to a good start particularly among business and parent groups and with system principals. The LH, assisted by outside business funding, started a Principals' Academy that volunteer principals could attend to become acquainted with various aspects of the RL initiative and ways they could foster literacy improvement in their schools. About 40 principals attended. Although some of the geographic district superintendents were involved in the selection process, no other involvement was asked of them. Also academy principals were asked to set specific objectives that they would implement in their schools, but there was no monitoring to ensure implementation.

In addition to the work with principals, the LH formed an Advisory Committee consisting of several business leaders, school board representatives, district superintendents, principals, and school district support personnel (e.g., the head of the Bilingual Language program). Everything was going well when, unfortunately, Superintendent A was fired and the System X School Board appointed an Interim Superintendent B. Superintendent B continued to support the goal of the Reading Literacy initiative because of the emphasis in the state of Texas and because of the strong, continuing support of the external business leaders.

At the request of the business leaders, the LH brought in a change management consultant to examine the process to date and suggest modifications or additions in the change process. The success of the RL curriculum and the achievement of the initiative's overall objective were being examined by the Curriculum and Instruction's research and evaluation group. Early indications were that the curriculum was having a positive impact on student test scores, the LRTs were a hit with all parties in their coaching roles, and the internal image of the initiative with other teachers as well as principals was quite good. There were a number of issues found with the change process, but the most important finding by the change consultant was that a student mobility factor outside the control of the RL initiative would probably have a tremendous impact on the success of the initiative. The *mobility factor* was defined in the district as the percentage of students who moved among schools in an academic year—about 30%. In essence, teachers were potentially *reworking* (reassessing, reteaching, etc.) 30% of the students each year.

Based on the results of the research and evaluation group, the LH revised the RL curriculum and made other changes to enhance success.

However, due to interdepartment strife, the LH resigned before Year 3 began. During Year 3, a permanent Superintendent C was hired by the system. He adopted the RL goal and, with the help of supporters within System X, convinced the former LH to return for Year 4.

Although the RL initiative had continued during Year 3, it had been in a maintenance mode. The LH began to restart the initiative including hiring additional LRTs. The new LRTs were given the same salary supplement as the older LRTs. A small cadre of RL personnel was aimed at new, experiential programs to deal with grades after Grade 3. Also the LH found that several district superintendents and some principals had begun to lobby for the LRTs to be assigned to their control, arguing that this would provide a greater impact. Yet during the fall of Year 4, the System X School Board fired Superintendent C, and a new Superintendent D was hired. This new superintendent requested that all programs and initiatives immediately deal with issues at all grade levels.

The research and evaluation group's RL initiative results clearly show that the initiative was having the desired impact. For example, Grade 3 student test scores under teachers who were RA graduates from the Year 2 cohort showed over 60% of their students reading at grade level (compared with 26% only 3 years before). Likewise, Year 3 RA teacher graduates showed over 55% of students reading at grade level and were expected to improve further as the teachers from this cohort further implemented the concepts and techniques. The rest of the system was at about 50%. Unfortunately, the results are not dramatic or rapid enough in the view of the new administration. The LH felt he had done what he could under the circumstances and resigned to take another position in a different organization.

CHANGE CONCEPTS: ROLES INCLUDING
SPONSORSHIP AND EARLY ADOPTERS

Armed with our case study facts, we can begin to develop our vocabulary of change concepts. There are many roles described in our case facts in a traditional sense (e.g., principals, LRTs, and others). However, in examining change, the following terms prove useful: *sponsors* (S), *change agents* (CA), *advocates* (AD), and *target audiences* (TA).

Sponsors (S) are persons who are the leaders of change efforts. They do not handle day-to-day change activities, but have money, authority, or formal power. Sponsors are motivated to identify and begin change. Further, sponsors see to it that change is implemented so that issues and problems are addressed. The most obvious sponsor in the case study is the Superintendent of School System X.

Change agents (CA) are designated by sponsors and have responsibility for both strategic and tactical activities. Change agents have resources and authority as delegated by the sponsor or may assume authority not challenged by others. Change agents handle the day-to-day activities of the change effort. The most obvious change agent in the case study is the LH.

Advocates (AD) can be key players in the change process because they have great need, may have money or other resources, but do not have formal authority or power. The obvious advocates in the case study are the external businesspersons.

Finally, the *target audience* (TA) is the group at which the change effort is aimed. This is the group whose behavior we are trying to modify. In our case study, students are an obvious target audience because it is their reading and writing literacy the system is attempting to improve. The change mechanisms used to assist students to change are K–3 teachers. The major change intervention is with the teachers as a TA using the RA curriculum followed by classroom support with the LRTs.

Confusing? Certainly because definitions depend on one's perceived role and perspective in the change process. Let us explore these definitions and relationships in greater detail. To begin, let us focus on the LH as change agent. From the perspective of the LH, possible sponsors are the superintendent, the district superintendents, the businesspersons (because the foundation provides the salary supplement), and principals. Yet the principals are also a target audience for the LH because the LH led the effort to educate the 40 principals in the Principal's Academy. We have already stated that the businesspersons are advocates because they have no formal power, but do have a lot of informal power. Many of the district superintendents and principals could be advocates. To further compound the situation, we could look from the LRTs' view and see that, for them, the principals could be sponsors in some situations or even advocates. Yet what is important is to identify the perspective we need to assume and understand why we need to take that perspective in various situations.

For those of us who wish to serve as change agents, it is important to identify sponsors to ensure we: (a) define our authority before embarking on the process, and (b) involve the sponsor appropriately in the process. Both of these steps became quite important in our case study because the overall sponsor, the system superintendent, changed so many times. This created attendant changes in needs and objectives. Second, it is easy for us as change agents to assume responsibilities we should not. In the case facts, it was easy for the LH to assume responsibilities that should have been left to the sponsor because of the LH's national reputation and the support of the business group. This was a major reason for the emergence of interdepartment strife under System Superintendent B. So Rule 1 for change agents is to make sure you have an understanding of roles and au-

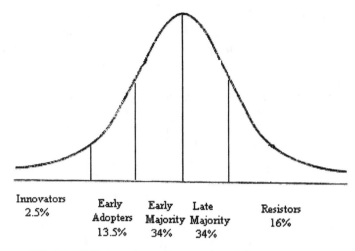

Innovators
2.5%
Early
Adopters
13.5%
Early
Majority
34%
Late
Majority
34%
Resistors
16%

FIG. 3.1.   Diffusion of innovations (Adapted from Rogers, 1983).

thority structures, and be sure that up front you define the situations where you must have the sponsor involved.[1]

Advocates can be most helpful in building good will for change programs. Advocates are generally well known by others and may have some control over resources. Yet change agents should map out exactly the role advocates should play because the exuberance of advocates generally leads them to overpromise what can be achieved in a given period of time. In our case, the LH may have overrelied on the businesspersons because of the ease of thinking of them as sponsors. Generally advocates' other areas of interest begin to dominate their time and their interest wanes.

In our case facts, one of the target audiences—K–3 teachers—was primarily a volunteer TA by design (i.e., not forced). A useful model for looking at target audiences comes from the diffusion of innovation literature (Rogers, 1983). Audiences can be looked at in a normal curve fashion as in Fig. 3.1.

- Innovators are 2.5% of the population or target audience. In the case study, the target audience was 3,000 K to 3 teachers so about 75 would be expected to be innovators. Innovators like risk and new

---

[1]One may argue that the change in overall sponsor had the biggest impact on the achievement of the RL stated goal of having 90% read at grade level. However, in a benchmark comparison of TAAS reading scores with a comparable system that used off-the-shelf materials and had the same system sponsor for the entire period, scores did not increase at any greater rate.

ideas. Their network or relationships tend to be outside the local environment in which they work. They do not worry too much about whether the innovation will be successful.

- Early Adopters are 13.5% of the target audience. They are considered leaders within their local networks and, thus, important to the adoption process. Because of this respectability, others tend to follow their lead, thus these are key persons in the change process. In our case example, many of the principals brought into the Principals' Academy should have been early adopters. Of course many of the teachers in the early audience of the Reading Academy should have been and probably were early adopters.

- Early Majority is 34% of the target audience. They are not leaders in the local system, but interact frequently with peers and, thus, are important to communication about the change and process. The early majority takes its time in totally adopting a new idea, but is earlier to adopt than the remaining majority (50%).

The decision process for these three groups tends to be positive at the beginning of a change. Yet they may raise tough questions about the change, its process, and outcomes. Often change agents (CA) misconstrue these questions as adversarial, particularly those of the early majority, because the questions may come late in the process. If approached as adversarial, rather than treated as positive information requests, some in these groups may opt out of the change and even become negative about it.

- Late Majority is 34% of the target audience. These persons are not negative about change, just skeptical. They tend to want lots of evidence about the need for and success of the change.

- Resistors are 16% of the target audience. They tend to focus on how things were done in the past and have little tolerance for ambiguity. They do not like change. Their decision process for change is slow. It is easy to think of Resistors as negative, but this is generally not the case. Resistors just see more disruption to their normal activities—the status quo.

Change agents should be aware that saboteurs could come from any of the groups. One can be negative about a change from the beginning. Negativity about change comes from one's perception of how disruptive the change will be in one's life. A teacher may start out positive about change, but become quite negative if they discern more disruption than they were told or thought. Change agents can use the diffusion model to think about their audience and plan strategies to address issues with each group as the change is implemented.

CHANGE CONCEPTS: TYPES OF CHANGE
AND GOAL OF CHANGE[2]

Now that we have established a beginning vocabulary about change roles, we can use it to discuss the types of change that occur. In a general sense, change is either planned or unplanned. Many believe unplanned change is easier to deal with because it has one characteristic that may make the entire target audience motivated to deal with it. *Unplanned change* is created by a crisis generally from outside or exogenous to the system in which change is needed. If all perceive a crisis and, therefore, the necessity for change of some sort, there is inherent motivation within the system. When TAAS was first introduced in Texas (i.e., high-stakes testing), many may have used this crisis as a motivator. However, this can get old if audiences perceive that crisis is manufactured in an attempt to produce change. Even if an audience is convinced of the crisis, there is no guarantee that it will buy into the sponsor's solution.

Planned change is generally classified into *minor* or *major* change, with a major change given a label such as *transformation*. In many organizations, quality process improvement was thought of as minor change, whereas many new strategic plans are labeled *system transformations*. Although all of this is nice and dandy, what is important is how the target audience feels. If the audience feels it would be too disruptive, then motivation is not positive.

We have mentioned disruption several times because it is the major barrier to change. Disruption generally causes loss of control, and most people do not like these feelings. So if disruption and attendant feelings of loss of control is *the* major barrier to change, what should be the goal of change?

Typically, the focus of change is to introduce an innovation that produces something better. Most change efforts fail because the emphasis is on the technical attributes and processes that produce the intended result. To a great extent, that is what our case study facts describe with the notable exception of the use of LRTs (coaches). In the next section, we discuss the technical change process—strategies and techniques for successful change. Please note that an important goal of change is to eliminate the barrier of feelings of loss of control. This is accomplished by ensuring that the change process does not focus on just the technical aspects of the solution intended to produce change, but also on the actors (sponsors, ad-

[2]Much of this discussion is adapted from Conner's (1992) *Managing at the Speed of Change*.

TABLE 3.1
Process of Change

Phase	State/Action	Goal Ending State
Preparation	Unawareness	Awareness
	Confusion	
Acceptance	Negative perception	Understanding
	Decision not to implement	Positive perception
Commitment		Installation
	Aborted after initial installation	Adoption
	Aborted after extensive installation	Institutionalization
Internalization		

vocates, and target audiences) that must deal with the change. Thus, the goal is to deal with making these persons more resilient[3] and able to continuously deal with change (and not make it a one-shot deal).

CHANGE CONCEPTS: CHANGE MODELS, STRATEGIES, AND TECHNIQUES

One can find many books on change. Some are in the bibliography at the end of the chapter. This section examines one change model, applies it to our case facts, and discusses the strategies and techniques used and others that might have been used. The steps or process in a change model can be described as in Table 3.1.

As the change agent began planning and implementing for the strategies and techniques in the case study, the prior model may have been used as a guide. The phases are not nice and smooth; they overlap on occasion. Some in the target audience(s) may move through these phases rapidly (Innovators), whereas others move more slowly or not at all.

All persons begin in a state of unawareness and the change agent must make them aware. In the case study, this occurred in several ways. First, there was the general activity by the state of Texas with the introduction of its high-stakes testing program (TAAS). Then the hiring of a LH with a strong, national reputation backed by local businesspeople to implement a program began initial awareness. The LH with the help of LRTs and others put together materials describing the plan, made speeches, ran short 1-day programs, and used other means to create awareness. Therefore,

---

[3]Developing resilient people should be the goal of all programs. The experience of the author in executive development programs was that this was paramount and began with creating feedback-seeking individuals. This begins with self-awareness. The key to examining one's self-awareness is to begin to look at moving or reshaping mental models or one's beliefs, values, and biases. The bibliography at the end of this chapter suggests one approach.

many in the target audience became aware. Yet being aware does not necessarily mean understanding; it can sometimes mean confusion. Many change agents go through this initial flurry of planning and activity and are then surprised and defensive when questions start being asked. Change agents should not become flustered with this state of confusion because target audience personnel are merely attempting to understand the possible impact of the change, thus moving into the acceptance phase. Even when the audience members understand, they may have a negative perception that the disruption to them could exceed the benefits gained.

In Year 2, the change agents in our case introduced a Reading Academy to provide details and knowledge of literacy techniques and approaches to increase understanding. LRTs were used to help teach these classes, and the classes simulated what the teachers would have to do on the job. All of this activity and the provision that LRTs would be available to help onsite were to show target audience personnel that disruption would be minimized. Most important, the Reading Academy was not imposed on the system, but was made a volunteer program. This ensured that the program attracted Innovators and Early Adopters who tolerate ambiguity well and are prone to try out new ideas. Early Adopters also contain the leaders who provide positive opinions. In addition, this helped get early, positive dispersion throughout the system, provided needed evidence that the approaches and techniques would work, and pilot tested the academy curriculum content. As we know from the case facts, all of this was seen as positive.

Unfortunately, two negatives arose. The change in major sponsor, the school system superintendent, led to new questions being asked about the initiative by new leaders. This is inevitable with sponsor changes. Change agents should realize this and adapt by going back into the preparation phase if necessary. Second, many in the change agent group assumed that they were moving into the commitment phase—a misunderstanding about the process. Other unknown negatives were also occurring. To continue the Reading Academy in Years 3 and 4 required more LRTs to support the additional 700 teachers while continuing to support the Year 2 group. These new LRTs were brought into the system with the same status as the more experienced LRTs. The conflicts this caused could not be dealt with adequately by the current RL organizational structure. In addition, the resource demands by continuing this strategy spread the change agent group thin.

Change agents typically want to leave the acceptance phase too quickly because they have adopted the quick dispersion approach of the case study facts. This quick dispersion approach only tests the technical ideas of most change efforts, but does not test the infrastructure of the system nor identify system barriers. In the case study facts, one system barrier—*student mobility factor*—proved critical. In addition, the dispersion gives a lot of evidence about individual success, but does not provide evidence that one can move the meter (student TAAS scores) on a system scale. In essence, this dispersion or diffusion approach is not focused enough.

To deal with all these issues, it is better to continue in the acceptance or experimental phase. The motto should be, *Go Slow to Go Fast!* The experiment should be more focused to test the system infrastructure. In the original Year 1 planning, the change agents in the case might have developed a plan that abandoned the expansion of numbers in the Reading Academy and focused efforts on a small part of the school system to test ideas. For Year 3, the LH could have selected three of the nine districts superintendents on whom to focus efforts. Within these districts, schools (and, therefore, principals and teachers) could be selected to test the Reading Academy ideas more thoroughly across all K–3 teachers and classes in the selected schools. The Year 2 approach had not really tested the ideas across all classrooms for Grades K–3. In some schools, for instance, teachers may have come from only the first grade. What impact did not having kindergarten teachers involved produce? To take an extreme example of what we are stressing, what happens when all kindergarten teachers are innovators and all Grade 1 teachers are resistors? By focusing on fewer schools, we could test the ideas more thoroughly, including establishing integrated objectives among the district superintendents, principals, and teachers within a district. In addition, reward structures and other factors such as mobility could be examined.

Two other benefits occur from a more focused approach. First, the schools selected really become research centers for looking at one variable in that school, but many variables are examined across all the involved schools. These research centers can then be used for publicity purposes and are of great help in the commitment phase when institutionalization is needed. The other benefit is that, by staying in this experimental phase, the LH can have a stronger argument with district superintendents and principals who are pushing for getting control of LRTs. These persons are pushing for control because it appears to them that the change is in the commitment phase.

The change model indicates that persons move from the acceptance phase into the commitment phase if they perceive that the benefits of the change exceed the costs of disruption. Rather than becoming negative about the change, persons choose to continue to try it out or install it. Yet even at this point further tryout can provide evidence that the change is too costly and should be aborted rather than adopted. Even if adopted, minds can change after extensive implementation, and a decision to abort the process can occur. If continued, steps should be taken to institutionalize the change, which involves making permanent those things about the change that were tried out—whether they be process changes or reward and punishment changes. In essence, the change becomes the norm. If the change has captured the hearts and minds of persons in the system, it becomes internalized or part of the persons' intrinsic motivation.

In the case situation, the continuation of the dispersion approach leads us out of the acceptance phase too quickly and sends the message that all are ready for commitment. Warning flags should go up about moving too quickly when one has this many changes in overall sponsor. The problem is compounded in this case because of the perceived power of the external businesspersons who were pushing for rapid implementation across the total system.

The Principals' Academy was a positive change approach for building advocates. However, it could have been more impactful if one of two approaches were used. It could have been used as part of the Year 3 plan in the focused approach suggested earlier. Whether it was used as detailed in our case study or as part of the Year 3 focused approach, an action-learning approach[4] should have been employed. Simply stated, action learning begins by focusing on a real-world issue that impacts both supervisor (district superintendent) and the supervised (principal). Objectives and goals are established between supervisor and supervised and monitored for proper implementation. The supervisor is not just involved in the selection of the participants, but continues to be involved as they would be in a real situation. Needed content knowledge is brought to participants as the need comes to bear on the real problem the group is addressing. By focusing on a real-world issue, motivation is high and the reward structure stays in play. In most classroom settings, reward structure is more remote.

CONCLUDING COMMENTS

When it comes to change, it is always great to have complete hindsight as we have in this case. Being in the line of fire makes all the difference in the world. However, knowing about the concepts and techniques introduced in this chapter can be most helpful for planning and thinking through the process of change.

The frequent sponsor changes in this case study made this a most difficult change effort. With such sponsor changes, it is always easier to continue present plans than to go back and replan. Commitments to current staff make it difficult to change plans. Strong advocates who believe you are on the right track can also make it difficult to change.

Finally, one must ask whether we addressed the right question to begin the change. In this case, it is highly unlikely that the solution provided

---

[4]Reg Revans of the United Kingdom is considered the developer of action learning. Early American proponents were Chris Argyris (Harvard) and Donald A. Schon (M.I.T.); see the bibliography.

would ever have been able to reach the targeted goal of 90% of students reading at grade level due to the student mobility issue. Once identified, perhaps we could have had the Principals' Academy work on this while the RL group continued to work on the achievement of the goal. It could have been great synergy. Change is tough!

REFERENCES

Conner, D. R. (1992). *Managing at the speed of change*. New York: Villard.
Rogers, E. M. (1983). *Diffusion of innovations*. New York: The Free Press.

BIBLIOGRAPHY

This chapter argued that the best way to deal with change was to develop resilient people. It is believed that the best, most effective method to do that is to help people become self-aware. To accomplish this, we must understand our values and biases that produce our overt behavior. In essence, we need to understand the lenses or mental models through which we view the world.

To begin this building of resiliency through self-awareness, we recommend becoming a feedback-seeking individual. We should always ask our clients, peers, supervisors, and subordinates about how we interact with them. We should not flinch (become defensive) when the feedback does not conform to our own self-image.

We recommend using anonymous feedback instruments such as the Myers–Briggs and custom-developed instruments that focus on the behaviors needed in your organization. We particularly recommend going beyond traditional 360 (supervisor, peer, subordinate) approaches to a 450 (client, supervisor, peer, subordinate) approach. Introducing explicit client feedback is powerful. We know that not all functions serve external clients, but all have at least internal clients. For example, in our case study, the lead reading teachers would have the following:

1. Clients: Principals, teachers they coach
2. Supervisors: Immediate supervisor and Head of the Literacy Initiative
3. Peers: Other lead reading teachers and others in district's curriculum group
4. Subordinates: Support personnel in the Reading Literacy Group (secretaries, etc.)

In addition to this focus on feedback seeking, the following books, articles, and Web sites may prove useful in your efforts to deal with change.

These are organized according to a model developed by the author to think about the process of change.

PROCESS OF UNLEARNING

Personal Mental Models (self-awareness)

Senge, P. M. (1990). *The fifth discipline*. New York: Currency, Doubleday.

Senge, P. M., Roberts, C., Ross, R. B., Smith, B. J., & Kleiner, A. (1994). *The fifth discipline fieldbook*. New York: Currency, Doubleday.

Covey, S. R. (1989). *The 7 habits of highly effective people*. New York: Fireside, Simon & Schuster.

Cultural Mental Models

Hofstede, G. (1980). *Culture's consequences*. Newbury Park, CA: Sage.

Trompenaars, F., & Hampden-Turner, C. (1998). *Riding the waves of culture*. New York: McGraw-Hill.

Change Management (moving mental models): General Analysis Models

Peters, T. J., & Waterman, R. H., Jr. (1984). *McKinsey 7-S Model, In Search of Excellence*. New York: Warner Books.

Burke, W., & Litwin, G. H. (1992). A causal model of organizational performance and change. *Journal of Management, 18*(3), 532–545.

Change Management (moving mental models): Specific Change Models

Kotter, J. P. (1995, March–April). Leading change: Why transformation efforts fail. *Harvard Business Review*, pp. 59–67.

Conner, D. R. (1992). *Managing at the speed of change*. New York: Villard Books.

Mink, O. G., Esterhuysen, P. W., Mink, B. P., & Owen, K. Q. (1993). *Change at work*. San Francisco, CA: Jossey-Bass.

Rogers, E. M. (1983). *Diffusion of innovations*. New York: The Free Press.

Hard Side of Change

*see above *The Fifth Discipline*: Chapters 5 and 6

Value-Based Leadership

O'Toole, J. (1995). *Leading change*. San Francisco, CA: Jossey-Bass.

TEAMING (CREATING POTENTIAL AND INNOVATION)

Foster, R. (1986). *Innovation: The attacker's advantage*. New York: Summit Books.

Katzenbach, J. R., & Smith, D. K. (1998). *The wisdom of teams*. Cambridge, MA: Harvard Business School Press.

Hughes, R. L., Ginnett, R. G., & Curphy, G. J. (1993). *Leadership: Enhancing the lessons of experience*. Homewood, IL: McGraw-Hill Irwin.

Katzenbach, J. R. (1998). *Teams at the top*. Cambridge, MA: Harvard Business School Press.

ORCHESTRATING CHANGE

Action Learning

Schon, D. A. (1987). *Educating the reflective practitioner*. San Francisco, CA: Jossey-Bass.

Argyis, C., & Schän, D. A. (1978). *Organizational learning: A theory of action perspective*. Reading, MA: Addison-Wesley.

Coaching

Mink, O. G., Owen, K. Q., & Mink, B. P. (1993). *Developing high performance people: The art of coaching*. Reading, MA: Addison-Wesley.

Dialoguing (Team Learning)

Bohm, D. (1990). *On dialogue*. Waltham, MA: Pegasus Communications.

Facilitation

Doyle, M., & Strauss, D. (1976). *How to make meetings work: The new interaction method*. New York: The Berkley Publishing Group.

Negotiation

Fisher, R., & Ury, W. (1981). *Getting to yes*. New York: Penguin Books.

Performance Measures

Kaplan, R. S., & Norton, D. P. (1992, January–February). The balanced scorecard-measures that drive performance. *Harvard Business Review*, pp. 71–79.

Reward Structures

Carrots, Sticks, and Self-Deception (an interview with Alfie Kohn). (1994, January). *Across Board*, pp. 39–44.

Zigon Performance Group: http://www.zigonperf.com.

CHAPTER FOUR

Challenges to Change: Implementing Research-Based Reading Instruction in Urban Schools

Kathleen S. Cooter
Texas Christian University

Robert B. Cooter, Jr.
University of Texas at Arlington

Large urban school districts in the United States are grappling with monumental challenges to the goal of universal literacy. In many city centers, fewer than half of third-grade children can read on grade level. For these youngsters, the picture becomes more grim as they progress in grade. Although one should use caution in generalizing about causal factors for such diverse populations, it seems clear that poor reading development is often the traveling companion of poverty, inadequate language development, high student mobility, and ineffective teacher preparation.

In 1996, the Dallas Independent School District (DISD) declared war on its own dismal reading rates in kindergarten through third grade. The first task was to better understand the challenges facing the district's 60,000 children in Grades K–3. Using a process created by the National Aeronautics and Space Administration (NASA) called *failure analysis*, the Dallas Reading Plan determined those critical elements of literacy that must be addressed if DISD were to achieve its goal of at least 90% of all children reading on grade level by the end of third grade (May & Rizzardi, 2002). An analysis of these results was presented in chapter 2 (this volume). As a result of the failure analysis, it was decided that the best way to address the needs of children was to ensure that there was a well-trained teacher in every classroom with deep knowledge and expertise in comprehensive reading instruction. Likewise it would be essential for principals to learn new research-proved ways to create and sustain schoolwide comprehensive reading programs.

Over the past several years, the Dallas Reading Plan created two state-of-the-art training programs for teachers and principals. For teachers, a 90-hour year-long Reading Academy was created to develop teacher capacity for consistently delivering comprehensive reading instruction. As of the spring of 2001, approximately 2,000 teachers had completed the voluntary Reading Academy. Student performance in reading has improved significantly as measured by the Stanford 9 Achievement Test (SAT 9) and the Texas Assessment of Academic Skills. Certainly these skilled teachers helped DISD make the greatest gains in 2001 of the eight largest school districts in Texas on these assessments.

School leaders (i.e., principals, assistant principals, and a few central office leaders) were offered a Principals' Fellowship to help them learn more about their role in sustaining effective reading programs. To date about 150 school leaders have completed the Principals' Fellowship. It is interesting to note that the schools enjoying the most rapid growth in reading in DISD were those having *both* a large percentage of teachers enrolled in the Reading Academy *and* a principal who has completed the Principals' Fellowship.

It is our belief that the Dallas Reading Plan provided one of the few longitudinal experiments in a large urban school district having the central aim of institutionalizing comprehensive reading instructional practices. Although data coming from the Dallas Reading Plan have indeed been encouraging over the years of its existence, and the trends were quite positive, the picture was not entirely rosy. Gains in reading were neither as rapid nor as robust as was originally hoped for. The purpose of this chapter is to summarize our findings concerning the challenges that have seemingly inhibited progress in Dallas. We also posit remedies and areas for future research that may prove promising.

DELIMITATIONS

Admittedly our viewpoint may have been affected to some degree by our participation in the project: one serving as creator of the Principals' Fellowship, and the other as assistant superintendent for the Dallas Reading Plan. However, findings reported here are well documented by quantitative analyses by internal (DISD) and external (state) agencies. Myriad triangulated qualitative data were also used in analyses presented herein. This includes literally hundreds of structured interactions with DISD teachers and principals (who command our deepest respect and appreciation). Thus, we present our findings, at least in part, as participant observers (Goetz & LeCompte, 1984).

Challenges to Change

We begin with the dominant challenges witnessed in this long-term intervention that had the potential to impede, if not destroy, systemic reform efforts in DISD. Although these challenges may not be applicable in all situations, they certainly appear to be rather commonplace maladies experienced by other leaders from large urban districts with whom we have compared notes.

Fragmented Instruction. Reading instruction can vary a great deal in a large urban district, both inter- and intraschool. Our classroom observation data, which have been gathered continuously from 1997 through 2001, verify that fact. Not only do you find vestiges of the Reading Wars still intact (i.e., entrenched American whole languagers vs. the phonics-first-and-only clan), but, worse yet, a near *majority* of teachers today (at least in Dallas) are emergency certified and/or alternatively certified. These are teachers holding forth armed, knowledge-wise, with little more than intuition and fond recollections of their own (usually) suburban schooling as the principal tool for helping youngsters learn to read.

A majority of the urban teachers we observed knew little about (a) the developmental milestones of reading and writing, (b) how to quickly and efficiently assess children's reading development, (c) how to group students effectively, (d) ways to adapt the curriculum to meet special needs, or (e) how to involve families in their child's learning. Critical reading skills, even when taught, are taught at different times of the year (a serious problem with highly mobile student populations), with vastly different methods and with generally poor results. Although there is usually some sort of reading program in place, it is so fragmented and full of holes that we have coined the phrase "Swiss cheese effect" as a descriptor.

Dearth of Teaching Materials. Most reading teachers would love to have a plentiful classroom library of teaching materials (e.g., leveled books, kits, assessment materials, etc.). A status study of some 146 elementary schools in Dallas having Grades K–3, the target population of the Dallas Reading Plan, consistently revealed a dearth of teaching materials available for balanced instruction. Simple mathematics proved it was economically impossible to stock 3,000 individual classrooms with the materials teachers would need for comprehensive reading instruction in English and/or Spanish. Further, with the rapid turnover of teachers and the shrinkage in classroom materials that usually occurs as teachers move about, replenishing these classroom libraries would be a formidable yearly expense. Another consideration is that individual classroom libraries make little sense when one considers that many of the books in such a library may only be used once in a school year and then put back on the shelf—a poor utilization of scarce resources especially during times of austere budgeting.

Politics and Power: The Wrong Agendas.   One of the disturbing realities we observed in a number of large urban school districts was the all-too-common driving force behind decision making at the top: a thirst for power. Although many upper level administrators love to chant the mantra, "we're in this for the kids," their actions sometimes belie the *libretto*. The dynamics that tend to spawn this form of leadership are rather easy to understand.

At the top of the power food chain we find state legislators, governors, commissioners, and others dictating high-stakes tests, mandated curricula, and the withholding of grant funds as a grand *baton* for noncompliance with the first two. Considering the dismal reading development of so many children from inner-city schools, we feel the political establishment is right to up the ante. Yet the intended result—better instruction and improved learning—is not happening (e.g., see results from National Assessment of Educational Progress, 2000).

At the next link in the power-broker food chain, we find school boards, often the dysfunctional small-scale replica of the state level. School board members often hire and fire school superintendents largely on their promise to make things happen quickly, *quickly* often being defined as 12 to 18 months. Because most board members have rarely served as classroom teachers, they tend to have little knowledge of change dynamics in a school that, conservatively, requires 4 to 7 years for substantive improvement. Hence, the average tenure of urban school superintendents has dwindled to only $2\frac{1}{3}$ years (Council of the Great City Schools, 2000). School board members are generally applauded, of course, for "holding those high paid superintendents' feet to the fire" and vociferously demanding (while the cameras are rolling) quick results.

Because superintendents and their cabinets feel pressured by school boards, they tend to make decisions about curricula and professional development based not on research data or expertise, but rather on rapidity of change in standardized test scores. It is the instinct of self-preservation and gives the public the appearance that something of substance is being done.

The ripple effect on the front lines of the literacy struggle—our schools—is much like a *tsunami*. Principals are accountable for implementing flawed decisions about curricula about which they had no voice. If they fail to implement the program of the year (or month), they are replaced. If they *do* implement a program, but it fails to achieve rapid improvement in test scores, the principal (not the curriculum director who made the original decision) can be removed—an educational Catch 22 at best.

Teachers, the only link that has consistently made a difference in reading research (not programs), get the final power-induced squeeze. It is the teachers who are expected to implement the latest and greatest reading program, often without adequate training or materials and under great pressure from several layers of administrators.

Turnover in the Superintendency.   DISD is infamous for high turnover in the superintendent's office. Since 1997, there have been five! Although that statistic is certainly beyond the pale, high turnover, as previously noted, is not at all extraordinary to that position in urban school districts. With each new leader comes a sense of mandate from the school board to change whatever went on before—regardless of whether it was working. Taking time to adequately assess the successes and foibles of the previous administration is time wasted, and the new *supe* (pronounced, coincidentally, as *soup*) usually jumps right in and implements whatever he or she feels are the universal cures to what ails schoolchildren academically. (Ranchers have known for centuries that you do not tear down a fence erected by the previous landowner until you figure out why it was installed in the first place. . . .)

This almost frenetic pace of change sans adequate assessment leads to instructional fragmentation, morale problems with teachers and principals, and, ultimately, poor student achievement in reading. Teachers begin to have a rueful "What's next?!" attitude toward reading programs/initiatives and fail to commit to any because they know from experience that the program is here today and gone tomorrow.

Student Mobility.   Students often move around in large urban centers. We have seen this phenomenon first hand—not only in Dallas, but also in the metropolitan schools of Chicago, Nashville, Toledo, Fort Worth, and St. Louis. It is usually an economic problem: The rent comes due and the primary caregiver, often a single mother, lacks sufficient resources to pay the bill. After 2 or 3 months of nonpayment, eviction is threatened, so she gathers up her children and moves to another apartment complex running a $99 move-in special. This pattern is repeated over and over because the parents' income remains in the poverty range. These dropin/dropout children, even with good teaching, miss consistent instruction on essential reading skills. They have an almost serendipitous education, and the literacy results are debilitating. According to the latest report of the National Assessment of Educational Progress (2000) for reading, children from poverty score significantly lower in reading proficiency than more affluent counterparts. High mobility as a result of poverty is unquestionably one of the primary culprits.

Nonstrategic Assignment of School Leaders. One of the most puzzling roadblocks to improving urban school literacy programs is the manner in which many principals and assistant principals are assigned. Many school districts seem to view the elementary principalship as the first (and lowest) rung on the career ladder for principals. Often we have seen our most troubled urban elementary schools assigned a first-year principal, which is an illogical placement, and some have *never* taught in an elementary school. Further, many new elementary principals served their only leadership apprenticeship as an assistant principal in either a middle or high school. The goal, if they are following the school district's tradition, is to somehow do well in the elementary school so they can be *promoted* (their words) to a middle-school principalship and, later, to a high school.

Reward systems are set in place to ensure the continuance of this mindset. Because elementary schools are viewed as the lowest rung in this paradigm, elementary principals are paid less. Thus, instead of encouraging and rewarding principals to stay in place and develop leadership expertise, they are encouraged to abandon young learners and their teachers as soon as a more prestigious middle-school principalship opens up— a leadership brain drain for urban elementary schools. In the end, schools that improve in student achievement end up losing the leader who took them there—somewhat analogous to replacing Winston Churchill *during* the Battle of Britain.

Teacher Mobility. The teacher shortage is already a harsh reality in urban schools. Aside from the problem of trying to find qualified teachers (there are nearly 200 unfilled teaching positions year round in Dallas), teachers already in urban districts leave in droves each year for the suburbs. In fact, DISD announced in the summer of 2002 that some 2,000 teachers were needed for the 2002–2003 school year or about one fourth of its teaching force. The suburban schools typically translate into better working conditions, less difficulties with poverty, and its effects on learning and often more attractive salaries for teachers. As one change management expert told us, "You win on talent!" The talent needed to win in schools is teachers. The constant retreat of qualified teachers from city to suburban schools makes it quite difficult to attain consistent quality and continuity.

Higher Education Inadequacies: Weak Entry-Level Teacher Preparation. Some of the challenges to improving reading instruction in our schools lie at the threshold of universities. Teachers colleges, even the most celebrated ones, have one-size-fits-all teacher education—the notion that there is one way to prepare teachers irrespective of their future teaching assignment. Clearly the challenges facing inner-city teachers are remarkably *dis*similar to those of teachers in the suburbs; although, interestingly, many of the obstacles faced by inner-city teachers are nearly identical to those faced by many rural teachers having children of migrant farm workers (e.g., high student mobility, large percentages of English Language Learners, a prevalence of poverty, limited family involvement).

Perhaps the genesis of this one-size-fits-all mentality in teacher education predates the famous *Brown* v. *Board of Education* decision in which the U.S. Supreme Court effectively outlawed the "separate but equal" doctrine in the education of minority children. However, it has taken five decades to (almost) achieve equality of concern for our nation's children. Before *Brown*, school districts need only be concerned about White children, and even then the more affluent families. A half century after *Brown*, many state-mandated proficiency tests, like the *Texas Assessment of Academic Skills (TAAS)*, must now include statistics from all sociocultural groups, including students enrolled in special education. This lifting of the student performance veil has revealed stark inadequacies in the development of young readers in our inner-city schools and, thus, the effectiveness of teachers in those settings.

What is needed is a greater degree of specialized preparation for those who will teach city kids. Urban education is withering in part due to the mere trickle of competent teachers to fill classroom vacancies. The talent pipeline for teachers (i.e., teachers colleges), therefore, must be considered in the equation for improving urban schools.

Higher Education Inadequacies: Preparation of Instructional Leaders. Just as most colleges of education have prepared all teachers in a homogeneous manner, they have typically prepared educational leaders with a single mindset as well. Few graduate programs for principals include training on ways to establish and maintain schoolwide reading/literacy programs. As corporate partners who contributed some $5 million for teacher and principal development in Dallas remarked, "We learned a long time ago that for any complex human enterprise to succeed, you *must* develop your building-level leaders in tandem with their professionals [teachers]."

The most common career path for central office leaders now presiding over reading and language arts curricula began in the classroom, followed by the earning of a master's degree in educational administration (or administrative credentials added to a curriculum-oriented master's), service as a principal, and then on to the central office. The problems associated with this route to leadership are many. First, as with other college of education programs, graduate programs for middle and upper school management (i.e., those intended for future directors, assistant superintendents, and superintendents) tend to treat central office leadership preparation in a single way as if being a director of special education is much the same as being in charge of school maintenance services.

Another problem is that the preparation of central office leaders via graduate programs is a lack of depth—much like the proverbial pond that is a mile long, but only a quarter inch deep. For example, school finance is generally covered in a single three-semester hour course. It is common in large districts now for an assistant superintendent of reading and language arts to administer yearly budgets of many millions of dollars. The annual budget for a top 10 urban district in the United States commonly exceeds $1 billion. Wisely managing these amounts of revenue requires expertise and skill. It is the difference between being *not competent* versus *incompetent*—in the former case, the person is improperly prepared (our current predicament); in the latter, he or she is unable to perform despite preparation.

Subterfuge by Vendors and Consultants.   Urban school districts have a great deal of money with which to work, and their budgets are public record. In Dallas, the annual Title I budget alone has typically exceeded $40 million. Such immense budgets, although we must remember that these budgets are intended to serve six-digit student populations, can motivate reading program vendors to promise much more than they can deliver to land a major contract. In DISD, there exists more than 15 years of internal program evaluation data showing that most reading programs purchased over the years have been ineffective, yet repeat purchases occur yearly due to either habit or subterfuge.

Vendors sometimes appear to be like the *snake oil* vendors of old— promises are made that their product can cure the reading ailments of all—from dyslexia to the boredom of the gifted. Just one expensive dose each day and your reading woes are banished. Because of pressure on new superintendents and their cabinets to deliver better test scores in 18 months or less, the frenzy to find quick solutions each year creates a kind of revolving door for the cure-all reading vendors. Because top-level administrators change every few years, the cycle is repeated over and over.

This problem seemingly grows worse each year as respected researchers create new products or sign on with vendors as senior authors for questionable but lucrative programs. The publishers' interest in celebrated researchers is that they bring an implied legitimacy to their product. We have witnessed egregious conflict of interest situations emerge, if not illegal conduct, in scenarios like the following: The reading researcher is first hired as a consultant by the school district at premium rates to conduct teacher training workshops. Next she or he energetically recommends a vendor's product (the vendor being their employer and/or they hold significant stock portfolios with the company). As an author of the program, the reading researcher turned vendor also, of course, receives royalties or other rewards. Usually the reading program introduced yields less than promised (see, e.g., Pogrow, 2002). Worse the reading needs of children and their right to a highly qualified and versatile teacher have again been compromised.

Rescuing Urban Reading Programs: Some Possible Solutions

Believe it or not, we actually feel optimistic about the future of urban reading instruction. Although there are many problems facing our schools, there are also many positive developments and viable courses of action for providing high-quality reading programs for city kids. Although space limitations do not permit us to describe all of the solutions witnessed in recent years, we summarize a few of the more workable ones that keep us hopeful.

Breakthroughs in Reading Research. Over the past few years, a number of important research reports have been released that show a high degree of agreement about the essential elements of comprehensive reading programs. Reutzel and Cooter (2003) summarized seven such reports (see Fig. 4.1) and their areas of agreement concerning reading pro-

- Flippo, R. F. (2001). *Reading researchers in search of common ground*. Newark, DE: International Reading Association.
- Snow, C. E., Burns, M. S., & Griffin, P. (1998). *Preventing reading difficulties in young children*. Washington, DC: National Academy Press.
- *Report of the Literacy Taskforce*. (1999). Wellington, New Zealand: Ministry of Education.
- American Federation of Teachers. (1999). *Teaching reading is rocket science: What expert teachers of reading should know and be able to do*. Washington, DC: Author.
- *Report of the National Reading Panel: Teaching children to read*. (2000). Washington, DC: National Institute of Child Health and Human Development.
- *Report of the National Education Association's Task Force on Reading 2000*. (2000). Washington, DC: National Education Association.
- *Every Child a Reader*. (1998). Ann Arbor, MI: Center for the Improvement of Early Reading Achievement.

FIG. 4.1. Seven landmark reading research reports.

- Family and Community Involvement
- Non-negotiable Skills and Instruction
- Teacher Competencies
- Schoolwide Practices
- Comprehensive Assessment
- Student Motivation
- Pursuit of a National Goal

FIG. 4.2.   Seven areas of agreement among reading research reports.

- Phonemic awareness; alphabetic principle
- Phonics
- Oral reading fluency
- Independent reading practice
- Exposure to a variety of reading materials
- Comprehension strategies
- Vocabulary instruction
- Guided reading instruction
- Oral language development
- Concepts of print instruction
- Spelling and word study skills
- Interactive read aloud
- Technology-assisted reading instruction
- Integrated reading, writing, and language instruction
- Adequate time for daily reading/writing instruction and practice

Note. These recommendations are minimal and do not speak to the many other needs of students, such as family involvement or adapting the curriculum to meet the needs of exceptional children.

FIG. 4.3.   Non-negotiable reading skills and instruction.*

grams and minimal reading skills to be learned (Figs. 4.2 and 4.3). This growing sense of concurrence in the field has the potential to help school leaders screen and select programs based on scientific research, assist colleges of education in updating and improving their programs for teachers and administrators, and create a framework for higher quality research.

Reading "Safety Nets" to Address Student Mobility.   One silver lining in the student mobility cloud is that urban students often stay within the same school district's boundaries. A viable solution is to cast a kind of reading safety net over the school district to prevent highly mobile students from falling through the cracks created by mobility-induced curriculum fragmentation. This can be accomplished by developing a curriculum calendar for the entire school district, such that on any given week in, say, third grade, *all* students in the school district would focus on a specific reading objective during a daily 30-minute lesson (as just one part of the teacher's daily reading instruction). We realize that some may consider this kind of regimented instruction heresy, but the consequences of *not* creating reading safety nets for highly mobile children are simply unacceptable. This kind of safety net only requires a small portion of the daily reading/language arts block and still allows for a great deal of teacher discretion.

This approach was implemented in the 2001–2002 school year in Dallas. Weekly lesson plans were developed by skilled lead reading teachers (LRTs) under a major grant from a private educational foundation. The lesson plans used teaching strategies confirmed as effective in the research reports cited earlier. Teaching materials in English and Spanish needed for implementing the reading safety net in Grades K and 1 were purchased under a second major grant and dispersed to the schools. Needless to say, teachers, especially those under emergency certification, were pleased to have structured daily lesson plans and abundant materials with which to teach. Safety net skills to be taught were correlated with required state objectives as well as those articulated by the school district's basal reading program. Safety net instruction can provide both the teachers and students with needed scaffolding for teaching and learning.

Providing Adequate Teaching Materials. Many urban classroom teachers have little with which to teach beyond the standard basal reading series. A common desire is to have one's own classroom library well stocked with a variety of genre and a range of reading difficulty levels. Frankly this is not a realistic goal in that to do so would be cost-prohibitive and an unwise use of resources.

Many schools are finding that they are better able to leverage limited resources and ensure that each child has access to high-quality reading materials by establishing a Reading Resource Room (Reutzel & Cooter, 2000). Title I funds and other district resources go into purchasing leveled books (English and Spanish), big books, pocket charts, easels, games, professional books, and other essential teaching materials. These materials are placed in a special Reading Resource Room and made available to all teachers for instructional needs. Books in the Reading Resource Room are not in general circulation to students for checkout to prevent them from being exposed to content prior to instruction. The chief advantage is that all teachers (and children) can have equal access to a full range of materials. Materials are also used more frequently because more than one teacher can access them. This is one cost-effective way to ensure that "every classroom is as good as our best" when it comes to the availability of instructional materials.

Stability in Leadership. It is tautology to state that great schools and school districts are built on stability and consistency in leadership. School boards must have the determination to stay with capable superintendents over time—preferably 5 or more years. Superintendents must revise their thinking (and the district's policies if need be) so that elementary and middle-school principals are rewarded for longitudinal service in their respective schools. There should be no difference in the reward system between elementary and high school principals, with possible exceptions made for principals leading larger campuses and faculties. Further, no one should be assigned as principal to an elementary campus unless he or she has had extensive and successful experience as a teacher at that level. It is clearly in the best interest of children to have strong, competent, and experienced principals helping their teachers to succeed.

Improved Incentives for Urban Teachers. If it is a truism that schools win on talent, then something must be done to improve the supply and quality of teachers for urban children. Most acknowledge that teaching in the inner city can be inherently more stressful than in other settings. Therefore, the reward systems for teachers must change accordingly if we are to recruit more teachers for city schools; they must be paid handsomely and supported with high-quality materials and professional development.

Teachers should be able to deepen and improve their expertise each summer through professional development, perhaps during the entire month of June, at full salary while they do so. It is common for leading corporations to allocate up to one third of their budget for professional development. The time is here for us to do as well for our urban teachers. Without this kind of support, we will be unable to recruit and retain the best and the brightest.

Higher Education: Retooling Teacher Education. Given that as many as half of new teachers leave the profession within the first 5 years, more so in urban schools, there must be some acknowledgment that entry-level certification programs for elementary and secondary teachers are falling short in providing requisite skills for urban classroom realities. Schools of education should consider overhauling entry-level teacher education programs using a *less is more* philosophy; *less content* presented as "survey" or *awareness* sessions (see chap. 3 for more information) and *more* attention paid to developing a reasonable degree of expertise in essential pedagogy.

Higher Education Retooling: The Instructional Leader. More must be done to prepare principals to deal strategically with urban school realities. As with teacher preparation, some rethinking about how principals and other school leaders are developed seems in order. Our data from 1997 through 2001 in Dallas confirms that the schools having the most significant and rapid improvements in reading typically have two things in common: teachers involved in deep and rigorous training over time, and principals likewise involved in professional development on ways to develop and sustain schoolwide comprehensive reading and writing programs.

Graduate programs for principals, in general, need to go far deeper into such areas as budgeting and finance, counseling, change management strategies, and certainly curriculum and instruction. For graduate programs to respond more effectively to the needs of children, they should also have areas of specialization including the needs of urban schools and the diverse students they serve, not to mention differentiation for those seeking to become elementary, middle-school, or high school principals. Because state certification criteria tend to precede innovation in these areas of the academy, legislatures likely need to consider new laws to make it so.

THE PRINCIPALS' FELLOWSHIP

Over the past 4 years, we have cotaught a special Principals' Fellowship aimed at building the capacity of principals in creating and sustaining comprehensive reading programs in their schools. This training was initially sponsored by Southwestern Bell, which recognized the need for educated school leaders and has been credited with moving a large number of schools from the state's low-performing list to acceptable rankings. Selected topics from the Principals' Fellowship are shown in Fig. 4.4. About 140 principals and assistant principals have now participated as fellows in this prestigious experience, and most petitioned for a Part II Fellowship. Fellows received three graduate hours of credit from a local university that can be applied to a graduate program if they so choose. Books, materials, and weekly refreshments were also provided in this weekly course. In recognition of the hectic and busy lives principals lead and, concomitantly, to help ensure full attendance, the Fellowship held its weekly 3-hour session on both Tuesday and Thursday evenings with the same content. Thus, if a scheduled Parent Night or other required activity for principals fell on

Principles of Balanced Literacy Instruction
Five (5) Strategies to Get the Ball Rolling Faster
Phonological Awareness, Alphabetic Principle, and Phonics: Research & Solutions
The Comprehension Workshop
English Language Learners
Guided Reading
Adapting Instruction for Special Needs Learners
Small-Group Instruction That Works
Classroom Management Strategies
Reading Recovery and Other Targeted Interventions
Involving Families and Volunteers
Developing Reading Fluency
Identifying and Obtaining External Funds for Literacy Programs

FIG. 4.4.   Selected topics of the Principals' Fellowship Training.

their usual class night, they could easily come to the alternate session that week. Attendance was near perfect.

SOME FINAL REFLECTIONS

As we look back over our experiences in Dallas, we see certain constants that seem to be at work when attempting to implement systemic literacy reform in urban schools. We offer some final reflections and proposals.

One should face systemic reform realistically. A key question should be: What must come first to achieve *consistent* comprehensive reading instruction? To answer that question, one must carefully review the research evidence to find what will matter most when trying to improve student reading ability districtwide. For example, in many urban settings, one may well see, as we have, fragmented and inconsistent instruction as a result of inadequate teacher knowledge about balanced instruction. The remedy (deep learning over time coupled with expert mentoring) may take years. Such a lengthy intervention cannot meet the needs of the thousands of children currently enrolled in our schools. Indeed, substantial research data from Tennessee (Sanders & Horn, 1995; Sanders & Rivers, 1996) indicate that a child placed with an ineffective teacher for just 1 year can be handicapped throughout their schooling, and a child placed with an ineffective teacher for 2 years is virtually *toast* in terms of ever reading on level. The first thing to do in such an extreme scenario as Dallas may be to put in place in Stage 1 a satisfactory basal program (not necessarily an oxymoron). This would serve to establish a consistent baseline program if implemented in a synchronized fashion using what we referred to earlier as a districtwide *curriculum calendar*. Although this notion is undeniably repugnant to many, it may be essential to stabilize instruction—a Stage 1 priority. Stability enables a school district to move into the next logical priority—teacher education.

We must establish a pipeline of training in the school districts so that everyone eventually has the same toolbox and vocabulary with which to teach. Comprehensive reading instruction, if implemented well, requires deep training over time, preferably coupled with expert mentoring. One does not gain true expertise in comprehensive reading instruction in even a 90-hour training program; it can take 2 or more years of careful study, practice in the classroom, and coaching from other more advanced colleagues. Therefore, as we begin to stabilize and make consistent classroom instruction in Stage 1 using a basal program as outlined earlier, we must simultaneously begin in earnest a massive teacher development program for our urban teachers. Entry-level training should include an introductory program of 90 or more hours for teachers on the most basic parts of a comprehensive reading program. Second stage training should be based on a careful assessment of each teacher's strengths and needs in the classroom; in other words, *individualized professional development* to achieve maximum effectiveness in the classroom over time. Professional development cannot stop here if our goal is to make "every classroom as good as our best"—we must include principals.

Principal training should begin with current principals and assistant principals as our building leaders. The emphasis, we think, should be on ways to ensure consistent implementation of the basal reader program as the first step and linked to ways they can support their teachers while involved in professional development on comprehensive reading instruction. When comprehensive reading instruction is a priority with the principal, it quickly becomes a school priority.

We must invite college of education faculties to reconsider their own *modus operandi* for teacher preparation and align with urban districts in more meaningful ways. A provost at a major university recently asked us, "Do you think colleges of education will ever be helpful to inner city schools in finding solutions to their problems?" "They *must* find ways to do so, if they are to survive," was our reply. Some rethinking of the Ed School milieu and tenure/reward system is certainly needed so that, for instance, expert inner-city practitioners can be hired as regular faculty (and *not* in some subpar designation like *instructor*) to mentor college students, inform other professors about the gritty realities of teaching in urban schools, and participate in the crafting of effective programs for teachers. It has been said by many that the abandonment of the normal school model (complete with laboratory/demonstration schools for educational research) in favor of less effective *faux* academic models was a disaster for children when it comes to their right to have access to a competent teacher. We feel there may be some validity to this proposition.

Finally, we must quit infighting. The literacy battle has many fronts and cannot be attacked long term without coordination. Turf disputes between departments in school districts, faculty in schools of education, and politicians must end. We are in this battle together, and the only victors or victims will be children.

REFERENCES

American Federation of Teachers. (1999). *Teaching reading is rocket science: What expert teachers of reading should know and be able to do*. Washington, DC: Author.

Council of the Great City Schools. (2000, March). Urban school superintendents: Characteristics, tenure, and salary. Second biennial survey. *Urban Indicator, 52*(2), 9.

Every Child a Reader. (1998). Ann Arbor, MI: Center for the Improvement of Early Reading Achievement.

Flippo, R. F. (2001). *Reading researchers in search of common ground*. Newark, DE: International Reading Association.

Goetz, J. P., & LeCompte, M. D. (1984). *Ethnography and qualitative design in educational research*. Orlando, FL: Academic Press.

May, F. B., & Rizzardi, L. (2002). *Reading as communication* (6th ed.). Upper Saddle River, NJ: Merrill/Prentice-Hall.

National Assessment of Educational Progress. (2000). *The reading report card*. Washington, DC: National Center for Educational Statistics.

Pogrow, S. (2002). *Success for All* is a failure. *Phi Delta Kappan, 83*(6), 463–469.

Report of the Literacy Taskforce. (1999). Wellington, New Zealand: Ministry of Education.

Report of the National Education Association's Task Force on Reading 2000. (2000). Washington, DC: National Education Association.

Report of the National Reading Panel: Teaching children to read. (2000). Washington, DC: National Institute of Child Health and Human Development.

Reutzel, D. R., & Cooter, R. B. (2000). *Teaching children to read: Putting the pieces together* (3rd ed.). Upper Saddle River, NJ: Merrill/Prentice-Hall.

Reutzel, D. R., & Cooter, R. B. (2003). *Strategies for reading assessment and instruction: Helping every child succeed* (2nd ed.). Upper Saddle River, NJ: Merrill/Prentice-Hall.

Sanders, W. L., & Horn, S. P. (1995). *The Tennessee Value-Added Assessment System (TVAAS): Mixed Model Methodology in Educational Assessment*. In A. J. Shinkinlfred & D. L. Stufflebeam (Eds.), *Teacher evaluation: Guide to effective practice*. Boston: Kluwer.

Sanders, W. L., & Rivers, J. C. (1996). *Cumulative and residual effects of teachers on future student academic achievement*. Knoxville, TN: University of Tennessee.

Snow, C. E., Burns, M. S., & Griffin, P. (1998). *Preventing reading difficulties in young children*. Washington, DC: National Academy Press.

PART TWO

OVERCOMING THE EFFECTS OF SABOTEURS

CHAPTER FIVE

Accountability in Texas: Fair or Foul

William J. Webster
Dallas Independent School District

THE TEXAS ACCOUNTABILITY SYSTEM

Texas has developed statewide content and student performance standards in reading, writing, mathematics, science, and social studies. The Texas Essential Knowledge and Skills (TEKS) designates the instructional objectives for each grade and subject.

The Accountability System currently holds students accountable for passing four high school end-of-course examinations or the exit level of the Texas Assessment of Academic Skills (TAAS). (The end-of-course examinations are scheduled to be phased out as a new, more difficult state assessment test is implemented in 2003.) It holds schools accountable for student performance and dropout rates. Its Academic Excellence Indicator System (AEIS) includes campus, district, and statewide performance data. AEIS matches demographic information with performance data in an attempt to measure academic progress among campuses and districts. AEIS includes TAAS results from special education and limited English-proficient students.

The Accountability Rating System uses two base AEIS indicators, TAAS performance and dropout rates, to calculate adequate yearly progress and categorize the performance of campuses and districts. The rating system is divided into four performance levels, which are determined by absolute performance primarily on the TAAS.[1]

The Exemplary performance level requires (a) 90% of the total students and each student subgroup (African American, Hispanic, White, and economically disadvantaged) to pass each subject, and (b) a dropout rate of 1% or less for all students and student subgroups. The recognized performance level requires (a) at least 80% of the total students and each student subgroup passing each subject, and (b) a dropout rate of 3.5% or less for all students and subgroups. The academically acceptable performance level requires (a) at least 55% of the total students and each student subgroup to pass each subject, and (b) a dropout rate of 6.0% or less for all students and subgroups. The unacceptable or low-performance rating is given when (a) less than 50% pass of all students and subgroups pass each test, and (b) the dropout rate is above 6%.

Texas administers the TAAS at Grades 3 through 8 and 10 in reading and mathematics; Grades 4, 8, and 10 in writing; and Grade 8 in social studies and science. It administers an exit-level assessment at Grade 10 required for high school graduation.

Strengths of the Texas Accountability System

The system is well documented and includes a 207-page manual that describes the accountability system. Generally speaking, the Texas Accountability System is seen as one of the best state accountability systems in the country (Webster et al., 2002). Its strengths include:

- The TAAS test is developed by an outside contractor within standards for test development established by the American Psychological Association (APA) and generally displays adequate reliability and validity. (There are volumes of technical data available on the TAAS if one asks.)
- A straightforward accountability manual that covers in detail the rules and regulations of the accountability system.
- Rigorous requirements of school districts with regard to reporting results to the public.

---

[1]The *Texas Assessment of Academic Skills (TAAS)* will be replaced in 2002–2003 by the *Texas Assessment of Knowledge and Skills (TAKS)*. Preliminary data on the *TAKS* suggests that it is much more difficult than the *TAAS* and exhibits severe differences in performance between various ethnic and socioeconomic groups. The comments in this paper are even more relevant to an accountability system based on *TAKS* than they were to *TAAS* because of the increased difficulty level and the differential performance registered by the different ethnic and socioeconomic groups.

- A well-designed academic excellence indicator report that aids in dissemination of results to the public.
- Professional scaling of the TAAS so that results are comparable from year to year.
- Progress toward reporting a longitudinal dropout rate that promises to be more revealing than the cross-sectional rate currently reported.
- The system includes specific rules for testing limited English-proficient students and provides TAAS tests in English and Spanish at Grades 3 through 6, which are aggregated into the accountability system.
- Provisions for measuring progress in special education are included.
- A statewide database so that students can be tracked from district to district.

Weaknesses of the Texas Accountability System

The Texas Accountability System has a number of weaknesses that it shares with many other state accountability systems. The most important of these weaknesses include:

- It is not fair to schools that serve high percentage minority and poor student populations.
- It has no valid value-added component.
- Accountability ratings are based on cross-sectional data.
- It is primarily dependent on one test. Actual classification of schools in the system is dependent on only two measures at the middle and high school levels (*TAAS* performance and dropout) and only one measure at the elementary school level (*TAAS* Performance).
- It defines continuous enrollment at the district rather than the school level and holds schools accountable for students who have been enrolled in the district for the requisite time yet may have only been enrolled in the school for a matter of days.
- It is administered like it is a game, not like it is a serious accountability system.

These weaknesses are discussed in the interest of improving the system, not in support of its elimination. Each of these weaknesses is discussed in turn.

Fairness. Systems, which employ unadjusted outcomes or testing programs as their basis for evaluation, produce results that are too highly correlated with context factors such as ethnicity, socioeconomic status

(SES), and language proficiency. As noted in Jaeger (1992) and Webster et al. (1995), these systems are biased against schools with larger proportions of minority, immigrant, and low SES students and are biased in favor of schools that contain larger proportions of White and higher SES students. The essence of these arguments is that with unadjusted outcomes schools are ranked primarily on the types of students they receive rather than on the education they provide. Use of unadjusted outcomes in the comparison of schools and programs confounds the differences in populations of students and how they are selected into their schools and programs with the difference the schools and programs make. Schools and programs, which draw on higher scoring students, receive the benefits of this bias before their students start their first lesson. Schools and programs that must deal with lower scoring students must overcome this bias before they can begin to show an effect. In short, the worst possible use of evaluative data for public reporting is the presentation of simple averages by districts and schools.

The following example illustrates this bias at the district level. The Dallas Independent School District (DISD) is often compared on unadjusted, cross-sectional TAAS scores to seven other districts in Texas that are considered to be other large urban districts. Published rankings on the TAAS cause great consternation among Dallas educators, as well they should, because Dallas consistently ranks seventh or eighth among the urban districts. As a result of these rankings, which are examples of the worst possible ways to report evaluative data, the DISD is thought to be one of the worst in the nation. Yet, is it really?

Of the eight urban districts in Texas, the DISD has the highest percentage of limited English-proficient students, the highest percentage of African-American students, the second highest percentage of economically disadvantaged students, and the second lowest percentage of White students. If one considers statewide averages, each of these factors is associated with lower achievement levels.

To examine this situation further, the author took statewide average percentages passing TAAS for limited English-proficient, Hispanic, African-American, and White students and multiplied the statewide passing rates by the percentages of each group in each of the eight districts. (Because I did not have individual student statewide data, I could not include low SES students—a factor that would have further exacerbated the differences.) Table 5.1 shows the results of this analysis.

The data in Table 5.1 suggest that, given statewide achievement patterns, if all districts are doing similar jobs of educating the students they receive, Dallas should rank eighth in reading and mathematics and seventh in writing. This analysis does not even take into consideration some other extremely important contextual variables, such as the number and percentage

TABLE 5.1
Adjusted Aggregate Sums and Projected (Ranks)
for Eight Texas Urban Districts

District	Reading	Mathematics	Writing
Austin	8327.06 (1)	8340 (1)	8416.62 (1)
Corpus Christi	8044.94 (2)	8227.57 (2)	8313.28 (2)
Dallas	7134.03 (8)	7371.84 (8)	7898.04 (7)
El Paso	7293.65 (6)	7702.01 (5)	8033.76 (6)
Fort Worth	7494 (5)	7659.68 (6)	8081.68 (4)
Houston	7246.52 (7)	7453.09 (7)	7886.38 (8)
San Antonio	7626.78 (3)	7917.47 (3)	8108.73 (3)
Ysleta	7502.63 (4)	7866.01 (4)	8071.4 (5)

of students in special education and alternative programs—variables that vary considerably among districts and carry testing exemptions.

This is not to suggest that Dallas educators should not be concerned that their students are not doing as well academically as the students of more demographically advantaged (from a test results perspective) districts. They should take these data and use them to improve instruction.[2] However, without a value-added component to lend fairness to the process, this system unethically brands as failures many educators who are making substantive improvements. Goals are nice for improvement, however an accountability system must be concerned with fairly assessing the impact of a teacher or school staff on important student outcomes.

Table 5.2 illustrates this bias at the school level by displaying the differences in school rankings on Dallas' value-added system, which takes the aforementioned variables into effect, versus the state's absolute system, which does not take them into effect for the top Dallas schools. Of the top 25 Dallas elementary schools on the value-added system, only those that had a relatively high percentage of White students (>50%), a relatively small percentage of African-American students (<20%), and a relatively low deprivation index ((%) ranked in the top 25 Dallas elementary schools on the state system.[3] The elementary school that ranked 1st on the Dallas system and 20th on the state system, an apparent anomaly because it was 98.9% African American and had a deprivation index of 87%, was subsequently disqualified for cheating by Dallas' Accountability Task Force.

---

[2]In fact a new superintendent to Dallas in 2000, Mike Moses, refocused the District on instruction, and the District has subsequently shown tremendous academic gains.

[3]For the year in question, district elementary percentages were 69% low SES, 16.1% White, 43.7% African American, and 38.2% Hispanic. Middle- and high school statistics are also listed under the district row in their respective tables.

TABLE 5.2
Demographic Characteristics of the Most Effective Schools Using
the Dallas' Value-Added System Versus the State's Absolute System

Elementary Schools

Rank	Grades	Enrollment	Percentage White	Percentage African American	Percentage Hispanic	Percentage DEP	Percentage LEP	State Rank
1	K-3	555	0.4	98.9	0.7	87	0.1	20
2	K-6	238	4.5	15.3	79.7	84	57.9	94
3	K-3	447	2.5	80.1	17.1	84	8.3	26
4	K-3	194	0	98.0	1.5	77	1.5	58
5	K-3	573	0.9	57.4	41.7	80	36.5	77
6	K-6	529	0.2	96.4	3.5	92	2.6	39
7	4-6	193	0.5	85.3	12.7	75	5.7	60
8	4-6	336	1.5	64.0	34.2	87	17.6	83
9	**K-6**	**518**	**64.5**	**18.5**	**10.2**	**20**	**2.7**	**11**
10	**K-6**	**462**	**54.4**	**16.2**	**28.4**	**33**	**3.5**	**4**
11	4-6	398	0.8	75.5	23.5	71	15.3	88
12	**K-6**	**539**	**51.9**	**11.0**	**31.4**	**40**	**15.6**	**8**
13	**K-6**	**656**	**50.0**	**27.5**	**21.7**	**36**	**13.4**	**9**
14	K-6	830	37.0	37.8	23.4	51	13.1	26
15	K-6	776	0	99.7	0.3	75	0	50
16	K-3	214	0.5	87.3	12.2	64	8.4	107
17	**K-6**	**630**	**63.3**	**7.8**	**26.0**	**27**	**15.3**	**12**

18	K–6	680	0.2	99.2	0.6	51	0	32
19	K–6	569	0.2	99.0	0.9	85	0	30
20	**K–6**	741	**58.6**	**11.0**	**20.8**	**36**	**12.0**	**17**
21	K–6	860	0.2	88.8	9.6	93	5.0	71
22	K–6	702	4.4	3.5	90.4	81	52.1	86
23	K–6	697	39.0	27.5	29.8	47	22.7	17
24	K–6	571	3.0	20.5	76.1	92	53.9	91
25	**K–6**	483	**55.4**	**11.3**	**30.9**	**18**	**3.5**	**3**
District	K–6	592	16.1	43.7	38.2	69	23.2	

Middle Schools

1	7–8	693	13.6	30.8	52.4	85	31.2	10
2	7–8	668	30.3	37.6	29.7	45	15.4	6
3	7–8	888	18.2	16.3	63.2	64	29.9	9
4	7–8*	367	24.4	50.4	22.4	38	0	2
5	7–8	863	7.0	75.4	15.7	30	1.3	5
District	7–8	703	15.2	48.6	34.3	55	13.2	

High Schools

1	9–12	1129	0.4	97.9	1.7	32	0	16
2	9–12	1004	36.7	37.7	23.3	24	13.0	4
3	9–12*	3567	18.5	43.7	32.9	22	4.8	5
4	9–12*	129	46.9	31.5	17.7	9	0	1
5	9–12*	623	48.4	34.3	15.6	9	0	2
District	9–12	1093	15.8	49.8	31.5	28	10.1	

At the middle-school level, where schools tend to have greater within-school variance than between-school variance, the rankings are closer. Of the 27 middle schools, both systems placed the top schools in the top 10.

At the high school level, arguably the best school in the district—one that has won numerous national awards—ranked 16 out of 21 comprehensive high schools. The reader should note that this school had a high percentage of African-American students and had a higher deprivation index than the other high schools in the top five.

Thus, a comparison of Dallas schools, ranked with a system that controlled for important background variables and those same schools ranked under a system that ignored context, clearly demonstrated that *effective schools*, as defined through a system that controlled for important context variables over which the schools had no control and also did well in the unadjusted system, had higher proportions of White students and affluent families. It also demonstrated that schools that were effective with their populations, but had high proportions of minorities and economically disadvantaged students, performed at lesser levels on the unadjusted system. Finally, a related study showed that correlations of school effectiveness rankings from an unadjusted system with important demographic factors were unacceptably high, ranging as high as .90 at the student level and .65 at the school level (Webster et al., 1995).

The point of all this is that context matters. This is not to suggest that systems should not establish appropriate, absolute goals, only that in addition to those absolute goals a supporting system should be established that takes context into consideration.

Value-Added Systems. Most state accountability systems, including Texas, are largely limited to the determination of whether students, teachers, or schools reach certain preset objectives. These objectives may be empirically set, although in many cases they are metaphysically established. Set goals are a necessary, but not sufficient component of an equitable accountability system.

Why go to the trouble of adding a value-added component to the accountability system? Again it is a matter of fairness. For explication, let us begin with examples of two unadjusted outcomes and the goals based on them. Assume for the first that a school has a dropout rate of 20% and a goal is set for the school to reduce it to 15%. Assume in the second that every school in a system has at least 50% of its students reading at grade level and a system goal is set for every school to have 60% of its students reading at grade level. On the surface, these seem like realistic uses of unadjusted outcomes and seem to make rational goals.

Now consider both examples further. Assume in the first example that the population of students on which the school draws has a general history of a dropout rate that ranges between 9% and 11%. Now the unadjusted outcome of 15% becomes undesirable and a goal of 15% too high a rate. A more appropriate goal for the school might be to reduce the rate to 8% in the first year and below 8% thereafter. In the second example, assume that in the past 2 years every school has had at some recent point 60% of its students reading at grade level. An unadjusted goal for every school might be to have at least 65% of its students reading at grade level every year.

The observant reader may note the caveats attached to each of these examples. The goals and outcomes are conditioned on the past performance of the underlying populations of students. Reconsider the two examples with different underlying conditions and these same unadjusted outcomes and their accompanying goals can rapidly become inappropriate for different reasons. In the first example, the school has held its dropout rate to 15% with a given population of students. If we now assume that the dropout rate for the population of students on which the school draws is 18% to 20% and that no other school has been able to reduce the dropout rate for a similar population to below 17%, the goal of 10% for that school may be unrealistic for a different reason (i.e., the school's rate of 15% may be an example of current best practice). In all likelihood, the unadjusted rate of 15% is an excellent outcome. The school is to be commended for keeping it at that rate and should be sharing its techniques with the remaining schools. The unadjusted rate of 15% remains an excellent outcome until it can be demonstrated that more effective techniques can reduce the underlying population rate below 15%.

In the second example, the system goal was 60% of students reading at grade level for every school. Yet now assume that this year is the first year ever that all schools have reached the goal of 50% of students reading at grade level. Assume also that several schools have never dropped below 75% of their students reading at grade level. Now the system goal of 60% may be more appropriately 55% for some schools and 80% for other schools.

Clearly in both of these examples pretreatment performance matters. Outcomes and goals must be considered in light of this pretreatment performance. As Glass (1978) argued, the outcomes and goals or standards developed from them are relative to the existing performance of their specific groups of students. This example also illustrates one of the major problems associated with unadjusted outcomes. Absolute goals based on these outcomes are established without any thought as to whether there is any probability of making the goals. Webster and Mendro (1995) discussed this problem at length. They showed that achievable goals can be set based on unadjusted outcomes. The most pressing problem is that the public or higher administration would like to see massive progress and typically feels that carefully constructed incremental goals present a problem of low expectations. Extreme, unrealistic goals, with little probability of attainment, are generally more satisfying to those outside of the school.

Regardless of how unadjusted data are used in goal setting, the question of evaluating educational progress in a fair and precise manner remains. How are we to determine the appropriate contexts for evaluating educational outcomes at the school level? How can we determine whether an outcome is actually improvement or is only the result of typical progress for a defined population? In other words, how can we be sure that we are evaluating the contribution that schools or teachers make to student progress, not just whether the student is progressing normally based on background and innate ability?

The answers to these questions and many like them lie in the rapidly developing field of value-added assessment of educational outcomes. With value-added systems, conditions outside of the control of a school are held constant for all schools in a group. The effects obtained by each school are measured on a common metric and the results compared. In essence, all schools in the group are set at a common baseline, and the critical element then becomes whether, relative to other schools, a school has had a positive or negative effect on its students. Has it added value to the base or subtracted value from the base? This common baseline helps answer the question of sorting out improvement from typical performance.

Value-added systems can be constructed with a variety of similar methodologies, all of which provide preferable alternatives to systems based on unadjusted outcomes. Although a system that has been carefully researched and fine tuned to eliminate many small biases is discussed later, most regression-based, value-added systems are far better than the alternative unadjusted systems. The essence of all of these systems is to eliminate known factors that affect school outcomes, but are not possible for the school to control. At that point, improvement can be identified. Further, when these systems are designed properly, they offer the best chance of adjusting for effects of variables at the student level that are not explicitly included in the known factors. In other words, they help control to some extent all factors that are not under the control of the schools. Thus, if designed appropriately, a value-added system can address both the fairness and previous achievement level concerns.

Cross-Sectional Versus Cohort Data.   The most publicized portion of the Texas Accountability System is based entirely on cross-sectional data. Cross-sectional data compare different students across time. Thus, for example, Year 2001 third graders are compared to Year 2000 third graders and pronouncements made about progress or lack of it. While this type of analysis, although not preferred, is still relatively interpretable on a statewide basis where there are hundreds of thousands of subjects in the population, it severely breaks down when one attempts to examine the progress of a small elementary school with less than 100 third graders. Cohort analysis would follow the same students from the third to fourth grades and examine gains or improvements.

The Texas Education Agency recognizes the need for cohort analysis and addresses this need through actual cohort analysis. Comparable improvement measures are published for students and are based on analysis of growth on the Texas Learning Index ([TLI] a scale score) for students who took the TAAS English version in reading and mathematics for 2 consecutive years. The TLI gain score analysis is then obliterated by an attempt to identify 40 like schools with which to compare individual school gains. Like schools are identified as having similar amounts of Hispanic, economically deprived, mobile, limited English proficient, White, and/or African-American students. Although this sounds good to the average superintendent in the state, 15 years of research into methodology for identifying more and less effective schools has demonstrated rather forcibly that there are no two schools that are exactly alike, let alone 40. Compromises must always be made that result in less than perfect matches.

The cohort analysis is also not an integral part of the accountability system. Schools are rated on absolute TAAS scores, not on improvement. Comparable improvement is treated as an afterthought. Schools are often classified into categories in the accountability system as a result of one student and, because of the rule that students must be continuously enrolled in the district not in the school, that one student is often a new enrollee in the school. Continuously enrolled status must be based on school enrollment, not district enrollment, when it is the school being rated. Failing that, at least cohort analysis would guarantee that the student would have been somewhere in the state and tested the previous year.

One Test. The issue of the system being based on only one test is more a criticism of Texas educator's response to the system than of the system. The general response to the accountability system by educators across Texas has been to drill and practice students on released test items. The Texas Education Agency resisted releasing previously used TAAS items, in some part, because it was afraid of exactly what has happened, but was forced to do so by a court order. In some cases, entire curriculums are made up of drilling released TAAS tests. Classroom observations of reading classes in one Texas district reveal far too much emphasis on lower level skills related directly to drilling and practicing released TAAS items (Denson, 1999, 2000). An entire cottage industry has sprung up around selling better ways to practice TAAS test items. This has resulted in claims that the achievement gains that Texas students have registered are not real (Clopton et al., 2000; McNeil & Valenzuela, 2000; Stotsky, 1998). In all fairness, however, there is evidence of pervasive achievement gains by Texas students on indicators other than TAAS (Charles A. Dana Center, 2002; National Center for Educational Statistics, 2000).

Although it is probably not practical to expand the number of tests in a statewide system, it would be appropriate for TEA or the Legislature to ban practice testing on released TAAS items. This action alone would improve the quality of instruction across the state and, with the advent of the newer more difficult state test in 2003, would erase any doubts that any registered gains are real.

Definition of Continuous Enrollment.   Under the rules of the system, a student is continuously enrolled at the district level if he or she is on the district's October PEIMS submission and still enrolled to take the TAAS. This is a logical definition of *continuous enrollment* at the district level because districts should legitimately be held accountable for children who have continuously enrolled since October. However, the system breaks down when, as long as the definition of continuous enrollment at the district level is met, it holds individual schools accountable for those students regardless of how long they have been enrolled in those schools.

The DISD has more intra- than interdistrict mobility. Many children are in more than three schools within the district in 1 year. A recent analysis of district data demonstrated that students continuously enrolled in their feeder patterns within the district outperformed students who were mobile between districts and in turn outperformed students who were mobile within the district. Thus, the lowest scoring students were those who frequently moved within the district. We are still studying this phenomena, but it is probable that these students are much more economically deprived than their peers and are also much more mobile. These students represent a challenge to the district and should legitimately be included in the district's accountability subset. However, to hold an individual school accountable for students who may have been enrolled in that school for a matter of days is not appropriate.

The solution to this problem is to have two different accountability subsets—one for the district and one for the school. Students who are continuously enrolled in the district, regardless of intradistrict mobility, would be ascribed to the district. Students who are continuously enrolled in individual schools would be ascribed to those individual schools.

Playing the Game.   The Texas Accountability System has a number of rules, some of which cause schools to be penalized through actions that were no fault of their own. An excellent example occurred in the DISD a few years ago. A relatively small elementary school that educated a student population that was predominantly poor and African American had worked hard to achieve excellence throughout the school year. When the ratings came out, they were rated as *Acceptable*. Staff was confused because, according to their calculations, their school was *Recognized*. They appealed to the Texas Education Agency. On investigation, it was discovered that another elementary school had mistakenly coded over 30 of their students to the would-be Recognized school. Without those 30 students, the first school achieved Recognized status. The Texas Education Agency determined that because they, the Agency, had not made the mistake, the results would stand. Thus, our Recognized school remained Acceptable with understandable resentment toward the system.

This is but one example of problems with the system. When one child's cross-sectional test score can make the difference between Low Performing and Acceptable status, between Acceptable and Recognized status, and between Recognized and Exemplary status, slipups occur. The system needs to include provisions for correcting these errors no matter who made them.

RECOMMENDED SYSTEM IMPROVEMENTS

The major recommended improvement for the Texas Accountability System is that it add a legitimate value-added component that (a) rewards growth, (b) is based on cohort analysis, (c) has a realistic definition of continuous enrollment in a school, and (d) controls for student contextual variables. Increasing the number of outcome measures would be a plus, but may not be realistic for a statewide system. The introduction of a legitimate value-added component would limit the impact of transient students and would make mistakes like those described earlier unlikely.

Possible Statistical Models

There are a number of statistical techniques designed to isolate the effect of a school's or teacher's practices on important student outcomes. The school effect can be conceptualized as the difference between a given student's performance in a particular school and the performance that would have been expected if that student had attended a school with similar context, but with practice of average effectiveness.

Investigators throughout the world have conducted and reported numerous studies aimed at identifying effective schools as well as estimating the magnitude and stability of school contributions to student outcomes. Good and Brophy (1986) provided an excellent review of this work. Researchers have been working for a number of years on appropriate methodology for adjusting for the effects of student and school demographic variables in estimating school effects. One approach has been to regress school mean outcome measures on school means of one or more background variables. This approach is only adequate to the extent that there is not much within school variance; that is, the school impacts all students similarly. Mendro and Webster (1993) demonstrated that this is generally not the case and that using school-level models to estimate school effects, although better than the common practice of reporting unadjusted test scores, produces extremely unstable estimates of school effects and, in case the reader is interested, devastatingly misleading estimates of teacher effects.

Fennessey and Salganik (1983) proposed a model for analyzing instructional program effectiveness within the context of gain scores. The rescaled and adjusted gain score (RAGS) index equalized aggregate net bias from responsiveness to instruction, regression to the mean, and boundary artifacts in all program groups. A crucial assumption to this approach is that any group of students with similar pretest scores will have similar rates of learning and will be subject to the same degree of regression to the mean. Although the RAGS procedure is appropriate for program evaluation, it would be difficult to apply in a situation where one is attempting to determine the relative effectiveness of schools or teachers with different student populations with differing learning rates.

Another approach—one that has received generally widespread acceptance among educational researchers—involves the aggregation of residuals from student-level regression models (Aiken & West, 1991; Bano, 1985; Felter & Carlson, 1985; Kirst, 1986; Klitgaard & Hall, 1973; McKenzie, 1983; Millman, 1981; Saka, 1984; Webster & Olson, 1988; Webster, Mendro, & Almaguer, 1994). These techniques can incorporate a large number of input, process, and outcome variables into an equation and determine the average deviation from the predicted student outcome values for each school or teacher. Schools or teachers are then ranked on the average deviation. Some advantages of multiple regression analysis over other statistical techniques for this application include its relative simplicity of application and interpretation, its robustness, and the fact that general methods of structuring complex regression equations to include combinations of categorical and continuous variables and their interactions are relatively straightforward (Aiken & West, 1991; Cohen, 1968; Cohen & Cohen, 1975; Darlington, 1990).

Finally, hierarchical linear modeling (HLM) provides estimates of linear equations that explain outcomes for group members as a function of the characteristics of the group as well as the characteristics of the members. Because HLM involves the prediction of outcomes of members who are nested within groups that in turn may be nested in larger groups, the technique is well suited for use in education. The nested structure of students within classrooms and classrooms within schools produces a different variance at each level for factors measured at that level. Bryk et al. (1988) cited four advantages of HLM over regular linear models. First, it can explain achievement and growth as a function of school or classroom level characteristics while taking into account the variance of student outcomes within schools or classrooms. Second, it can model the effects of student characteristics, such as gender, race/ethnicity, or SES, on achievement within schools or classrooms and then explain differences in these effects between schools or classrooms using school or classroom characteristics. Third, it can model the between- and within-group variance at the same time and thus produce more accurate estimates of student outcomes. Finally, it can produce better estimates of the predictors of student outcomes within schools and classrooms by using information about these relationships from other schools and classrooms. HLM models are discussed in the literature under a number of different titles by different authors from a number of diverse disciplines (Bryk & Raudenbush, 1992; Dempster, Rubin, & Tsutakawa, 1981; Elston & Grizzle, 1962; Goldstein, 1987; Henderson, 1984; Laird & Ware, 1982; Longford, 1987; Mason, Wong, & Entwistle, 1984; Rosenburg, 1973).

Criterion for Judging Models

The criterion that should be used to judge the appropriateness of statistical models designed to rank schools is *fairness*. That is, a school's estimated effectiveness level should not be capable of being predicted by the individual or aggregate composition of its student body. Variables over which the school or teacher have no control should not be correlated with the school's effectiveness rating. These variables include such things as student pretest score, ethnicity, SES, mobility, gender, and limited English-proficient status. The models proposed in this chapter produce results at the school and student level that correlate zero with these important school- and student-level contextual variables.

It is obviously also important that there be a school effect. If there is none, one is reduced to ranking schools based on random error. This methodology must be part of a comprehensive accountability system that provides valid data for decision making and improvement as well as for accountability purposes (Webster, 2002). It cannot be emphasized enough that a system designed to help schools and teachers improve as well as to provide accountability information must have both absolute and relative components. Absolute goals should be established and monitored for improvement, but accountability must include a value-added component.

Relevant Results From Alternative Models

All studies summarized in this section examined correlations between indexes produced by various statistical models and those produced by the
methodology of choice as well as correlations with individual student
background and classroom and school contextual variables. The methodology of choice for producing school effectiveness estimates is a two-stage,
two-level, student–school HLM model. Formulae for this model are specified later in this chapter. Results are discussed in relation to the model of
choice to limit the statistics presented and simplify the discussion. Detailed backup data are contained in the various referenced papers, particularly the one, by Webster et al. (1997a, 1997b).

School-Level Effects. Individual student background variables include gender, SES (free or reduced lunch), ethnicity, limited English-proficient status, and pretest scores. Parental income, family poverty index,
and parental education level can also be used if census data are available.
Aggregate school variables include percent student mobility, percent over-
crowded, percent economically disadvantaged (same variables as specified earlier), percent limited English proficient, percent African American,
percent Hispanic, and percent minority. The majority of studies were
done at Grades 4 through 6, although additional studies were conducted
at Grade 8. Conducting studies at the different grade levels is significant
because the elementary levels (Grades 4 through 6) have large numbers of
relatively homogeneous schools, whereas the middle-school level (Grade
8) has a small number of relatively heterogeneous schools.

At the school level, six questions were investigated through a series of
studies (Mendro & Webster, 1993; Mendro et al., 1998; Webster, 1998;
Webster & Mendro, 1997; Webster, Mendro, & Almaguer, 1993, 1994;
Webster & Olson, 1988; Webster et al., 1995, 1996, 1997a, 1997b; Weerasinghe, Orsak, & Mendro, 1997). The questions are:

- Is there any practical difference between effectiveness indexes produced by two-stage versus one-stage models? (Two-stage models are
  models that regress student demographic variables on pre- and posttest variables in Stage 1 and employ the resulting residuals in a Stage
  2 model predicting posttest from relevant pretests.)
- Is there any difference between effectiveness indexes produced by
  HLM models assuming fixed versus random slopes?
- Does a three-level HLM model that uses student gain scores as the
  outcome variable produce results similar to those produced by status-
  based models?

- How free from bias relative to important student- and school-level contextual variables and pretest scores are the various models?
- Can a longitudinal student growth curve approach to predicting school effect produce bias free results?
- Although not explicitly stated, is there a best model for estimating school effect?

Before discussing a number of thoughtful methodologies for estimating school effect, it is important to reiterate that ranking schools based on unadjusted student test scores or gain scores is neither particularly informative nor fair. The results produced by these systems correlate poorly with the results produced by the model of choice ($rs \leq .508$ for unadjusted test scores, $rs \leq .732$ for gain scores) and produce results with unacceptably high correlations with student background variables and school aggregate variables (as high as $r = .648$ with parental education level; Webster et al., 1995). Evidence suggests that this type of reporting under the guise of determining school or teacher effect does severe injustice to teachers and schools that serve poor and minority student populations. It is important to note that the backbone of most state accountability systems is unadjusted test scores or student gain scores, often not even based on cohort data.

Ordinary least squares regression (OLS) models improve reporting significantly over those models discussed in the previous paragraph as long as the models use data at the individual student level. Using OLS models with aggregated school-level variables produces results that correlate poorly with results produced by the model of choice ($r \leq .58$) and correlate highly with student- and school-level contextual variables. Too much information is lost when student data are aggregated to the school level prior to analysis. The greater the within-group variance of the individual schools, the poorer the estimates produced by the aggregate models (Mendro & Webster, 1993).

OLS models that include all of the individual student demographic variables presented earlier, as well as relevant pretest scores, produce results moderately correlated with the model of choice ($r \leq .8637$) and are relatively unbiased at the individual student level (most $rs \leq .02$). Correlations with background variables become higher than desired at the school level, with the correlation with percentage of African American reaching $-.1225$. If one looks at a grade with relatively few schools (<30) with high within-group variance, such as Grade 8 in this series of studies, the school-level correlations explode to $r \geq .40$ for most SES indicators (Webster et al., 1997a, 1997b).

Implementing a two-stage OLS regression model with student demographic variables regressed on pre- and posttest variables in Stage 1 and the resulting residuals used in a Stage 2 model predicting posttest from relevant pretests significantly improves the equations. Correlations between the indexes produced by the one-stage versus two-stage models consistently hover around $r \geq .95$, and the results from the two-stage model correlate much higher with the model of choice ($r \geq .97$). However, correlations with important school-level contextual variables were not improved (Webster et al., 1995, 1996, 1997a, 1997b). The reason for the development of the original two-stage OLS equations was ease of explanation, not statistical parsimony.

The final series of OLS regression equations examined in these series of studies utilized individual student growth curves based on 2, 3, and 4 years of data. No demographic data were included in the equations because it was believed that the individual student growth curves would serve as a surrogate for student background variables. These equations produced results that correlated poorly with the other OLS regression models ($r \leq .85$), more poorly with the model of choice ($r \leq .75$), had unacceptably high correlations with student ethnicity (r as high as $-.3587$ with African-American students), and registered unacceptable correlations with school-level contextual variables (r as high as $.4621$ with percentage African American). Thus, it seems obvious that individual student growth curves utilized in a standard regression model do not contain all of the information necessary for nonbiased prediction. As an aside, the results produced by using 4 years of prediction correlated $.9992$ with the results produced using 3 years of prediction and included about 5% more of the student population (Webster & Olson, 1988; Webster et al., 1997a, 1997b).

Moving to hierarchical linear models (HLM), a number of questions were investigated across a series of studies. The first involved whether the use of a two- or three-level HLM model would produce improved effectiveness indexes—that is, indexes that were not correlated with student- or school-level contextual variables. It is important to note that the correlation between comparable two-stage OLS regression models and two-stage, two-level HLM models was $r \geq .97$. Both models (OLS and HLM) produced minimal correlations with student-level background variables ($r \leq .01$), but the OLS regression model produced correlations with school-level contextual variables as high as $-.1794$, whereas the HLM model caused all of those correlations to be zero (Webster et al., 1995, 1996, 1997a, 1997b). All HLM models were centered on the grand mean.

The basic three-level HLM model designed to include comparable student- and school-level contextual variables would not run in either a one- or two-stage form. Although several models were attempted, major problems were encountered with the algorithms for solving them. In short, to successfully run a three-level HLM status model, many important contextual variables had to be eliminated from the equations resulting in models that produced unacceptably high correlations with noncontrolled contextual variables (Webster et al., 1995).

A three-level HLM model using gain scores as the unit of analysis instead of pre- and posttest scores was also examined. The results obtained from comparable two-level student-school pretest–posttest HLM models with those obtained from three-level gain score–student–school HLM models were compared. Virtually identical results ($rs \geq .98$) were obtained. Two-level models are more convenient and efficient than three-level models because they can accommodate more Level 1 student and Level 2 school contextual variables and are not nearly as sensitive to multicollinearity and low variance in conditioning variables as are three-level models. Whether fixed or random slopes are assumed, the number of second- and third-level conditioning variables are severely limited in the three-level model. The inability to accommodate sufficient conditioning variables in the three-level HLM gain score model causes results that correlate poorly with the model of choice ($r \leq .40$) and produce correlations as high as .1887 with important student background variables, as well as producing results highly correlated with important school contextual variables that the models are not able to accommodate (rs as high as .4747; Webster et al., 1997a, 1997b; Weerasinghe et al., 1997).

Throughout the course of the various studies, several other important issues were investigated. The issue of one- versus two-stage models—be they OLS regression or HLM—is moot. Correlations between and among one- versus two-stage models consistently hover around $r \geq .95$ for comparable models, and generally there is no practical difference when results are correlated with background variables (Webster et al., 1997a, 1997b). However, the correlations of residuals produced by one-stage HLM models with student-level contextual variables suggest that one-stage HLM models carry suppresser effects not found in two-stage HLM models or OLS regression models. When this result is coupled with the inability to include important school-level contextual variables in one-stage HLM models because of limitations of the models resulting in unsatisfactory correlations with those contextual variables, two-stage models are the models of choice.

The final issue investigated in this series of studies was the fixed versus random slopes issue. Correlations between and among comparable models assuming fixed versus random slopes were generally around $r \geq .98$. Models studied were all two-stage HLM models because three-stage HLM models, including a full array of contextual variables and assuming random slopes, could not be solved. These models produced low correlations with student-level background variables and, when school-level conditioning variables were added, zero correlations with school-level variables. Because the fixed model is much easier to compute and both models produce similar results, our models are fixed slope models.

PROPOSED FORMULAE FOR ESTIMATING
STATEWIDE SCHOOL EFFECT

Based on the analyses conducted through the series of studies reported in this chapter, an HLM two-stage, two-level, fixed model with a full range of student- and school-level contextual variables produces the most bias-free estimates of school effect. This, in conjunction with the current state accountability system, would eliminate many of the inequities of the system described in this chapter.

Student-level variables that could be easily included in statewide HLM models are:[4]

Y_{ij} = Outcome variable of interest for each student i in school j.

X_{1ij} = African American English-Proficient Status (1 if African American, 0 otherwise).

X_{2ij} = Hispanic English-Proficient Status (1 if Hispanic, 0 otherwise).

X_{3ij} = Limited English-Proficient Status (1 if LEP, 0 otherwise).

X_{4ij} = Gender (1 if male, 0 if female).

X_{5ij} = Free or Reduced Lunch Status (1 if subsidized, 0 otherwise).

X_{kij} = Indicates the variable k of ith student in school j for $i = 1, 2, \ldots, I_j$ and $j = 1, 2, \ldots, J$.

School-level variables that could be easily included in statewide HLM models are:

W_{1j} = School Mobility.

W_{2j} = School Overcrowdedness.

W_{3j} = School Percentage on Free or Reduced Lunch.

W_{4j} = School Percentage Minority.

W_{5j} = School Percentage African American.

W_{6j} = School Percentage Hispanic.

W_{7j} = School Percentage Limited English Proficient.

---

[4]If census data can be cross-indexed to existing databases, then family education, income, and poverty indexes can be added at both the student and school levels.

STAGE 1:

$$Y_{ij} = \Lambda_0 + \Lambda_1 X_{1ij} + \Lambda_2 X_{2ij} + \Lambda_3 X_{3ij} + \Lambda_4 X_{4ij} + \Lambda_5 X_{5ij} + + \Lambda_6 (X_{1ij} X_{4ij}) +$$
$$\Lambda_7 (X_{2ij} X_{4ij}) + \Lambda_8 (X_{3ij} X_{4ij}) + \Lambda_9 (X_{1ij} X_{5ij}) + \Lambda_{10} (X_{2ij} X_{5ij}) +$$
$$\Lambda_{11} (X_{3ij} X_{5ij}) + \Lambda_{12} (X_{4ij} X_{5ij}) + \Lambda_{13} (X_{1ij} X_{4ij} X_{5ij}) + \Lambda_{14} (X_{2ij} X_{4ij} X_{5ij}) +$$
$$\Lambda_{15} (X_{3ij} X_{4ij} X_{5ij}) + r_{ij}$$

STAGE 2:

Level 1:

Criterion Variable_R_01$_{ij}$ $= \beta_{0j} + \beta_{1j} R_1\_00_{ij} + \ldots + \beta_{nj} R_n\_00_{ij} + \delta_{ij}$

Where:

Criterion Variable_R_01$_{ij}$ = posttest residual from Stage 1

R_n_00 = n^{th} pretest residual from Stage 1

$\overset{iid}{\delta_{ij}} \sim N(0, \sigma^2).$

Level 2:

$$\beta_{0j} = \gamma_{00} + \gamma_{01} W_{1j} + \gamma_{02} W_{2j} + \ldots + \gamma_{07} W_{7j} + u_{0j}$$
$$\beta_{kj} = \gamma_{k0} + \gamma_{k1} W_{1j} + \gamma_{k2} W_{2j} + \ldots + \gamma_{k7} W_{7j}$$
$$\text{for } k = 1, 2, \ldots, n.$$

$$E[u_{kj}] = 0, \text{ Var/Cov}[u_{kj}] = T, \text{ and } u_{kj} \perp \delta_{ij}$$

$$SEI_j^* = u_{0j}^*$$

SUMMARY

This chapter examined the Texas Accountability System's strengths and weaknesses. It also described possible improvements and statistical models for estimating school effect that could be used to supplement the current system by adding a legitimate value-added component. It summarized 15 years of research on developing these models and specified a recommended model for statewide use.

Weaknesses enumerated include that the system (a) is not fair to schools serving high percentages of minority and poor student populations, (b) has no valid value-added component, (c) is primarily dependent on one test and cross-sectional data, (d) defines continuous enrollment at the district rather than the school level but holds schools accountable, and (e) is administered like it is a game, not like it is a serious accountability system.

This is not to say that the Texas Accountability System has no strong points. Strengths include that (a) the TAAS test is developed by an outside contractor within standards for test development established by the APA and generally displays adequate reliability and validity, (b) there is a straightforward accountability manual covering in detail the rules and regulations of the accountability system, (c) the system includes rigorous requirements of school districts with regard to reporting results to the public, (d) it includes a well-designed academic excellence indicator report that aids in dissemination of results to the public, (e) it features professional scaling of the TAAS so that results are comparable from year to year, (f) there is progress toward reporting a longitudinal dropout rate that promises to be more revealing than the cross-sectional rate currently reported, (g) includes provisions for testing limited English-proficient and special education students, and (h) features a statewide database so that students can be tracked from district to district.

There is some evidence that the Texas Accountability System has been associated with significant increases in achievement among Texas school children (Charles A. Dana Center, 2002). However, with the implementation of the new Texas Assessment of Knowledge And Skills (TAKS), a test that all indications suggest is going to be much more difficult than the TAAS, it is crucial that educators who work with high-minority, high-poverty student populations receive credit for the good work they do. The current accountability system will not reward outstanding performance in schools that serve predominantly impoverished minority children, particularly if those children start well below the established standard.

REFERENCES

Aiken, L. S., & West, S. G. (1991). *Multiple regression: Testing and interpreting interactions.* Newbury Park, CA: Sage.

Bano, S. M. (1985). *The logic of teacher incentives.* Washington, DC: National Association of State Boards of Education.

Bryk, A. S., & Raudenbush, S. W. (1992). *Hierarchical linear models: Applications and data analysis methods.* Newbury Park, CA: Sage.

Bryk, A. S., Raudenbush, S. W., Seltzer, M., & Congdon, R. (1988). *An introduction to HLM: Computer program user's guide* (2nd ed.). Chicago, IL: University of Chicago.

Charles A. Dana Center. (2002). *The Texas Statewide Systemic Imitative.* The University of Texas.

Clopton, P., Bishop, W., & Klein, D. (2000). *Statewide mathematics assessment in Texas.* http://mathematicallvcorrect.com/lonestar.htm.

Cohen, J. (1968). Multiple regression as a general data-analytic system. *Psychological Bulletin, 70,* 426–443.

Cohen, J., & Cohen, P. (1975). *Applied multiple regression/correlation analyses for the behavioral sciences* (1st ed.). Hillsdale, NJ: Lawrence Erlbaum Associates.

Darlington, R. B. (1990). *Regression and linear models.* New York: McGraw-Hill.

Dempster, A. P., Rubin, D. B., & Tsutakawa, R. V. (1981). Estimation in covariance components models. *Journal of the American Statistical Association, 76,* 341–353.

Denson, K. (1999, August). *Final evaluation of the 1998–99 Dallas Reading Plan* (Evaluation Report REIS99-147-2). *Dallas Independent School District*, 318 pp.

Denson, K. (2000, August). *Final evaluation of the 1999–2000 Dallas Reading Plan* (Evaluation Report REIS00-147-2). *Dallas Independent School District*, 367 pp.

Elston, R. C., & Grizzle, J. E. (1962). Estimation of time response curves and their confidence bands. *Biometrics, 18,* 148–159.

Felter, M., & Carlson, D. (1985). *Identification of exemplary schools on a large scale.* In G. Austin and H. Gerber (Eds.), *Research on exemplary schools* (pp. 83–96). New York: Academic Press.

Fennessey, J., & Salganik, H. L. (1983). Credible comparison of instructional impact: The RAGS procedure. *Journal of Educational Measurement, 2*(3), 13–17.

Glass, G. V. (1978). Standards and criteria. *Journal of Educational Measurement, 15,* 237–261.

Goldstein, H. (1987). *Multilevel models in educational and social research.* New York: Oxford University Press.

Good, T. L., & Brophy, J. E. (1986). School effects. In M. C. Wittrock (Ed.), *Handbook of research on teaching* (3rd ed., pp. 570–602). New York: Macmillan.

Henderson, C. R. (1984). *Applications of linear models in animal breeding.* Guelph, Canada: University of Guelph.

Jaeger, R. M. (1992). Weak measurement serving presumptive policy. *Kappan, 74*(2), 118–128.

Kirst, M. (1986). New directions for state education data systems. *Education and Urban Society, 18*(2), 343–357.

Klitgaard, R. E., & Hall, G. R. (1973). *A statistical search for unusually effective schools.* Santa Monica, CA: Rand.

Laird, N. M., & Ware, H. (1982). Random-effects models for longitudinal data. *Biometrics, 38,* 963–974.

Longford, N. T. (1987). A fast scoring algorithm for maximum likelihood estimation in unbalanced mixed models with nested random effects. *Biometrika, 74*(4), 817–827.

Mason, W. M., Wong, G. Y., & Entwistle, B. (1984). Contextual analysis through the multilevel linear model. In S. Leinhardt (Ed.), *Sociological methodology* (pp. 72–103). San Francisco: Jossey-Bass.

McKenzie, D. (1983). School effectiveness research: A synthesis and assessment. In P. Duttweiler (Ed.), *Educational productivity and school effectiveness* (pp. 28–50). Austin, TX: Southwest Educational Development Laboratory.

McNeil, L., & Valenzuela, A. (2000). *The harmful impact of the TAAS system of testing in Texas: Beneath the accountability rhetoric.* Unpublished manuscript.

Mendro, R. L., & Webster, W. J. (1993, October). *Using school effectiveness indices to identify and reward effective schools.* Paper presented at the Rocky Mountain Research Association, Las Cruces, NM.

Mendro, R. L., Jordan, H. R., Gomez, E., Anderson, M. C., & Bembry, K. L. (1998, April). *Longitudinal teacher effects on student achievement and their relation to school and project evaluation.* Paper presented at the annual meeting of the American Educational Research Association, San Diego, CA.

Millman, J. (Ed.). (1981). *Handbook of teacher evaluation.* Beverly Hills, CA: Sage.

National Center for Educational Statistics. (2000). *NAEP Performance.* www.nces.ed.gov/nationsreportcard.

Rosenburg, B. (1973). Linear regression with randomly dispersed parameters. *Biometrika, 60,* 61–75.

Saka, T. (1984, April). *Indicators of school effectiveness: Which are the most valid and what impacts upon them?* Paper presented at the annual meeting of the American Educational Research Association, San Francisco, CA. (ERIC ED 306 277)

Stotsky, S. (1998). *Analysis of the Texas reading tests: Grades 4, 8, and 10, 1995–98.* http://www.taxresearch.org/read.htm.

Webster, W. J. (1998, April). *A comprehensive system for the evaluation of schools.* Paper presented at the annual meeting of the American Educational Research Association, San Diego, CA.

Webster, W. J. (2002). A comprehensive school and personnel evaluation system. *Journal of School Research and Information, 20*(1), 36–46.

Webster, W. J., Almaguer, T., & Orsak, T. (2002). State and school district evaluation in the United States. In D. Stufflebeam & T. Kellaghan (Eds.), *International handbook on educational evaluation* (pp. 929–949). New York: Kluwer.

Webster, W. J., & Mendro, R. L. (1995). An accountability system featuring both value-added and product measures of schooling. In A. J. Shinkfield & D. L. Stufflebeam (Eds.), *Teacher evaluation: Guide to effective practice* (pp. 350–376). Boston: Kluwer.

Webster, W. J., & Mendro, R. L. (1997). *The Dallas value-added accountability system.* In J. Millman (Ed.), *Grading teachers, grading schools* (pp. 81–99). Newbury Park, CA: Sage.

Webster, W. J., Mendro, R. L., & Almaguer, T. D. (1993). *Effectiveness indices: The major component of an equitable accountability system.* ERIC TM 019 193.

Webster, W. J., Mendro, R. L., & Almaguer, T. (1994). Effectiveness indices: A "value added" approach to measuring school effect. *Studies in Educational Evaluation, 20,* 113–145.

Webster, W. J., Mendro, R. L., Bembry, K., & Orsak, T. H. (1995). *Alternative methodologies for identifying effective schools.* Distinguished Paper Session, American Educational Research Association, San Francisco, CA. *(ERIC EA 027 189)*

Webster, W. J., Mendro, R. L., Orsak, T. H., & Weerasinghe, D. (1996, March). *The applicability of selected regression and hierarchical linear models to the estimation of school and teacher effects.* A paper presented at the annual meeting of the American Educational Research Association, New York, NY.

Webster, W. J., Mendro, R. L., Orsak, T., Weerasinghe, D., & Bembry, K. (1997a). Little practical difference and pie in the sky: A response to Thum and Bryk and a rejoinder to Sykes. In J. Millman (Ed.), *Grading teachers, grading schools* (pp. 120–130). Newbury Park, CA: Sage.

Webster, W. J., Mendro, R. L., Orsak, T. H., & Weerasinghe, D. (1997b, March). *A comparison of the results produced by selected regression and hierarchical linear models in the estimation of school and teacher effect.* Paper presented at the annual meeting of the American Educational Research Association, Chicago, IL. Accepted for publication in *Multiple Linear Regression Viewpoints.*

Webster, W. J., & Olson, G. H. (1988). A quantitative procedure for the identification of effective schools. *Journal of Experimental Education, 56,* 213–219.

Weerasinghe, D., Orsak, T., & Mendro, R. (1997, January). *Value added productivity indicators: A statistical comparison of the pre-test/post-test model and gain model.* A paper presented at the 1997 annual meeting of the Southwest Educational Research Association, Austin, TX.

CHAPTER SIX

Deep Training + Coaching: A Capacity-Building Model for Teacher Development

Robert B. Cooter, Jr.
University of Texas at Arlington

Many urban school districts in the United States fail in carrying out their primary mission: to help *all* children become fully literate. The central reason, at least from my perspective, is that the initial training of teachers in colleges of education, and the subsequent professional development (i.e., inservice training) provided by school districts for practicing teachers, lack sufficient depth to ensure the development of expertise or capacity in essential teaching methods. In this chapter, we first examine some of the causal factors for this failure in capacity building by teachers colleges and school districts. Later a model for effective professional development is offered that could be applied to each venue.

UNPLUGGED: WHY MANY TEACHERS COLLEGES FAIL URBAN CHILDREN

In 1997, I arrived at the Dallas Independent School District (DISD) to assume duties as the assistant superintendent for reading and language arts instruction. My colleagues and I soon thereafter conducted a status study of some 3,000 kindergarten through Grade 3 classrooms that provided us with some interesting insights. Among many other things, we discovered that the knowledge and skill level of approximately 75% of the teaching force was inadequate. That figure was not difficult to calculate: If approximately three fourths of the children were unable to read on level at the end of third grade, the effectiveness level of our efforts must be directly correlated to that number. I also became concerned when learning of the incredibly high teacher burnout/turnover rate and the utter paucity of teaching materials.

As a veteran teacher education professor, I had assumed colleges were doing a good job of preparing teachers for our nations schools. Yet it was clear that the least affluent of our children were being short changed in their literacy education. How could my university colleagues and I have been so out of touch with inner-city realities? How could we have become so *unplugged* from the needs of poor children?

To assist in our teacher training efforts in DISD, I invited college of education faculty and their leadership from the five area universities who provided most of our teachers to discuss the literacy emergency in our schools and seek systemic solutions. After all teachers colleges are our pipeline for teachers, I reasoned, and DISD was one of their biggest customers. Further, all but one were public universities supported by taxpayer funds. Certainly the public should be confident that their public schools are staffed with fully trained teachers ready to meet the needs of their children.

I began our first meeting by summarizing test data and other student performance indicators from DISD in reading and writing. I shared my belief that we—the school district and teachers colleges—were inextricably linked in the mission to provide successful and high-quality literacy education to all urban children. Feeling passionate about the vocation of literacy education, I suggested that when children fail to become literate, the problem is jointly shared by the school district and colleges that trained the teachers. We concluded the initial presentation by agreeing that the war on illiteracy was winnable if we locked arms and worked together to produce teachers armed with the requisite knowledge and skills.

As the meeting came to a close, I was heartened by several voices of genuine concern and pledges of support, but I was also troubled by the rather tepid response of the majority. Most professors and deans seemed to feel it was inappropriate for them to be held accountable for producing teachers skilled in such areas as effective classroom management, meeting the needs of English language learners, teaching practices that lead to demonstrable learning outcomes, and assisting students having serious learning difficulties. Indeed, many actually stated that to hold college of education faculty accountable for the actual performance of the teachers they trained would surely be an infringement on their academic freedom. Imagine, if you will, other professional schools taking this attitude. Consider medical school faculty refusing to be held responsible for graduating physicians who are unprepared to treat even the most basic ailments of strep throat or bronchitis, a law school consistently graduating attorneys unable to draw up a simple contract, or a business school whose graduates continually caused Enronlike failures. It appeared to me that a reexamination of education colleges and their responsibilities to children was in order. How did education colleges become so unplugged from their service constituents?

Perilous Homogeneity

Public education has generally been thought of as being reasonably effective for the masses since its inception. Only in the past three decades have school district leaders seen a growing spirit of discontent, particularly in urban centers. Perhaps one reason is that the public has greater access than ever before to hard data.

The landmark *Brown v. Board of Education* Supreme Court decision outlawing the "separate but equal" doctrine, coupled with the effects of the civil rights movement of the 1960s, gave Americans from lower socioeconomic groups a voice they had not previously enjoyed. With the implementation of the federal *Elementary and Secondary Education Act* in the 1970s, and subsequent reporting of student achievement by racial group via the National Assessment of Educational Progress (NAEP), families became much better informed about how well their children were doing in acquiring literacy and numeracy skills. The veil was being lifted from the eyes of many city-dwelling Americans in the 1970s, and the image was bleak—*too many of their children were weak in reading and writing and dropping out of school in record numbers, whereas children of the more affluent were doing reasonably well.* Pressure was brought to bear as these stakeholders gained greater political access in the coming decades.

The literacy gulf between poor and more affluent children does not appear to be the result of some sort of insidious plot, however, but the outcome of an overly homogeneous education system. Here is how this kind of dysfunctional homogeneity has developed. The majority of people who become teachers come from the middle class. They typically attend public suburban schools and are taught by middle-class teachers from similar backgrounds and value systems as themselves. Most new teachers speak English as their only language. When these young people go off to university, they are mostly taught by middle-class professors who have a background quite similar to their own. Their student teaching and other field experiences are usually in (where else?) middle-class suburban schools under the guidance of a middle-class teacher. It is not surprising, then, that most new teachers flock to middle-class suburban school districts for jobs (where they feel most comfortable) instead of inner-city schools. It is worth noting, however, that even this system of teacher preparation fails to serve suburban schools well: About 50% of new teachers leave the profession in the first 5 years (Easley, 2000) even when they are matched to a school that closely matches their heritage. Thus, comparatively few new teachers choose to teach in an inner-city school district (MacDonald, 1999).

Having gone through the experience myself early in my career, I can attest to the stress a new teacher sometimes feels when his goal of serving urban children collides with a degree of culture shock. I found that some of the issues that can affect a new teacher's success include verbal communications (e.g., English language learners [ELL], dialect, misunderstandings about body language), establishing family communications, maintaining order in the classroom when one does not really understand what *normal* behavior looks like with different populations, and establishing trust and mutual respect. Thus, a teacher viewing life through middle-class lenses can quickly become frustrated in an urban setting unless extensive capacity building has occurred in that environment. Further, principals and teachers who attempt to operate an urban school (whose student population is highly mobile and has significant language needs) like a suburban school (whose population is comparatively homogeneous and stable) will almost certainly fail.

Colleges of education tend to operate from an ultrahomogeneous, one-size-fits-all paradigm. This is true whether we consider the preparation of teachers, principals, or superintendents. For example, if a college student wishes to one day teach in a suburban school, she gets the college of education's "teacher preparation program." If another student plans to teach in an urban school, he gets the identical program, just as a student who wants to dedicate her career to serving rural children. Teacher educators have known for many decades that children—the target population for their profession—have different needs regardless of socioeconomic background, yet college faculty typically train teachers with little or no differentiation. It is easy to conclude that a middle-class child is far more likely to have a teacher who understands his needs than is a child from an urban center who lives in poverty.

Lack of Accountability

The question remains: How do we provide better, more effective teachers for urban children? One remedy would be to recruit more future teachers into our colleges who are indigenous to the urban centers. The problem with this proposition is that many inner-city residents who are able to attend college, especially those from lower socioeconomic groups, are actually discouraged from becoming teachers by their peers. The teaching and nursing professions were virtually the only professions open to poor and minority citizens until the latter half of the 20th century, so urban families

often encourage college-bound children to seek the more high-dollar/
high-prestige professions. Besides even if we were able to quadruple the
number of indigenous urban teachers over current levels, we would still
be terribly short in filling yearly vacancies. Further, if we were to continue
to prepare all teachers using the same one-size-fits-all paradigm, the indigenous teachers would be rendered almost as ineffective as their middle-
class counterparts. A better solution would be the complete restructuring
of teacher education programs using special career paths focusing on
meeting the specific needs of specific populations (e.g., a major in "Urban
Education"), coupled with a much improved model for expertise development in key pedagogical areas.

WHY SCHOOL DISTRICTS OFTEN FAIL IN THEIR RESCUE EFFORTS

Literacy education rescue efforts seem to fail in urban school districts
largely as a result of an interaction of three variables: precipitous re-
sponses by superintendents to political pressure, anemic efforts at capacity building, and overreliance on scripted programmatic solutions. Because a discussion of scripted programmatic solutions was presented
earlier (chap. 2, this volume), I focus here on the first two roadblocks to
urban literacy reform mentioned before.

Precipitous Responses to Political Pressure

School boards in most locales primarily have only one card they can play
in school reform: hiring and firing the superintendent (i.e., they have no
direct authority over school personnel). This partially explains why the average tenure of superintendents nationally is less than 3 years: Students in
urban centers perform poorly on state or national tests, school board
members get pressure from special interest groups and parents in their
precinct, and then school board members exert pressure on the superintendent to do something. This knee-jerk response by school board members can and does happen even if a multiyear intervention has recently
been put in place and was approved by school board members previously.
In the case of the DISD, this sort of dysfunctional school board pressure
contributed greatly to the district's problem of keeping a superintendent;
from 1995 to 2001, DISD had 5 superintendents and one interim superintendent, all of whom felt pressured to come up with a new literacy plan
for school board members demanding change. *Change*, at least in this instance, may be defined as having the appearance of addressing hot button
issues *immediately*.

Anemic Capacity Building

Teachers, as with other professionals in business, medicine, and science, require high-quality and ongoing professional development to remain on the cutting edge of effectiveness. As E. F. Baskin once remarked in a DISD Reading Department meeting, "You win on talent!", meaning we must invest in the betterment of a school district's *talent*—teachers. Without this piece of the rescue puzzle, school districts cannot break through the performance glass ceiling they experience when relying on programmatic solutions alone. Second language learners, students with special needs, and above average children require idiosyncratic and flexible instructional adaptations that commercial programs are unable to address. Further, many average and below average city kids fail to respond to commercial programs and need alternative learning strategies delivered by a well-trained teacher.

In school districts where the superintendency turns over regularly or where school boards stymie leadership efforts by creating dysfunctional pressure on the superintendent and her staff, analytic-sequential-scientific interventions are surrendered to a quick-fix mentality because the message to superintendents is, "do something about our problems, or else. . . ." *Success* in this pressure-cooked arena is not necessarily defined as getting positive results, but on having the appearance of doing something quickly. Small wonder the route urban superintendents steadfastly follow is to take a programmatic approach and limit capacity building to the anemic inservice model even when they are aware that the chances of achieving substantial improvement is unlikely.

High-quality capacity building, although capable of obtaining major systemic results over time, is not quick or simple. Complex problems often require complex solutions. Complex solutions usually take many months and years to achieve. So what does effective capacity building involve?

A CAPACITY-BUILDING MODEL
FOR TEACHER DEVELOPMENT

During the 20th century, a number of educational researchers (Bloom, 1956; Vygotsky, 1962) described ways in which learning occurs. Whether the learning is by urban children acquiring basic literacy skills or teachers becoming proficient in a new instructional methodology, the learning curve is both predictable and constant. Figure 6.1 presents a capacity-building model for teacher development reflecting the fundamental stages of learning drawn from the earlier work of Vygotsky (1962), and Bloom (1956).

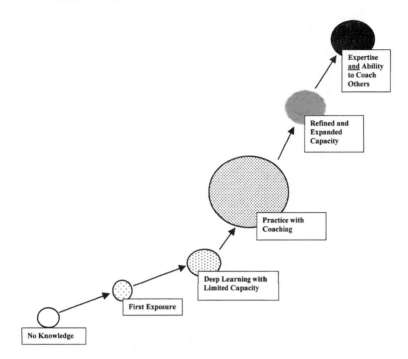

FIG. 6.1.   Capacity-building model for teacher development: Deep training
+ coaching.

A key feature of this capacity-building model for teacher development is
distributed learning over time. It acknowledges that neither cognitive development of new knowledge nor field practice is sufficient. Rather, both
elements—new learning developed over time combined with extensive
practice under the guidance of a more knowledgeable coach—is the most
effective combination.

Professional development for teachers usually begins and ends, sadly,
with what I term *awareness-level* or *first-exposure* training. One- or two-
day inservice workshops for teachers or, for that matter, college classes
where numerous aspects of reading and writing instruction are introduced during the semester and are awareness-level experiences. These experiences create little more than simple awareness of a pedagogical construct. As the model indicates, first-exposure training is a critical first step
in the development of new expertise, but is never sufficient. Many a
school administrator has invested in inservice training in an area of great
student need only to become frustrated when no positive improvement
occurs. Inservice workshops are almost invariably incapable of doing
more than creating a working knowledge about a topic. One colleague
calls the exclusive use of inservice training for teacher capacity building a

"spray and pray" strategy—spray the teachers with lots of information and then pray that some of it will somehow take root and produce change.

Here is an example of first-exposure training from my own experiences. Guided reading (Fountas & Pinnell, 1996), as the reader may know, is a structured approach for small-group reading instruction that helps early readers develop fluent reading habits and strengthen their vocabulary. Over a 3-year period in the Dallas Reading Academy, we found that the basic components of guided reading could be learned in several 3-hour awareness-level/first-exposure sessions, much like the way the approach is introduced in college classes. However, it soon became clear that much more study and practice was needed for teachers to internalize the information and implement the strategy in their classrooms. We had to go deeper in our capacity-building efforts if we were to produce positive change in our classrooms.

The next level of teacher capacity building is *deep learning with limited capacity*. This level involves significant study of the new topic or strategy beyond the awareness level, coupled with the teacher's first attempts at classroom application. In the case of helping Dallas teachers use the guided reading approach (Fountas & Pinnell, 1996), teachers were required to read the *Guided Reading* textbook (Fountas & Pinnell, 1996) in its entirety and demonstrate their knowledge of key concepts. Demonstrations of their learning occurred in two venues: in subsequent Reading Academy classes, and during one-on-one coaching sessions with expert mentor teachers called *Lead Reading Teachers*. Their knowledge of the rudiments of guided reading was further crystallized in a special session with co-author Gay Su Pinnell who lectured on the basics of her approach. Thus, at the deep learning with limited capacity level, teachers deepen their knowledge about the topic or strategy, but have only experimented with the pedagogy with students thus far.

Practice with coaching is the essential next step in teacher capacity building and requires massive classroom practice over time with the aid of an expert coach. Actual coaching sessions should focus on improving the quality of implementation and dealing with substantive issues experienced by the teacher in training. Lead reading teachers in the DISD initiative frequently modeled guided reading lessons for Reading Academy teachers in their own classrooms. They also observed academy teachers as they taught lessons and coaching sessions afterward, then recommended next steps for the academy teachers to try. This powerful stage of development ensured implementation because the Academy teachers knew their lead reading teacher/coach would visit their classroom regularly expecting to see specific strategies demonstrated with students. We also discovered, as have others (Southeast Center for Teaching Quality, 2002), that providing mentor teachers to assist teachers in training not only ensured implementation of new methods, but also helped retain these teachers in hard-to-staff schools.

In the final two stages of the model, teacher capacity continues to deepen appreciably. *Refined and expanded capacity* occurs as the teacher fully understands most elements of the new pedagogy and regularly uses them as part of her usual protocol of instruction. Dallas teachers in the first cohort of the Reading Academy generally reached refined and expanded capacity with the guided reading approach by the third semester of implementation. Strategies began to feel natural and automatic, and student performance in reading improved appreciably on all measures (Cooter, 2002). Lead reading teachers (LRTs) were now able to speak with the first year Reading Academy graduates (called *laureates*) as peers comparing notes to refine classroom practice—LRTs were now in a maintenance or collegial mode.

Expertise and ability to coach others is the final stage in the teacher capacity-building model. Relative mastery of the new pedagogy has been achieved, and the teacher, if needed, is capable of coaching others on the strategy. The term *relative mastery* is used here because any complicated pedagogical method requires a great deal of time and practice to master. Teachers using guided reading as a strategy, for example, often discover they are able to do such things as select appropriate books for instruction and conduct guided reading lessons with ease, yet may feel less confident about their ability to conduct and interpret running records as a diagnostic tool. On the whole, however, the teacher has reached a level of proficiency and expertise using the method.

Is it possible for a teacher to be considered an expert while still having areas needing further development? Vygotsky would have responded in the affirmative. He felt that with any complicated task, we are continually at some stage of learning; we reside permanently in what he termed the *zone of proximal development*. That is why master teachers everywhere continue to burn the late night oil pursuing ever more effective ways to help children learn. The true benchmark for expertise in teaching is this: *Urban children becoming more literate than ever before and at greater levels of proficiency*.

IMPROVING TEACHER DEVELOPMENT IN TEACHERS COLLEGES AND SCHOOL DISTRICTS

There are several implications of the capacity-building model for teacher development. Colleges of education, particularly those serving as a pipeline to urban schools, might well review the effectiveness of their existing teacher development programs in terms of how well the *students* (i.e., public school children) of their graduates do on assessments of literacy, mathematics, and other critical academic skill areas. This would require a different mindset and level of accountability than has traditionally been the case. If they found that graduates of their programs had consistent problems helping children achieve as expected, professors might consider contrasting the capacity-building model for teacher development with the manner in which they typically structure their classes so as to better provide potent deep learning and coaching experiences. They would also need to consider the socioeconomic and mobility patterns of the children to be served in constructing their curricula for effectiveness.

Because deep training plus coaching takes much more time to accomplish than mere awareness-level/first-exposure training, professors need to adopt a less-is-more strategy in rebuilding their curricula. In other words, what are the most essential knowledge and skills one *must* have as a beginning teacher in an urban school? The answer to this question should fit within the twin parameters of (a) available time in a baccalaureate program for teachers, and (b) requirements of a capacity-building model for teacher development. It is likely that only about one third of the traditional curriculum for elementary teachers can be developed to an expertise level.

The capacity-building model for teacher development can also be of benefit to urban school district leaders. For districts having extreme difficulties with literacy education (e.g., I would define this as more than 15% of students reading below grade level by third grade, dropout rates in excess of 10% when comparing 9th-grade enrollment to the 12th-grade graduation figures), a two-stage approach is recommended. First, implement a basal program having the best track record in other demographically similar districts. This should be determined using norm-referenced test score summaries from the comparison districts as opposed to high-stakes state tests. The program should be mandated in the district for a 2-year period while the second stage of the remedy is put into place (see chap. 2, this volume) for a broader explanation of this Stage 1 approach).

Stage 2 would be to develop and implement a vigorous program of teacher development following the protocol described in the capacity-building model for teacher development. Our research in DISD revealed that a 90-hour professional development program for teachers (80 hours is the minimum time needed for results) is sufficient to raise the basic competency level of teachers to the early stages of the refined and expanded capacity level shown in Fig. 6.1.

For best results, a second tier of training should be developed in specific areas of need for each teacher. This would involve principals reviewing the performance of students in each of her teacher's classrooms over a period of at least 3 years, determining any problem areas for each teacher's students, then providing each teacher with deep training and expert coaching in their specific need area(s). If, for example, the students in Ms. Spencer second-grade class over the past 5 years have consistently performed poorly on measures of reading vocabulary, then Ms. Spencer would be required to attend a 6-week/18-hour program of deep study and coaching on methods of improving students' reading vocabulary. A teacher/mentor with an exemplary record of success in vocabulary instruction or a district-provided LRT would follow up with Ms. Spencer to assist her in implementing the new teaching strategies. Ideally the bulk of the training would occur in late July or early August, and the teacher would have an extended contract to pay her a proper per diem for her time. This would enable her to begin implementation at the beginning of the school year when the new ideas were still fresh—a kind of just in time model of delivery. Other short-term modules could be offered for teachers needing specific help in such instructional areas as phonemic awareness, phonics, reading comprehension, fluency, or writing. In summary, the idea is to provide broad-brush training for all teachers to establish good basic instruction in all classrooms, followed by specific and ongoing need-based advanced training.

Once the two-stage model has had a chance to gain purchase in the district, many benefits can occur. In DISD, for example, we found that the attrition rate of teachers who had attended our Reading Academy ($n = $ ~2,200), which was based on this capacity-building model for teacher development, dropped to nearly zero. (DISD typically has to replace 1,000–2,000 teachers per year. The national average for teacher attrition in elementary schools is about 11% [Easley, 2000; MacDonald, 1999].) This convinced us that when teachers receive professional development opportunities targeted specifically to their teaching needs, they are less likely to leave their assignment. Most important, student performance on all measures improved significantly, although we were only permitted by the various superintendents to develop Stage 2 of the recommended plan noted previously.

MOVING THE NEEDLE

A corporate change management expert and advisor to the Dallas Reading Plan, Dale Kesler, once remarked that we must find new ways to "move the needle in the right direction." The preeminent catalyst for positive change in urban schools (i.e., moving the needle) is improved teacher capacity. The capacity-building model for teacher development presented offers one research-based explanation as to how we can move the literacy needle in the right direction for urban children and the teachers who serve their needs.

REFERENCES

Bloom, B. (1956). *Taxonomy of educational objectives*. New York: David McKay.

Cooter, R. B. (2002, May). Systemic reform efforts in a large urban school district: Implementing balanced literacy instruction. Keynote address presented at the Balanced Reading Special Interest Group session, 47th annual conference of the International Reading Association, San Francisco, CA.

Easley, J. (2000). *Teacher attrition and staff development for retention*. East Lansing, MI: National Center for Research on Teacher Learning. (ERIC Document Reproduction Services No. ED 446054)

Fountas, I., & Pinnell, G. S. (1996). *Guided reading*. Portsmouth, NH: Heinemann.

MacDonald, D. (1999). Teacher attrition: A review of literature. *Teaching and Teacher Education, 15*(8), 835–848.

Southeast Center for Teaching Quality. (2002). *Recruiting teachers for hard-to-staff schools*. Chapel Hill, NC: University of North Carolina Press.

Vygotsky, L. S. (1962). *Thought and language*. Cambridge, MA: MIT Press.

CHAPTER SEVEN

An Alchemist's Tale (or . . .
The Marriage of Technology
and Literacy in Trying Times)

Lee Allen
Dallas Independent School District

PROLOGUE: IN THE COURT OF THE CRIMSON QUEEN

In a land not so far away and in a time not so long ago lived a Queen. Now this Queen had ruled only a short time in this troubled land for this land had many factions, each struggling for its voice to be heard among a great deal of shouting. One side claimed the Queen as one of their own, whereas the other side saw her as an enemy. There was another side, the advisors, but they kept their cards close to their vests for fear of revealing their hands.

At this time, the Queen was assembling her new Court because her old Court turned out to be filled with saboteurs who scorned her and considered her their enemy. Some who continued to advise her also scorned her, but they dared not show this in her presence. Instead they continued to flatter her and pretend to be admirers while they conspired to overthrow her. In assembling her Court, the Queen sent word out far and wide to find those whom she could trust and would support her ideas. One of these was a Guru of Alchemy, who arrived from the mountains. He had encountered the Queen once before, and she agreed with his ideas regarding alchemy and trusted his knowledge of the arcane arts.

Another arrival from afar was the Czar of Literacy, who came from the woodland and was a prolific scribe, having written many tomes on his art. He, too, arrived with new ideas. The local gentry also supported this Czar, and they filled the coffers to offer him abundant resources to pursue his vision because it was also *their* vision. The vision they shared was that one day all the children in this troubled land would be able to read and be knowledgeable in all things. Unlike his predecessors, this Czar of Literacy had a plan—a Master Literacy Plan.

A WOODSMAN—A WORDSPLAN

This Plan was detailed and filled with the sorts of strategies that sometimes only the knowledgeable could appreciate. Because of this, some in the Queen's Court did not understand the Czar's Plan and thus disliked and mistrusted him. Part of this detailed plan involved the services of the Guru of Alchemy. This would involve the combined wisdom of the leaders of literacy and the best alchemists available. They were to formulate a plan of their own, coinciding with the Master Literacy Plan, and include the mystical elements of alchemy. It was to be a marriage between the magical properties of the computing devices and the essential mechanics of literacy. It was deemed (by those bestowed with such wisdom) that an opportune moment in a child's secular upbringing would be the time when the child had entered the third year of primary learning. Thus, it was given a name: Aim Thrice! This designation indicated that it was a goal targeting the children in the third year of learning.

LUCRE MUST BE LOCATED!

The first task was to locate a source of lucre to fund such a noble endeavor. This would prove difficult because, alas, no one in the Court had set aside sufficient funds to buy the expensive devices and lesson modules needed to help the children learn to read and cipher. So a search for funds began. Some thought to petition the Queen for an official handout while others inquired whether the Grand Council might appropriate the requisite coin. Neither of these possibilities was deemed likely to succeed, in the end, because almost all of the monies were already dispensed.

The Czar of Literacy and the Guru of Alchemy met to determine from whence the funding could be derived. An elder suggested that a closer look at the Book of Official Entitlements might offer some recourse—that was it! The Book of Official Entitlements spoke of monies that could be utilized for the learning modules and devices required to operate them. There was one problem: The Official Entitlement monies would only go so far in covering the needs of the third year of primary schooling. In fact, the funds would only allow for one third of these classrooms to be appropriately outfitted. There was actually another problem: There were a few third year classrooms that did not meet the requirements for Official Entitlements, and they could not be endowed in the same manner as the others.

What could these seers do to accomplish their goal of granting all the children in the third year of primary schooling a magical computing device and accompanying incantations to assist in their acquisition of literacy adeptness? Their answer came mathematically and most logically: Aim Thrice would be a *4-year* plan. This plan could accommodate one third of the third year children who were allowed to partake of the Official Entitlements; the subsequent year another third of similarly blessed children; the third year the last third of these; and on the fourth year, those other children who were not fortunate enough to receive an Official Entitlement using other moneys carefully saved for that purpose.

With the plan thus created, it was placed into action. First, the special guides for this project had to be identified. The finest alchemists well versed in the learning arts were chosen, along with masters of literacy. Next a person who best understood literacy was chosen to be the Primary Literacy Guide. The Primary Guide would represent the Czar of Literacy in enacting Aim Thrice and seeing the edict carried forth throughout the land. The 4-year plan was set into motion!

LET THEM EAT FURNISHINGS

All was well and good for a short while, but soon the fickle Hand of Fate began to alter the course of events in a most terrible way. One version of this infamous legend has it that the flatterers and panderers among the Queen's entourage conspired with her enemies to trick her into committing a crime, thus ensuring her downfall. Others tell a tale of a woefully naïve Queen who began to believe in the illusion that she was omnipotent and could not be harmed. In any event, her downfall did come, and whether she succumbed to malevolent witchery or her own utter folly it did not matter—the Queen was dethroned and cast into the dungeon never to be seen or heard from again.

Her enemies greeted this development with delight, but her recently arrived advisors, the Guru and Czar, were extremely dismayed. What would become of the kingdom's children and their literacy needs—the quest that had brought them from afar? Would a newly installed potentate accept their theories and methods? Time would surely tell. . . . In the meantime, Aim Thrice was in progress—the Official Entitlements were being distributed, the mechanisms and tomes gathered, the pedagogues enlightened. The academies that were to be the first recipients were excited. The stage was set, and then the Primary Guide had a change of heart. Perhaps those who had entrusted him with this magnificent task had a change of heart.

Anyway, another who would act as Primary Guide for Aim Thrice replaced him. She arrived with a pedigree as a merchant. This was not a bad thing, but some viewed her arrival as Primary Guide with much skepticism. Others decided to wait and see what the outcome would be. It would not take long.

While the pedagogues were being enlightened, the devices delivered, and the manuscripts unfurled, the Primary Guide was charged with the disbursement of the Official Entitlements. Disburse them she did because the Official Entitlements fund was rather large, and the Primary Guide of Aim Thrice at this time answered to one with little interest in how coin was spent. In fact spending from the Entitlement was often, well, curious. The Primary Guide acquired lavish furnishings for her occupational quarters, made of fine wood with many trappings, and she engaged her friends and confidantes to perform duties as hostesses at gloaming gatherings, all in the name of Aim Thrice, of course. Many modules for the Aim Thrice devices were also obtained, so many, in fact, that soon those who served under the Primary Guide could not find rooms to fill with them. So the modules were placed wherever there was space: under stairwells, in cupboards and cloakrooms, and stacked unopened in unused amenities. There were LOTS of modules for devices, but the devices were being placed in the great halls of the pedagogues who did not know that they were to receive this wealth of materiel. They were not to receive these modules for a very long time.

AIM HIGH—BUT STAY BELOW THE KEEP

In the meantime while Aim Thrice was in progress, the Grand Council had anointed the new potentate. He was not quite King, but had similar powers and bore a striking resemblance to the ruler of fabled Lilliput. He was a kindly man, not ill intentioned, but he knew little of Literacy and Alchemy. The Czar and Guru were subsequently summoned to the potentate's quarters, where they were informed, along with others in the Court, that they were to answer to the newly appointed Grand Vizier. Now the Grand Vizier was not at all like the potentate, and he eyed all the advisors with deep suspicion. He called them all to his quarters, one by one, to let each know that he expected loyalty and submission to his views, whether they were views based on knowledge or unproved speculation—he was, after all, Grand Vizier! Well some in the Court were not at all pleased by this development, and several of them left the Court to strike out on their own destiny. One was the highly regarded Court Statistician, and his loss was viewed by many as insurmountable. One of his minions was designated as his replacement in the Grand Vizier's court, and this person had the demeanor and bearing of a lapdog. Things did not bode well for the Czar of Literacy and the Guru of Alchemy.

With the passing of days, the Primary Guide of Aim Thrice continued to spend the Entitlement coin in an improvident manner, but grew increasingly bored with her lifestyle. She made the decision to return to the ways and life of a merchant. It was left to others to discover what had become of the devices, modules, lavish furnishings, and trappings with which she had surrounded herself, and this was to be no small chore. A replacement Primary Guide was hurriedly appointed to assume the helm of Aim Thrice and immediately set out to locate the many missing articles with admirable vigor. She and others tasked to assist her began to retrace the mazelike path of the Entitlement funds from the source to the many articles acquired with them. She began to catalog the items as they were eventually located: under stairwells, in cupboards and cloakrooms, and stacked unopened in unused amenities. This endeavor took over three phases of the moon, but eventually all the missing items were located and sent to the halls of learning where they truly belonged. The pedagogues with Aim Thrice were pleased with this event even if it had taken over an entire planting and harvest cycle to arrive. The replacement Primary Guide even discovered unspent coin in the coffers, and this was used to expand Aim Thrice and its reach into the halls of learning and the little ones for whom it was designated. For now all was well with Aim Thrice.

However, not all was well back in the Court. The original vision and the Master Literacy Plan seemed anathema to the new order and were in the process of being dismantled despite the protests of the supportive gentry. The Grand Vizier had so imposed his will and views on the advisors that eventually the Czar of Literacy, like the Court Statistician before him, decided to leave. The Guru of Alchemy was saddened to see this advisor, who had arrived in this land at almost the same time as he, depart, but he understood. The Grand Vizier at times appeared intolerable, and he was granted immense power by the potentate who so resembled the ruler of fabled Lilliput. It was believed that at some point the Grand Vizier might consolidate his power with the Grand Council and eventually succeed the sitting potentate. Yet this was not to be because, during this time, the Grand Council had sent forth seekers to find a true king to replace the fallen but not forgotten Queen. The Council wanted to be certain that the seekers located one deemed truly worthy of the royal mantle because they were somewhat shamed in many of the populace's view for their trust in the Queen and in their general tendency to bicker endlessly. Also the Council had apparently found it necessary to forfeit vast amounts of currency in settling various legal conundrums brought about by former members of the Court. This did not sit well with the town criers, who visited the Council often and spoke poorly of their decisions and public behavior.

With such a burden of unwanted scrutiny, the Grand Council was certain to deliberate long and hard before they would select a new King from among those they allowed the professional seekers to deliver to them. So the process would be long, slow, and deliberate. Until the Council encountered the King from the rich harbor . . . whom they ordained immediately as the successor to the throne.

This sudden ordination came as a surprise to many among the populace and even had the town criers so bewildered that they momentarily dropped their writing quills. Who was this new King? From whence had he arrived? Had he left behind a kingdom happy with his reign? Most important, why was he chosen so suddenly when it appeared that the Grand Council would take as long as it deemed necessary to select the best to rule their land? All of these questions meant little to Court because it had become evident from the start of his reign that this new King would do things his way. The former Statistician returned to the Court, and the Guru of Alchemy was to answer to the King's Commander of Alchemy, who bore a striking resemblance, both in appearance and temperament, to a legendarily ill-tempered antipodean marsupial.

As the new King assumed control of the land, changes were occurring in Aim Thrice. The Master Literacy Plan had been all but abandoned, and its initial vision was so hopelessly blurred by the incompetent hands of the successors as to render it myopic. It was decided that, to survive and fulfill its initial promise and deliver its primary goals, Aim Thrice would reside in the Order of Alchemy. The replacement Primary Guide was well versed in Alchemy and, indeed, resided comfortably among their ranks. She was also a caring steward of the literacy legacy and maintained scrupulous oversight of the Official Entitlement coffers. This Guide proved hardworking and diligent in maintaining the goals set nearly three harvest cycles ago. The devices and mechanisms, with their mysterious incantations and modules, the various scrolls and manuscripts, all had been distributed to the Official Entitlement halls of learning, and all that remained were those halls in which resided those not able to partake of the Entitlement's bounties. The remaining pedagogues were being prepared and enlightened in the ways of alchemy and literacy and at last the dream seemed close to completion.

Other developments ensued in the Court. It began to slowly dawn on the Grand Council that perhaps it had made too hasty a decision in anointing the new King. He tended to be brash and short with certain members, and he issued royal decrees without, they felt, the proper consideration due the Grand Council. He berated, belittled, and derided them in public forums, and this did not sit at all well with the Council members, who were rather sensitive about their image. The populace and certain members of the Council also questioned his association with merchants, especially when an edict was announced that mandated certain halls of learning to be ruled by one of these merchants.

The Grand Council began to plot the removal of what they now viewed as a terrible mistake (again) on their part—a tyrant and despot so despicable that his continued reign could not be allowed. The King's every move was now watched and scrutinized at every moment—like a cat observes its prey and awaits the appropriate moment to pounce on it. Eventually the Grand Council found its moment and, of course, the King was deposed. Again the Grand Council appointed an interim ruler and attempted to explain to the populace and town criers how they had been mesmerized and hypnotically induced to crown the former King, how he had cast spells and used trickery to fool them into allowing him to reign. The interim ruler was another derived from the ranks of the Court and was a benevolent monarch, although not fully empowered by the Grand Council, as was the previous interim ruler. He was empowered enough, however, to request the return of the Czar of Literacy, and this was welcomed by the populace and the Court (mostly) as an appointment beneficial to the goals of the land.

In the meantime, the Primary Guide of Aim Thrice had made such a commendable effort in maintaining the integrity of its goals that the Czar requested her return to the Ministry of Literacy. This deeply saddened the alchemists, but they realized they had nearly completed their goals. Indeed, 4 years had passed—the initial goals and objectives of the Aim Thrice mission had been nearly accomplished. Although many felt that all the work was yet to be completed, the time had arrived to let others determine the fate of Aim Thrice. What had Aim Thrice accomplished during these tumultuous 4 years? It had survived a Queen and three Kings and the departure and return of the Czar of Literacy; tremendous changes in alchemy over the 4-year span; 564 pedagogues prepared and enlightened in the art of meshing alchemy and literacy, and their charges beneficiaries of the wonderful devices, modules, and scrolls; and, as its legacy, new aggregates in the tertiary level of primary learning would have the gifts of literacy and alchemy bestowed on them yearly.

What of the land that serves as the setting for this tale? A new King has since been crowned, and the stories relayed by travelers to the land tell of the populace's renewed faith in his rule. The Czar of Literacy has departed again to dwell in other halls of knowledge and learning. The Guru of Alchemy? Well, it is said that he remains awaiting the next chapter in this story, but that is another tale yet to be told.

CHAPTER EIGHT

Changing Lives
on the Boundaries

Jeanne Gerlach
University of Texas at Arlington

Manny Bustos awakened when the sun cooked the cardboard over his head and heated the box he was sleeping in until even a lizard could not have taken it, and he knew, suddenly, that it was time. This was the day. He would make the crossing today.

Juarez, Mexico, was never quiet. As a border town it was made of noise—noise that filled all the hours of the day—but the noises changed, and he listened to them now without thinking. Honking horns, the market starting to fill with people trying to get fresh goat cheese or the thick coffee, people yelling insults and curses at each other—a hum of noise. Mornings were the best time, not a good time—there were no good times for him—but the best. He lived on the street, moving, always moving because he was fourteen and had red hair and large brown eyes with long lashes, and there was danger if he did not move—danger from men who would take him and sell him to those who wanted to buy fourteen year-old street boys with red hair and long eyelashes.

So now he rolled out when the sun warmed the cardboard of his lean-to, wiped his mouth with a finger, and stood to begin moving for the day. Another day in Juarez. But this time it was different. This day would change it all; he would leave. This day he would cross to the north to the United States and find work, become a man, make money, and wear a leather belt with a large buckle and a straw hat with a feathered hatband.

Hunger was instant, had never gone. He went to bed hungry, slept hungry, awakened hungry, had hunger every moment of the day, and could not remember when he did not have hunger, even when he was small, a baby in the back of the Church of Our Lady of Perpetual

Sorrow where his unknown mother had left him in a box and the sisters had tried to feed him, there was hunger. It was almost a friend, the hunger, if something could be a friend and be hated at the same time, and he set out now to find the first food of the day.
—Paulsen (1987, pp. 3–5)

I read Paulsen's *The Crossing* in 1987 and was shaken by his portrayal of young Manny Bustos. The young boy's daily activities of searching first for food and then for a place to sleep remained in my mind long after I finished the book. Over the years, I have read excerpts from the book to students in my classes and adults in conference audiences. Even today I continue to think about Manny and his struggle for survival.

Now I must point out that for many years I have been keenly aware that hunger among children is a major problem worldwide, and I have seen hungry children in North America, Europe, Asia, Australia, and New Zealand. However, through Manny Bustos, Paulsen brings all of those children to the forefront of my mind. Manny actually lived on the boundaries of Mexico and the United States, whereas all the hungry children I have seen and known often live on the boundaries of life and death. Moreover, children who suffer from hunger and homelessness exist everywhere—in big cities, small towns, farms, reservations, and even suburban areas. Manny, of course, is a young Mexican boy living in Juarez, but trying to cross the border into El Paso. He is willing to risk his life to move from one urban area to the other for the promise of a better life—one where hopefully he can have a home, regular meals, and an education.

Although to Manny life in El Paso appears to be more desirable than life in Juarez, we know that often children living in large urban areas are not provided with minimum educational opportunities to rise out of poverty. The picture remains the same regardless of the city—El Paso, Dallas, New York, Chicago, Sydney, Auckland, or Berlin. In his book *Savage Inequalities*, education reformer Jonathan Kozol (1991) explored the educational inequalities in urban areas, including unequal school financing, poor teacher and administrator training, low pay scales, mistreatment of students, and outdated school buildings. His account of urban schooling in America points out the horrors faced by students, parents, teachers, administrators, and staff. Others (e.g., Jean Anyon) have provided readers with systematic accounts of the historical, economic, social, political, and sociological issues surrounding the difficulties of reforming urban schools. In her book *Ghetto Schooling: A Political Economy of Urban Educational Reform*, Anyon (1997) questioned whether there is an appropriate pedagogy for urban children. For example, do African-American and Hispanic-American children need a pedagogical practice that recognizes their special and unique needs and learning styles? Do best practices work for all children? Is there research that supports either of these stances? Anyon argued that there is not one factor that explains student underachievement, nor is there any one solution to the problem. Others including Stanford Professor Larry Cuban (2001) believe that the key assumptions of current school reform policies, especially those focusing on accountability and testing and one-size-fits-all practices are inapplicable to urban schools. Cuban asserted that, "Equating inadequate urban schools with all public schools has encouraged sloppy thinking about American education. When it comes to criticism of American schools, for the last half-century, the urban tail has wagged the public school dog" (p. 1). What is it that we are doing wrong then? Cuban believes that comparing poor, racially isolated schools with all other schools ignores the numerous achievements of the students and teachers in schools where students are achieving excellence, including the ones in urban areas. Further, he feels that diversity among cities is being ignored. Finally and perhaps most important, Cuban noted that blending of urban, suburban, and rural schools encourages educators and political and business leaders to design curricula, tests, legislation, and community activities that become a one-size-fits-all model. If we agree with Cuban and others who believe that urban education needs more than the No Child Left Behind plan, where the emphasis is on annual testing as a cure all for educational ills, we must be willing to look for alternate ways to meet the needs of a diverse mix of students, teachers, and communities.

When considering the prior information concerning urban educational needs, one necessarily asks what can be done to ensure that all children in urban schools receive the kind of education they need to become whatever they want in life. What will it take for Manny Bustos and other children living in urban areas to become teachers, lawyers, or doctors? Kozol (2000) reminded us that, "We owe it to these children not to let the doors be closed before they're even old enough to know how many rooms there are, how many other doors there are beyond the one or two that they can see" (pp. 290–292).

How do we reform urban schools so that doors can be opened for all children? This question is one that I continually asked myself when I came to the University of Texas at Arlington (UTA) as Dean of Education in 1997. My charge from President Robert E. Witt and Provost George C. Wright was to build a school of education that would address the needs of the school children in the Dallas/Fort Worth Metroplex—home to more than 4.5 million people and the second fastest growing area in the United States. It is helpful to note Metroplex demographic data here. The area includes 180 independent school districts, with a combined student population approaching 1 million and representing 25% of Texas' public school enrollment. Dallas Independent School District (DISD) is the largest district in the area, with a pre-K–12 enrollment of more than 160,000 students, followed by Fort Worth (78,650), Arlington (56,000), Garland (49,000), and Plano (45,560). An additional 13 districts with student populations exceeding 10,000 also lie within a 60-mile radius. The region's public and charter schools employ more than 68,000 teachers and administrators.

The University of Texas at Arlington (UTA) with an enrollment of over 21,000 is the largest university in the Metroplex and the second largest campus in the University of Texas System. Although 78% of all UTA students come from eight Texas counties in the immediate area, other students represent 46 U.S. states and more than 100 nations. Interestingly enough, UTA alumni stay in the Metroplex area; more than 80% of the university's 94,433 graduates live and work in the Dallas/Fort Worth area.

Given that demographic information, I knew that UTA needed a school of education that could take a leadership role in addressing urban education needs while addressing the needs of suburban and rural school districts within the North Texas region. Because the Center for Professional Teacher Certification (the designation before school status was granted January 1999) seemed to be addressing the needs of the suburban and rural areas more effectively than the needs of the urban districts, and because I was charged with developing a school of education that would become known as a Center of Excellence for Urban Education, I set out to understand the complex interrelationships among schools, families, higher education institutions, communities, and businesses in the Metroplex.

To begin to understand the needs of the schools, teachers, and administrators, I knew I had to spend time visiting with all players; listening to their stories; observing classrooms; talking to the students, teachers, and parents; and, finally, reflecting on my experiences. During my first year (1997–1998), I visited schools in most districts in North Texas; I met with teachers, principals, and administrators; I listened to their stories of success, but I also heard their concerns about failing test scores, poor school attendance, students' low self-esteem, and little parent participation. I must pause here to tell the reader that I was reminded many times by teachers and administrators to use the term *caregiver* rather than *parent* because a large percentage of the young people live with a grandparent or family member other than a parent. Often those students who do live with parents rarely see them because most moms and dads work, sometimes at more than one job. As a matter of fact, I soon realized that in many of the low-performing schools, there was little if any connection among parents, schools, and communities. Further, I noticed that many of the students who were not doing well in school did not have family or parental support. Some of the students told me about belonging to gangs and groups who became like a family for them.

Here I think of Walter Dean Myers' (1988) novel, *Scorpions*. Myers constructed a believable plot and realistic characters that deal with urban life that is frightening to contemplate. The young protagonist, Jamul, is having trouble at school; everyone (including his teachers and principal) is giving him a hard time. Home life is not any better. His brother, Randy, is in jail, and his mother is always yelling at him. One day Jamal is asked to take over as leader of the Scorpions and run crack. Jamal really does not want to join the gang, let alone be the leader. However, he realizes that it is the only way to get money for Randy's appeal. Myers' dialogue is so realistic that it is frightening:

> "That ain't real," Dwayne said.
> "Come on," Jamal said. There was the taste of blood in his mouth. "You gonna see it's real."
> Dwayne didn't move.
> Jamal held the gun pointed at Dwayne. He could hear the sound of his own breathing and Dwayne's even heavier breathing.
> "That ain't nothing but a cap pistol," Dwayne said.
> "The Scorpions don't have no fake guns, Jamal said.
> "You ain't no Scorpion."
> "I'm the leader of the Scorpions." (Myers, 1988, p. 106)

Although Myers' story is fictional, it is a story that many of the students whom I met could tell as truth. *Scorpions* is a novel that mirrors the lives of some of the students who are turning to gangs to replace the family unit. Although there are lessons to be learned from reading this novel and others like it (i.e., novels that deal with student problems and concerns), many of the students do not have the skills necessary to read and comprehend the work. They do not have basic literacy skills. Interestingly enough, research has linked incidents of students' misbehavior to illiteracy. One such study in Orange County, Florida, focused on middle-school students who had been suspended 30 days or more. The researchers discovered that all students had reading comprehension scores below the 25th percentile on the Stanford 9 Achievement Test. The middle-school students reported that they had developed coping strategies to avoid reading, including misbehavior.

Literacy—one of the major aims of the American educational system—refers to the integration of thinking, reading, and writing skills. In its limiting definition, *literacy* is the ability to read and write. Literacy, in a broader context, is about using language to learn. When defined in this way, it is central to all content and school curricula; it recognizes the expertise of the science teacher, art teacher, and history teacher. The value of literacy, then, is its ability to help the student discover and make knowledge. Traditionally, as stated earlier, we have thought of literacy as simply the ability to read and write. Often that meant the ability to decode and write simple sentences. It is not simply that. Rather, literacy is the ability to think critically and creatively about any subject.

When thinking about literacy as learning, we realize that every teacher must teach literacy to learn. Literacy is needed to succeed in every subject. Such a position is based on two observations. First, language/literacy is what every subject has in common. Teachers all use language to teach. We are all language teachers in the sense that each discipline uses a particular language to represent a way to view our world. According to Langer (1969), "sense data are constantly wrought into symbols, which are our elementary ideas" (1969, p. 42). We need to create visual, musical, mathematical, and linguistic symbols to think at all. The symbol systems become the language through which we study and understand. We use language to learn. If this is so, then guiding students to attend to literacy/language to learn should be shared by all teachers. Second, students who use literacy/language to learn are more likely to succeed in school and in life.

From what has just been said, we can begin to sense the importance of literacy. Literacy is a process fundamental to the life-long course of connecting and integrating thoughts and ideas. Through reading and writing, we discover our ideas and discover meaning. We realize the need to analyze, synthesize, organize, apply, and evaluate—all of which are tools of learning—to express ourselves, communicate our ideas and feelings, and demonstrate an understanding of our subject matter. Through reading and writing, we learn what it is we know or do not know.

Literacy as learning has implications for using reading and writing in all content areas, for through language students can clarify the categories and relationships already in their minds as they grapple with new information and ideas. In addition, when students read and write, they may become actively involved in the subject about which they are reading or writing. For example, when students have trouble retaining facts in a science class, their teacher can encourage them to record in their own words what they have learned or what confuses them. Periodically, the teacher can read the journals to clear up any inaccuracies and praise well-written entries. Similarly when a group of students has studied a piece of literature, instead of testing their knowledge with a fill-in-the-blank or multiple-choice questionnaire, the teacher could have them write about it from the point of view of the different characters in the work.

These examples are only two of the many ways in which teachers can facilitate literacy to learn—to discover knowledge in the content areas. Students must know how to read and write to understand content information, synthesize and organize information with their own ideas, and put them into a form that others can examine and understand. In this way, literacy becomes a vehicle to enable the learner/student to discover knowledge. Literacy helps a student make knowledge. Students use reading and writing as a heuristic for conceiving the relationship among facts and ideas designated as important knowledge of the content areas. Mayher (1983) reminded us that no matter how the curriculum is organized, learning takes place only when learners make active connections between what they need to learn and what they already know, understand, and believe. Being able to read and write helps learners make active connections between what they need to learn and what they already know, understand, and believe. Being literate helps learners make connections, realize whether they have made them, and bring together the results of the observations, abstractions, and generalizations. Reading and writing helps one discover what one thinks, believes, and means. Literacy is bound up with the processes of discovery and learning. We cannot separate what we know from language in which we have come to learn it and the language with which we express that knowledge. To do all that, we must be able to read and write—we must be literate.

Wisell (2000) reminded us that the literacy demands placed on students today are greater than at any other time in history. Students must be able to read critically and creatively, solve problems, and utilize technology. For example, today students need to be technologically literate. They need to know how to use the word processor, they need to know how to send and receive e-mail, they need to know how to *surf* the Web, they need to know how to do library searchers online, and they even need the skills to take online courses. Further, she contended, this means that parents and caregivers must play a major role in the literacy development of their children. Numerous researchers have demonstrated that children who read and write at home often have higher achievement in school (Anderson, 1994; Benjamin, 1993; Chall & Snow, 1982; Darling & Hayes, 1989; Greer & Mason, 1988; Mansback, 1993; Mundre & McCormick, 1989; Nurss, Mosenthal, & Hinchman, 1992; Ostlund, Gennaro, & Dobbert, 1985; Wells, 1986).

It is not surprising that the movement for family literacy is becoming one of the most visible educational concepts in American schooling today. "Teach the parent, reach the child" is the slogan of the National Center for Family Literacy. The Center, created over a decade ago, provides programs and classes where adults and children learn to read and write together. Centers base their practice on research that indicates that young children who can read and write have the keys to success.

Thus, staff at these Centers as well as K–12 educators and faculty in colleges and universities are forming partnerships that focus on literacy and language to learn. These educators realize that the language arts—reading, writing, listening, speaking, viewing, and thinking—are necessary components of learning. Although this awareness exists, educators know that, to be successful, they must elicit the help of two other groups—parents and administrators. Thus, the question becomes how can all stakeholders—parents, teachers, administrators, community, and business leaders—work together to help all students become literate so that they may be successful in school and in life?

Literacy, when thought about in these ways, becomes a vehicle for helping urban students improve their lives. It becomes a pathway to social reconstruction. The teachings of social reconstructionists, such as Harold Rugg, George Counts, and Theodore Brameld, add to our understanding of how literacy contributes to social change, including political, economic, and social development of society. These educators believe that school curriculum should be developed in an effort to aid students in identifying societal problems and appropriate solutions. Another well-known social reconstructionist, Paulo Freire (1970), believed that being literate is a pathway to liberation from economic and political oppression. Friere contended that many students in urban schools face problems that are a result of living in poverty. Poverty coupled with illiteracy is often the reason that students drop out of school. Thus, the cycles of poverty and illiteracy continue, and society as a whole continues to suffer the consequences.

Given this information about the importance of fostering literacy, I began to work with School of Education faculty who were interested in building partnerships with urban school districts, parents, and community businesses and organizations to search for ways to positively impact students' literacy development. Research tells us that literacy is not the responsibility of the schools alone. Rather, it must be shared by the school, community, and family (Fredericks & Rasinski, 1990; Rasinski, 1995). As a matter of fact, Marjoribanks (1972) found that more than half the variance in children's IQ scores could be attributed to the learning environment in the home. Postlethwaite and Ross (1992) agreed that family involvement is the most critical factor in children's literacy development. Finally, family involvement in a child's literacy development has been found to have a positive effect on regular school attendance, school completion rates, and self-esteem and health (Anderson, 1994; Benjamin, 1993; Chall & Snow, 1982; Darling & Hayes, 1989; Greer & Mason, 1988; Mansback, 1993; Mundre & McCormick, 1989; Nurss, Mosenthal, & Hinchman, 1992; Ostlund, Gennaro, & Dobbert, 1985).

Influenced by this information, I and three reading professors—Sylvia Vardell, Nancy Hadaway, and John Jacobson—partnered with the DISD to develop a collaborative effort to foster family literacy. We worked with the Director of the Dallas Reading Plan, school principals, parents, community members, and students to support the district's reading initiative to have all students reading at grade level by the end of third grade. Our work, described by Gerlach, Hadaway, Jacobson, and Vardell (2000), included collaborating with all stakeholders to design a project focusing on building a frame of reference on family literacy for all participants. Additionally, we developed, modeled, implemented, and evaluated family literacy projects. Some of the projects included Saturday parent clinics, cultural awareness days, storytelling workshops, book talks, and puppet theater instruction and presentation. For us, our work was a meaningful connection among all stakeholders who worked collaboratively in an effort to find ways to foster children's literacy.

Building on our collaborative efforts to foster family literacy, we then became one of the university partners that contributed to a state-of-the-art training program for teachers and principals in the DISD. For teachers, a 90-hour, year-long Reading Academy was initiated to help teachers learn to deliver balanced reading instruction to students in Grades 1 to 6. Similarly, principals were offered fellowships to help them learn more about their role in sustaining the literacy programs (for a detailed discussion of the projects, see Cooter & Cooter, 2001).

Faculty at UTA now have worked to train over 3,000 DISD teachers to teach reading. In addition to working with DISD, the faculty collaborate with K to 12 teachers and administrators in other districts, including Arlington, Forth Worth, and Hurst, Euless, Bedford to offer high-quality reading instruction to students, teachers, parents, and the community.

Other School of Education literacy-related projects include the development of a Master Reading Teacher certificate for those teachers wishing to continue their coursework in reading. The School is also home to the North Texas Writing Project, a local arm of the National Writing Project. Through its annual summer invitational institute and other inservice teacher/administrator training programs, participants in the Writing Project work toward their own development as writers and learn to teach writing to their students; they have opportunities to work in a supportive environment to examine the theory, research, practice, and challenges of teaching writing. Similarly, the Center for Bilingual Education's mission is to provide literacy education for bilingual and ESL learners. Through bachelor's and master's degree programs, effective teaching practices for language-minority students are discussed, modeled, and implemented.

Although the faculty of the School of Education (SOE) are committed to training practicing teachers to teach reading and writing to students in urban schools, they realize that preparing preservice teachers to teach in inner-city, multicultural contexts requires the preservice teachers to have knowledge in their content areas as well as pedagogical knowledge. Equally important is their need to understand and interact with urban schools and communities. Howey (1999) believed that preservice teachers should engage in activities designed to (a) elicit both scholarly analyses and first-hand knowledge of sociocultural/political factors that influence learning by youngsters in and out of school in inner-city contexts, (b) help them understand forms of bias and discontinuity in curriculum materials and classroom interactions (linguistic bias, stereotyping, limited frames of reference, (c) encourage them to examine their own cultural norms and behavioral patterns in relation to another's, (d) help them examine the interactions and relationships among language, learning, and culture, (e) acquire an understanding of youth and family services, (f) assist them in becoming advocates for all students especially those who do not have equal opportunities, (g) orient them to the particular background experiences of youngsters' lives outside of school, and (h) reinforce in them a commitment to valuing cultural pluralism, social justice, and equal opportunity for all.

Howey continued to note that if schools and colleges are to effectively prepare teachers to teach successfully in urban schools, faculty must be willing to help recruit, prepare, and retain urban teachers. Although students in inner cities have challenges that are different than those students in suburban and rural areas, they also have many strengths and successes. They are resilient and can succeed academically. Teachers need to be trained to understand how to help young people deal with and overcome poverty, drug use, violence of every kind, and behavior and beliefs that are in opposition to both academic and personal successes. This means that university faculty must understand the same and along with the understanding must come action. The SOE faculty are taking the action necessary to help students in the Metroplex urban districts succeed.

Just as the SOE faculty is preparing teachers to face the challenges of teaching in urban schools, they are also preparing administrative leaders who understand that poor, culturally/ethnically diverse children need principals and superintendents who are prepared to make instructional and budgetary decisions based on particular urban needs. Thus, the Educational Leadership and Policy Studies faculty offer a research-based curriculum that applies the principles and theories of educational leadership to real-world situations. The curriculum emphasizes site-based decision making and strategic planning, supervision and human resource development, collaboration and communication, organizational management and fiscal responsibility, and instructional leadership development focusing on urban leadership needs. Coursework prepares students for a master's degree and qualifies them for a principal's certificate. Candidates who choose to do so may earn a superintendent's certificate as well. A PhD in Public and Urban Administration with an Educational Administration Emphasis is available through a collaborative doctoral program between the SOE and the School of Urban and Public Affairs. The coursework prepares students for key administrative positions in public and private schools, teaching and research positions at the college and university level, and policy analysis and development positions in the public and private sectors. Graduates will have an understanding of urban education as well as urban economics, transportation, housing, and city planning needs. Students in leadership and policy studies programs, like the students in teacher preparation programs, focus on the characteristics and needs of urban communities. They not only participate in coursework, but many of them work as administrators while completing their degree and certificate requirements. Equally important, they are required to participate in service-learning activities that are tailored to help them learn firsthand about contemporary classrooms by assisting at-risk students. Research indicates that students who participate in service-learning projects gain awareness about the importance of individual and social characteristics, which influence educational development of students (Hamm et al., 1998).

The Department of Kinesiology faculty is also implementing service-learning projects into its curriculum as it prepares students for successful careers in teaching, fitness management, and the allied health sciences. The Department trains students to make contributions to their areas of specialization through basic and applied research in the cultural, biomechanical, physiological, neuromotor, psychological, and educational principles of human behavior. Kinesiology students are prepared to work with urban schools to promote students' individual and collective well-being. The program for physical education emphasizes the promotion of learners' physical, affective, social, and cognitive development and implementation of physical education programs at the appropriate level. Although our focus is preparing teachers and administrators to focus on the academic, cultural, and social needs of urban school children, students who are prepared by the Kinesiology faculty learn to focus on their students' wellness and physiological needs. We realize that we must build strong minds and strong bodies. As we have learned, children in urban areas often live in substandard housing (often on the street) and suffer from continual hunger. These children go to school to get a meal or to have a warm place to be. Their major concern is for physical survival, not on learning content and social skills. Kinesiology students subscribe to the precept that all children must be feed, clothed, and housed to have a chance to be physically fit. They work with their peers in Curriculum and Instruction and Educational Leadership to address the needs of children in urban schools. In turn, they all work with their professors, the K to 12 teachers and administrators, parents, business leaders, and citizens from the community to ensure urban children have opportunities for educations.

Realizing that *it takes a village* to educate a child (borrowing liberally from Hillary Clinton's [1996] book title, *It Takes a Village*), I agreed to serve as cochair of the UTA's K to 16 Council. UTA Provost George C. Wright and Hurst, Euless, Bedford Independent School District Superintendent, Gene Buinger, are the other cochairs. Our charge is to work with university faculty and administration, 2-year college faculty and administrators, K to 12 teachers and administrators, business and corporate employees and leaders, and community leaders to provide quality education opportunities for all students in the North Texas region so they will eventually have access to higher education. Our areas of focus include: (a) getting all students into and through a college preparatory curriculum, (b) aligning standards for high school exit and college entry, (c) identifying instructional strategies that work for students who arrive behind—in early childhood, middle school, high school, or college, (d) transforming counseling from gate keeping to eliminating barriers, (e) improving teacher effectiveness, (f) developing strategies for getting elementary children and their families focused on college opportunities, and (g) planning for interactions with policymakers and legislators. The K to 16 Council is tackling these seven issues head on in an effort to provide access to an education for all students in the North Texas area.

As Dean, then, I have collaborated with the faculty, staff, and administration to build an SOE that is *the heart of urban education.* We continue our work as we began it—listening to the voices of K to 12 teachers, administrators, and students and to the beliefs, ideas, and questions of parents and community/business representatives. We believe that all efforts to educate urban students must begin with listening, not telling, and we must value all voices and all views. Further, we feel that the success of our work will be based on our efforts to ensure all students cannot only read and write, but can use literacy/language to think critically and creatively. Our work is based on the belief that literacy/language is the basis for all learning and for *changing lives on the boundaries.*

REFERENCES

Anderson, J. E. (1994). *Families learning together in Colorado.* Denver, CO: U.S. State Department of Education, Office of Adult Education.

Benjamin, L. A. (1993). *Parents' literacy and their children's success in school: Recent research, promising practices, and research implications.* Washington, DC: Office of Educational Research and Improvement.

Chall, J., & Snow, C. (1982). *Families and literacy: The contributions of out-of-school experiences to children's acquisition literacy.* (ERIC Document Reproduction Service No. ED 234345)

Clinton, H. R. (1996). *It takes a village: And other lessons children teach us.* New York: Simon & Schuster.

Cooter, R., & Cooter, C. (2001). Challenges to change: Implementing balanced reading instruction in an urban district. *Balanced Reading Instruction, 8,* 8–26.

Cuban, L. (2001). *Urban school leadership—different in kind and degree*. Washington, DC: Institute of Educational Leadership.

Darling, S., & Hayes, A. (1989). *Breaking the cycle of illiteracy: The Kenen family literacy model program*. Louisville, KY: National Center for Family Literacy.

Fredericks, A. D., & Rasinski, T. V. (1990). Working with parents: Factors that make a difference. *The Reading Teacher, 4,* 76–77.

Freire, P. (1970). *Pedagogy of the oppressed*. New York: Herder & Herder.

Greer, E., & Mason, J. (1988). *Effects of home literacy on children's recall*. Urbana, IL: Center for the Study of Reading, University of Illinois.

Hamm, D., Dowell, D., & Houck, J. W. (1998). Service learning as a strategy to prepare teacher candidates for contemporary diverse classrooms. *Education, 112,* 196.

Howey, K. (1999). Preparing teachers for inner city schools. *Theory Into Practice, 38.*

Kozol, J. (1991). *Savage inequalities*. New York: Crown.

Kozol, J. (2000). *Ordinary resurrections*. New York: Crown.

Langer, S. (1969). *Philosophy in a new key* (3rd ed.). Cambridge, MA: Harvard University Press.

Mansback, S. (1993). *A series of solutions and strategies: Family literacy's approach to dropout prevention*. Clemson, SC: National Dropout Prevention Center at Clemson University.

Marjoribanks, K. (1972). Environment, social class, and mental abilities. *Journal of Educational Psychology, 63,* 103–109.

Mayher, J. (1983). *Learning to write; Writing to learn*. Montclair, NJ: Boynton/Cook.

Mundre, L., & McCormick, S. (1989). Effects of meaning-focused cues on underachieving readers' context use, self-corrections, and literal comprehension. *Reading Research Quarterly, 24,* 89–113.

Myers, W. (1988). *Scorpions*. New York: HarperCollins.

Nurss, J. P., Mosenthal, & Hinchman, K. (1992). *Blalock FIRST: A collaborative project between Georgia State University and the Atlanta public schools*. Final Report. (ERIC Document Reproduction Service No. ED 355, 408)

Ostlund, K. E., Gennaro, E. D., & Dobbert, M. (1985). A naturalistic study of children and their parents in family learning courses in science. *Journal of Research in Science Teaching, 22,* 723–741.

Paulsen, G. (1987). *The crossing*. New York: Dell.

Postlethwaite, T. N., & Ross, K. N. (1992). *Effective schools in reading: Implications for educational planners*. The Hague: The International Association for the Evaluation of Educational Achievement.

Rasinski, T. V. (Ed.). (1995). *Parents and teachers: Helping children learn to read and write*. Fort Worth, TX: Harcourt Brace.

Vardell, S., Hadaway, N., Gerlach, J., & Jacobson, J. (2000). Linking schools families and communities: A family literacy project. *American Reading Forum Yearbook, XX,* 55–71.

Wells, G. (1986). *The meaning makers: Children learning language and using language to learn*. Portsmouth, NH: Heinemann.

Wisell, D. (2000). Taking the initiative: Dallas teachers as parent mentors in the literacy development of children. *English Leadership Quarterly, 22,* 9–10.

CHAPTER NINE

Minimizing the Effects of Student Mobility Through Teacher and Administrator Training

Katy Denson
Dallas Independent School District

Student mobility is an increasing problem now recognized as a detriment to student learning. *Mobility* is defined as a measure of the number of times a student changes schools, excluding changes due to single grade-level promotions (U.S. Department of Education, National Center for Education Statistics, 1995). Mobility has not always been pinpointed as a cause of poor achievement because it is frequently found in combination with other at-risk characteristics such as poverty, limited English proficiency, substandard health and living conditions, and changes in family structure. However, not only mobile students, but also nonmobile students, teachers, schools, and entire districts also suffer the impact of mobility.

In the Dallas Independent School District (DISD), student mobility and associated at-risk factors have been a threat to student achievement and the institutionalization of innovative teaching practices. In this chapter, the effects of student mobility on reading achievement are defined and discussed. A brief review of the research literature is followed by an analysis of the problem of student mobility in the DISD. Last, the effect of an innovative staff development effort for both teachers and principals on mobile students is identified.

DEFINING THE MOBILITY PROBLEM

It is sometimes difficult to discuss mobility and compare mobility figures across districts because there are varying ways in which mobility rates are calculated. After studying mobility formulas in 93 districts, Ligon and

Paredes (1992) identified five dimensions of mobility that should be considered when selecting a method of calculation: (a) level of analysis (i.e., school, district, state), (b) term of analysis (i.e., length of time for which the analysis occurs), (c) frequency of moves, (d) nature of moves made, and (e) cause of change (i.e., family structure, economic, health).

Mobility Nationwide

The National Center for Education Statistics produced student mobility data in 1995 (U.S. Department of Education, National Center for Education Statistics, 1995). Based on a nationwide survey of the eighth-grade class of 1988:

- 31% of the students had changed schools two or more times since entering first grade, and by spring 1992, 10% had changed schools two or more times again.
- White students were less likely to change schools than Asian, Hispanic, or African-American students.
- Students who lived with their mother and father were less likely to change schools than were students living in other types of families.
- Students in low-income families (under $10,000) were more likely to change schools two or more times after entering first grade than were students whose family income equaled or exceeded $20,000.

School Instability

In a study of urban student mobility in the Chicago Public Schools, Kerbow (1996) calculated a stability rate indicating the percentage of students who remained in a school from year to year. This produced a clearer meaning of the level of mobility within a school because it eliminated students who entered and exited during the year. Using September 1993 to September 1994 data, the school stability rates within the district varied considerably. Eleven percent of the schools had stability rates of less than 70, indicating that these schools lost approximately 10 students from a classroom of 30. Only 7% of the schools had stability rates of 90 or greater. Instability became even more apparent when stability was calculated over a 4-year period. On the average, only 46% of the students who began in the school were present after 4 years. Thus, the typical Chicago school had more new students than continuing students.

However, mobility histories of individual students revealed that instability was actually related to a small number of students who changed schools several times. Of the students who were new to a school in September 1993, 87% moved from a school within the Chicago Public Schools system. Of those students who moved during the school year, 82% were from another Chicago school within the system. The median distance that students moved was 2.4 miles.

In a similar study conducted in Minneapolis, most of the student moves were within a fairly confined area of the city (Kids Mobility Project, 1998). Families usually remained in the same or a neighboring community, with 66% of the families included in the study moving less than 2 miles. In Rockville, Maryland, half of the *highly mobile* students, defined as having changed schools three or more times, moved from another school within the county, many 4.5 miles or less from their previous school (Montgomery County Public Schools, 1998).

The U.S. Census Bureau (Schachter, 2001) confirmed that moving short distances is still the current nationwide pattern. Between March 1999 and March 2000, 56% of movers reported moving within the same county, 20% moved from a different county within the same state, 19% moved from a different state, and 4% moved from a different country.

EFFECTS OF MOBILITY ON MOBILE STUDENTS

Academic Achievement of Mobile Students

Research conducted primarily before 1980 frequently found that mobility had statistically insignificant effect on academic achievement (Black, 1972; Black & Barger, 1975; Cramer & Dorsey, 1970; Evans, 1996; Gilchrist, 1970). It is troubling that all of these studies focused on sixth-grade students' reading scores because generalization is limited.

With the exception of a few studies from the 1960s and 1970s, most studies since the 1980s have concluded that mobility can be a factor in predicting student achievement (Abramson, 1974; Audette & Algozzine, 2000; Clark, 2001; Dilling & Farrell, 1973; Faunce & Murton, 1965; Hefner, 1994; Mehana & Reynolds, 1995; Reynolds, 1991; Sewell, 1982; Temple & Reynolds, 1999; Wasserman, 2001; Waters, 1996). However, Kerbow (1996) pointed out that little of the research distinguished between inter- and intracity mobility, such as that previously described, or between one-time movers and frequent movers, who have proved to have different academic growth patterns. Even less work has been done on the long-term cumulative effects of mobility on academic growth.

Frequency of Moves

These data appear to indicate that frequent rather than occasional mobility is more detrimental to student achievement.

One Move.   In a longitudinal analysis of the mathematics achievement of two groups of students on the Iowa Tests of Basic Skills (ITBS), it was found that the students who moved only once were behind students who had not moved (Kerbow, 1996). Prior to moving, the mobile students were about 11% of a year behind the nonmobile students. After moving, the mobile students were 21% of a year behind their nonmobile counterparts. If they remained in the same school for the third year, the mobile students recovered to about where they were before they moved (about 10% of a year behind). The fact that mobile students were behind even before they moved suggested that other factors frequently associated with mobile students affected achievement. These included low socioeconomic status (SES), attendance problems, family structure, and limited family resources.

Examining the ITBS scores of fourth and fifth graders in New Jersey, Waters (1996) found that there was little difference among students who had attended the same school and those who had moved only once. Significant differences in reading scores were found among students who had moved three or more times and those who had not moved or only moved once. Evans (1996) found that sixth-grade students who had never changed schools did not score significantly higher in reading or mathematics on the ITBS than students who had transferred one or more times. Nevertheless, the study indicated that students who had attended the same school for 5 to 6 years did better than students who had only attended the same school 1 to 2 years.

More Than One Move.   After controlling for students' SES, Kerbow (1995) estimated that the difference in students' achievement levels increased as the number of school changes increased. Students who made four or more moves during a 5-year period were approximately 1 full year of growth in mathematics achievement behind those who had not moved.

In Minneapolis, average reading scores for students with three or more moves were nearly 20 Normal Curve Equivalents (NCEs) lower on the California Achievement Tests than those of students who had not moved (Kids Mobility Project, 1998). Students who had moved only within the district scored nearly 5 NCEs lower in reading and 8 NCEs lower in mathematics than nonmobile students. In a study in Cleveland, Clark (2001) analyzed fourth-grade students' test scores on the Ohio Proficiency Test from 1997 to 1999. Students who changed schools one or more times during the school year scored 3.5 and 7.5 points lower in reading and mathematics, respectively, than their stable classmates.

In Rockville, Maryland, fifth graders who had attended three or more schools in the Montgomery County Public Schools (1998) averaged 32 points lower on the California Reading Test than classmates who attended one school. Students who received free or reduced lunch and had moved three or more times by the end of fifth grade scored an average of 52 points lower than nonmobile students. In addition, fifth graders with only 1 or 2 years in the school system scored 23 points lower on the California Reading Test than students who had been there all 6 years (K–Grade 5). However, fifth graders who had been in the system 3 to 5 years scored almost as high as students who had never moved provided that they remained in the same building.

EFFECTS OF MOBILITY ON NONMOBILE STUDENTS, TEACHERS, AND SCHOOLS

Nonmobile Students

Even students who do not move frequently suffer the effects of high mobility. Kerbow (1996) found that teachers tended to increase their review of curricula already covered instead of introducing new material for which transferring students would not have the background. This decreased the opportunity for all children to learn, not only those who moved frequently. The collective impact across grades was that, each year, further review and a reduction in instructional pacing were necessary to accommodate the discrepancies in student learning. Kerbow (1996) called this overall effect a *flattening* of curricular pacing. For students in highly mobile schools, instruction and pacing was as much as a year behind that of students in more stable schools.

Teachers

Instructional changes in a highly mobile school means that student mobility also affects teachers. Teachers in highly mobile schools reported less collaboration with peers, less collective focus on student learning, and less interest in the use of innovative instruction (Sebring et al., 1995). Long-term instructional planning becomes difficult because teachers are uncertain of their students' needs. Assessment of the impact of instruction also suffers when teachers are unable to observe the effects of their strategies and techniques. Teachers in Chicago reported that 50% of students joining their class after the beginning of the year were unable to work at the level at which they were teaching (Kerbow, 1996). Sixty-eight percent of the teachers structured portions of their lessons specifically to the review of material for new students.

Teacher mobility may also be related to student mobility. In Maryland, schools with the highest student mobility also had the highest teacher turnover (Montgomery County Public Schools, 1998). Forty-two percent of teachers in stable schools had 15 or more years teaching experience, whereas in the highly mobile schools, only 27% of teachers had similar experience. Keeler and McCall (1972) found that more experienced teachers in San Diego moved to more attractive schools—those with more stability and higher achieving students. In their study, teacher turnover was negatively related to students' reading ability.

Schools

High student mobility puts added stress on schools. Decisions regarding teaching assignments and program commitments are likely to change throughout the year due to a change in student population. If high teacher mobility is also a problem, administrators must take time away from other duties to work with new faculty members. Districts that place emphasis on long-range planning based on previous student performance may find the exercise meaningless when student membership and its needs change yearly (Neuman, 1988). The stress of initiating a new program in a district or school is compounded when high student mobility is an issue. It may become difficult to adopt new practices or programs because teachers are unable to evaluate the results.

DEFINING THE MOBILITY PROBLEM IN THE DISD

Patterning after the work by Kerbow (1996) in Chicago, mobility in the DISD was examined at the student and classroom levels. Four of the five dimensions of mobility identified by Ligon and Paredes (1992) were considered: (a) level of analysis (student, classroom, district), (b) term of analysis (the 2000–2001 school year), (c) frequency of moves, and (d) nature of moves made. Cause of change was impossible to determine from the district database.

Methodology

A district-maintained database recorded transactions for every student move, including the student identification number, date of the transaction, sending school, and receiving school. This transaction database, combined with a student test score database, provided a record of students who had remained in the district for the April 2001 norm-referenced testing. Only Grades K to 3 students with achievement test scores on the Stanford 9 or its Spanish counterpart, the *Aprenda*, were included in the analyses (Kindergarten, $N = 5,544$; Grade 1, $N = 10,252$; Grade 2, $N =$

10,864; Grade 3, $N = 11,180$). This does not totally define the number of students who actually moved in and out of a school because many students withdrew before testing.

Transactions were coded for these analyses to describe four types of moves that occurred: (a) Beginning of the Year—when the move was on or before the first day of school, (b) Within District, No Absences—when the move was within the district with fewer than 7 calendar days between withdrawal from the sending school and enrollment in the receiving school, (c) Within the District, Absences—when the move was within the district, but there were more than 7 calendar days between withdrawal from the sending school and enrollment in the receiving school (no knowledge of whether the student was enrolled in an out-of-district school in between), and (d) Same School, Absences—when students reenrolled in the same school from which they had withdrawn, but there were more than 7 calendar days between withdrawal and enrollment in the same school (no knowledge of whether the student was enrolled in an out-of-district school in between). There were no "Beginning of the Year" moves for Kindergarten students.

The Mobility Problem

Mobility and Ethnicity.   The ethnic makeup of the Grades K to 3 students enrolled in the district at the time of testing was 30% African American, 63% Hispanic, 6% White, and 1% other ethnicities (Asian and American Indian). Across Grades 1 to 3, about 84% of the students were stable— that is, they remained all year long in the same school they had attended the previous year. Of those students who did move, most moved either at the beginning of the school year (9% African American, 6% Hispanic, 4% White, and 4% Other) or at some other time during the year (10% African American, 6% Hispanic, 5% White, and 2% Other; Fig. 9.1). Greater percentages of African-American students had two, three, or more moves than

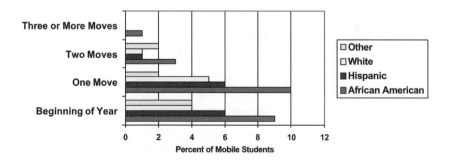

FIG. 9.1.   Student mobility by ethnicity for Grades 1–3.

other ethnicities. Kindergarten students had slightly fewer moves than students in Grades 1 to 3.

Types of Moves. There were definite ethnic differences when the types of moves were examined. Because percentages were similar for each grade, Fig. 9.2 shows the aggregated percentages of types of moves for Grades K to 3 students who changed schools during the year. Hispanic (44%), African-American (42%), and Other (43%) students were more likely to enroll in a new school at the beginning of the year than White students (36%). African-American (44%) and Hispanic (38%) students were also more likely to move within the district without an absence between withdrawal and enrollment in a new school. White students were more likely to move within the district with absences between withdrawal and enrollment (12%) and to reenroll in the same school (22%) than African-American and Hispanic students. Hispanic students (11%) were nearly twice as likely to reenroll in the same school than African-American students (6%).

Date of Moves. Other than at the beginning of the school year, first moves occurred throughout the year, with highest percentages in September (15%), October (16%), November (12%), January (18%), and February (12%). Most second and third moves occurred in January (21%). Students' fourth moves occurred primarily in February and March (29%). Fewest moves occurred during December and April.

Mobility in Classrooms. The percentage of mobility in classrooms was based on the number of students tested in April who had moved at some time during the year, including those that had changed schools at the beginning of the year. Only 14% of the Grades K to 3 classrooms in the district tested only students who were stable. Twenty-one percent of the classrooms tested one or two new students, and 16% and 12% tested three

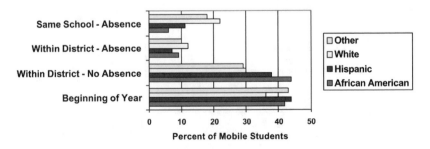

FIG. 9.2.   Types of student mobility by ethnicity for Grades K–3.

TABLE 9.1
Number and Percentage of Schools by Mobility Rate

School Mobility Rate	Number of Schools	Percentage	Cumulative Percentage
3%–5%	3	2	3
6%–10%	42	23	25
11%–15%	54	38	63
16%–20%	35	25	87
21%–25%	14	10	97
More than 25%	4	3	100

or four new students, respectively. Another 14% of the classrooms tested five to seven new students and 2% tested eight or more new students.

Mobility in Schools. Mobility in schools was computed by dividing the number of new Grades K to 3 students tested by the total number of students enrolled in the school. The greatest percentage of schools (38%) had school mobility rates of 11% to 15% (Table 9.1). Another 23% and 25% had mobility rates of 6% to 10% and 16% to 20%, respectively. Cumulatively, 63% of the schools had mobility rates of 15% or less.

Summary

The five indicators of mobility that were examined indicate that the mobility problem in the DISD was similar to that of Chicago, Minneapolis, and Rockville, Maryland. That is, most of the student population was relatively stable, with 84% of the students remaining in the same school they had previously attended all year. If students did change schools, the greatest percentage changed at the beginning of the school year. Only about 7% of the students changed schools once during the year, 2% had two moves, and less than 1% had three or more moves. Only 14% of the Grades K to 3 classrooms were unaffected by student mobility, and only 25% of the school had mobility rates of 10% or less.

Greater percentages of African-American and Hispanic students changed schools, no matter when or how often, than White students. Over 40% of the moves made at the beginning of the school year were by African-American and Hispanic students. Of those students who moved, most enrolled in a new school almost immediately on withdrawal from the previous school, indicating short moving distances. However, greater percentages of White students reenrolled in the same school, although absences between withdrawal and enrollment may have occurred.

EFFECT OF STUDENT MOBILITY
ON ACHIEVEMENT SCORES

With student mobility clearly established as a current problem in the DISD, the effects of movement on reading comprehension achievement scores were then analyzed.

Methodology

Reading Comprehension Achievement Scores.   Similar methodology was used for analyses of reading comprehension scores on both the Stanford 9 and the *Aprenda*. The scores of students who tested off level were excluded. The effects of gender, ethnicity, special education participation, English proficiency status, and family income level (based on free- and reduced-lunch status) were removed from reading comprehension Normal Curve Equivalent (NCE) scores using a multiple regression procedure by grade. The multiple regression design controls statistically for any initial differences in the students that might have been present and might have confounded differences among groups. This allowed the research to focus on the effects of mobility rather than other high-risk factors. Adjusted (residualized) scores were converted to an NCE-like scale. Grade equivalent (GE) scores were standardized using the adjusted NCE scores.

Analyses.   Analyses of variance (ANOVAs) were used to ascertain whether the number, types, and dates of moves had a statistically significant effect on reading comprehension standardized grade equivalent scores. All analyses were conducted by grade.

Effect of Number of Moves

The number of moves that a student made during the year significantly affected the standardized grade equivalent score at each grade, K to 3 (Fig. 9.3). Grades 1 and 2 students who moved at the beginning of the year scored about the same as students who had not moved, losing about 1 month at Grade 1 and 2 months at Grade 2. Yet by Grade 3, students who moved at the beginning of the year were almost 4 months behind those who had attended the same school as the year before.

The effect of one or two moves was relatively the same at Grades K and 1, but the differences increased significantly at Grades 2 and 3. The reading comprehension grade equivalent scores for Grades K to 2 students who moved three or more times during the year were about 5 months lower than students who had made no move. By Grade 3, the difference was more than a grade level (GE = 4.1 for students who had not moved, GE = 2.9 for those who moved three or more times).

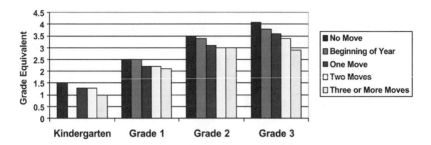

FIG. 9.3. Effect of mobility on reading comprehension grade equivalent scores by grade.

Effect of Types of Moves

The effect of the types of moves was statistically significant at each grade, K to 3. At Grades 1 and 2, the grade equivalent scores of students who made no move and those who moved at the beginning of the year were almost the same (Fig. 9.4). By Grade 3, students who moved at the beginning of the year were about 3 months behind those of students who were attending the same school as the previous year.

At Grades K to 2, students who moved within the district, but had more than 7 calendar days between withdrawal and enrollment, had the lowest grade equivalent scores. In Grades 2 and 3, reading comprehension grade equivalent scores of students whose final move was to reenroll in the same school scored almost as well as students who enrolled in a new school at the beginning of the year.

Effect of Dates of Moves

The date of students' last move was statistically significant at each grade. For students who only moved once, the difference in reading achievement

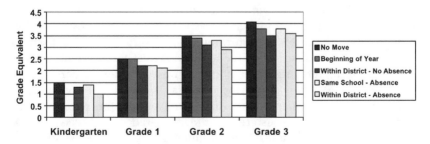

FIG. 9.4. Effect of type of move on reading comprehension grade equivalent scores.

between students who moved in August or September was as much as 5 months higher than those who moved in April. Particularly at Grades 1 and 2, the later in the school year students moved, the lower their reading comprehension grade equivalent scores.

Effect of Classroom Mobility

The number of students who had transferred into the classroom before testing was a significant factor in reading achievement at all grade levels. On average, Kindergarten classes with five to seven new students scored almost 4 months lower (GE = 1.2) than classes that had only one new student (GE = 1.6). At Grade 1, classes with five to seven new students scored 2 months lower (GE = 2.3) than classes that had only one new student (GE = 2.5). At Grades 2 and 3, the differences were even larger. Classes with eight or more new students scored 7 and 6 months lower, respectively, than classes with no new students.

Summary

Much of the mobility research in the DISD parallels the findings of other large urban districts, such as Chicago and Minneapolis. Similar to Waters' (1996) work, in Dallas there was little difference between the scores of students who moved once, particularly if the move was at the beginning of the year, and those students who were stable. Whereas Kerbow found that fifth-grade students who had made four or more moves in a 5-year period were a grade level behind, in Dallas third-grade students who made four or more moves in a 1-year period were more than a grade level behind students who had not moved that year. This may have been caused by at-risk factors other than moving, such as change in family structure or economic hardships for which there was no information in the database.

The fact that students who returned to the same school from which they had withdrawn had higher scores than those who moved to a new school within the district was further indication that stability of schools, even with a time lapse in between, was essential for academic growth.

Although no verifying observations of instruction were conducted in classrooms in Dallas with varying degrees of mobility, it appeared that Kerbow's findings related to the impact of mobility on nonmobile students and teachers were also relevant for the Grades K to 3 classes in Dallas. It is conceivable that teachers modified their curriculum somewhat to meet the needs of mobile students, thus holding back students who had not moved.

EFFECT OF PARTICIPATION IN THE ACADEMY
AND FELLOWSHIP

In an effort to assist teachers and principals in implementing a new balanced literacy initiative, a Reading Academy for teachers and a Principals' Fellowship were offered. Beginning in the 1998–1999 school year, Reading Academy participants received graduate credit for participation, which included deep training and continued coaching. Although the training for principals was not as intense as that for teachers, the Fellowship taught principals to effectively manage schoolwide balanced literacy programs and provide assistance to teachers participating in the academy.

There are two questions related to mobility and participation in the academy and the Fellowship: (a) After removing the effects of student mobility, what was the effect of participation in the Reading Academy and Principals' Fellowship? (b) Did teacher participation in the Reading Academy have an effect on students who were mobile?

Methodology

The mobility and test score database only provided knowledge of the teacher in whose class students were enrolled at the time of the norm-referenced achievement testing (April 2001). Analysis of the effect of teacher participation in the academy and principal participation in the Fellowship was, therefore, based on this information.

Teachers were coded based on their participation in the Reading Academy. Those who completed the academy in 1999 (Laureates 1999) had been practicing balanced literacy instruction for 3 years, those who completed the academy in 2000 (Laureates 2000) for 2 years, and so on. By spring 2001, there were still a number of teachers who had never attended the academy (Non-Laureates).

It is important to note that the Non-Laureate group was not a pure research control group. During the past 5 years, all teachers in the district were exposed to information regarding balanced literacy—the focus of the Reading Academy. It was shown through classroom observations that many Non-Laureates conducted balanced literacy activities in their reading classes (Denson, 2000, 2001). Therefore, differences in student outcomes between Laureate and Non-Laureate classrooms, based on that coding alone, may have been greatly diminished.

Schools were coded based on the principal's or assistant principal's participation in the Principals' Fellowship. In contrast to the academy, a Fellowship II was offered to principals who had completed Fellowship I. Therefore, schools were coded as *No Fellowship*, *Fellowship I*, or *Fellowship II*.

Stanford 9 and *Aprenda* reading comprehension grade equivalent scores were recomputed, removing the effects of mobility (using the number of moves a student had made) as well as other demographic characteristics. ANOVAs were used to ascertain whether participation in the academy and Fellowship had a statistically significant effect on reading comprehension standardized grade equivalent scores. All analyses were conducted by grade.

Results

After removing the effects of mobility from reading comprehension grade equivalent scores, there were statistically significant differences among groups based on combinations of academy and Fellowship membership. Because it is too laborious to examine each combination of academy and Fellowship membership, the only comparisons discussed here are those of the two extremes, the Laureate 1999 and Fellowship II group, which is called *Full Dallas Reading Plan* (Full DRP), with the Non-Laureate and non-Fellowship group, which is called *No Dallas Reading Plan* (No DRP) at each grade level.

At Kindergarten and Grade 1, the Full DRP group scored 2 months higher than the No DRP group (Fig. 9.5). At Grade 2, the Full DRP group scored about 1 month higher. However, at Grade 3, the Full DRP group scored 9 months higher than the No DRP group, placing the Full DRP students more than a full grade above grade level (GE = 5.0).

The second question assessed effect of teacher participation in the academy on students who were mobile. The scores of students who moved twice during the year were compared based on whether their teacher at the time of testing was a Laureate 1999 or a Non-Laureate. Group sizes for students moving three or more times were too small to analyze. Differences were statistically significant only at Kindergarten and

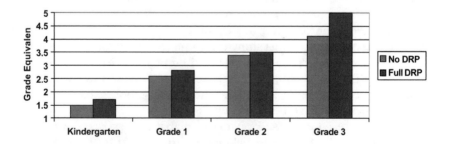

FIG. 9.5.   Comparison of grade equivalent differences between students with teacher and principal participation in training and those with no teacher and principal participation in training.

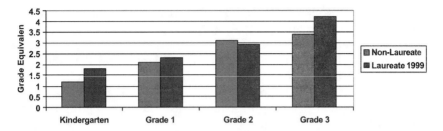

FIG. 9.6.   Comparison of grade equivalent scores of students who moved twice during the year by academy participation.

Grade 3. Kindergarten students who moved twice during the year to a Laureate 1999 teacher's class scored 6 months higher than students who moved to a Non-Laureate's class. At Grade 3, there was a 9-month difference, meaning that students who moved to a Laureate's class scored a grade level higher than students who moved to a Non-Laureate's class.

CONCLUSIONS

When conducting educational research, the researcher can statistically remove the effect of mobility or any other at-risk factor from students' achievement scores to better study the contribution of that factor to achievement. In real life, however, educators cannot remove that factor from children. A student's ethnicity, SES, or mobility rate cannot be altered. Consequently, when a factor significantly contributes to or detracts from educational progress, the question becomes: What can we as educators do to counteract the effects of that factor? The first step is to acknowledge that the problem exists.

This research in the DISD corroborated findings from other districts that student mobility is a significant issue. In Dallas, most students were stable. African-American and Hispanic students moved more frequently than White students. More moves occurred at the beginning of the school year than any other time. Of those students who moved, most moved only once during the year and typically enrolled immediately in another school. Less than 20% of the Grades K to 3 classrooms in the district tested only students who had the same teacher all year.

Also it must be acknowledged that mobility affected students' educational performance. The effects were less dramatic at Grades K to 2. However, by Grade 3, students who moved four or more times during the year were more than a grade level behind students who did not move or moved at the beginning of the year. Absences caused by moving greatly affected students' performance. Students who quickly enrolled in a new school scored higher than students who did not. Students with absences reenrolling in the same school scored higher than students changing schools. The number of new students that came into a class had an impact on the scores of all students, not just those who moved. Classrooms with higher mobility rates had lower average grade equivalent scores than those with lower mobility rates—sometimes as much as 5 to 7 months lower.

The second step in counteracting the problem is to initiate support measures. In other districts, these measures have included both community and school district solutions. The Kids Mobility Project (1998) worked with apartment owners and managers informing them about the effects of mobility on student achievement in an effort to cut down on local moves. School attendance boundaries were flexible so that students could remain in the same school until the end of the year. Counseling parents against moving unless absolutely necessary and having special support for students who did move (Evans, 1996) have also been successful strategies. The role of mandated curriculum calendaring to ensure constancy in reading development for intramobile students was discussed by Sewell (1982). Training for urban teachers and administrators to work with highly mobile minority students is also a support measure.

The Dallas Reading Academy and the Principals' Fellowship provided an innovative staff development program to teachers and administrators. Although specific mobility issues were not the focus of the training, students who were mobile were more successful in classes in schools where teachers and principals had attended the academy and Fellowship. Unfortunately, the innovative teaching practices taught in these courses were never institutionalized across the district.

Contrary to the Sebring et al. (1995) findings, academy participants and Laureates reported more collaboration with peers, a more collective focus on student learning, and a much greater interest in the use of innovative instruction (Denson, 1999, 2000, 2001). Principals also enjoyed a more relaxed atmosphere of collaboration. Many of the techniques taught in both courses focused on continued informal assessment procedures, such as running records and small-group instruction, which was more likely to meet all students' needs. It is possible that it was easier for an academy teacher to assess new students and begin serving their individual needs without taking away from the needs of more stable students.

Were the Reading Academy and Principals' Fellowship the answer to the problem of student mobility in the DISD? Probably not. However, the fact that mobile students in a mobile district scored higher with Dallas Reading Plan-trained educators makes it an option worthy of consideration.

REFERENCES

Abramson, J. (1974). *The effect of continuity of school environment on reading achievement of fifth grade pupils.* (ERIC Document No. ED120318)

Audette, R., & Algozzine, B. (2000). Within district transfers and student achievement: Moving ahead by staying in one place. *Special Services in the Schools, 16*(1-2), 73–83.

Black, F. S. (1972). *The relationship between pupil mobility and reading achievement in high-mobility-low-income elementary schools*. (ERIC Document No. 065860)

Black, F. S., & Bargar, R. R. (1975). Relating pupil mobility and reading achievement. *Reading Teacher, 28*(4), 370–374.

Clark, S. (2001, March–April). Mobile students score lower on state test. *Catalyst for Chicago Schools*.

Cramer, W., & Dorsey, S. (1970). Are movers losers? *Elementary School Journal, 70*(7), 387–390.

Denson, K. (1999, August). *Final evaluation of the 1998–1999 Dallas Reading Plan* (REIS99-300-03). Dallas, TX: Dallas Public Schools. Division of Evaluation, Assessment, and Information Systems.

Denson, K. (2000). *Final report. Reading and language arts grades K–6: 1999–2000* (REIS00-147-2). Dallas, TX: Dallas Public Schools. Division of Evaluation, Assessment, and Information Systems.

Denson, K. (2001). *Final report. Reading and language arts grades K–6: 2000–01* (REIS01-147-2). Dallas, TX: Dallas Independent School District. Division of Evaluation, Assessment, and Information Systems.

Dilling, H. J., & Farrell, M. A. (1973). *An investigation of factors related to reading achievement*. (ERIC Document No. ED119103)

Evans, D. (1996). *The effect of student mobility on academic achievement*. (ERIC Document No. ED400048)

Faunce, R. W., & Murton, B. J. (1965). *Student mobility in selected Minneapolis schools. Report Number 1, Mobility of elementary school children in high and low delinquency areas*. Minneapolis, MN: Youth Development Project.

Gilchrist, M. A. (1970). *Reading achievement and geographic mobility*. (ERIC Document No. ED041699)

Hefner, M. (1994). *What is the effect of the rate of transfer on the academic achievement of fourth grade students?* (ERIC Document No. ED364866)

Keeler, E., & McCall, J. (1972). *Simultaneous estimation of teacher mobility and reading scores*. (ERIC Document No. ED075358)

Kerbow, D. (1995). *School mobility, neighborhood poverty, and student academic growth: The case of math achievement in the Chicago Public Schools*. Paper presented at the Workshop on the Study of Urban Inequality, University of Chicago, IL.

Kerbow, D. (1996). Patterns of urban student mobility and local school reform. *Journal of Education for Students Placed at Risk, 60*(1), 147–169.

Kids Mobility Project. (1998). *Kids mobility project report*. Available at http://www.fhfund.org/Research/Kids.htm. Minneapolis, MN: Family Housing Fund.

Ligon, G., & Paredes, V. (1992, April). *Student mobility rate: A moving target*. Paper presented at the American Educational Research Association annual meeting, San Francisco, CA. (ERIC Document No. ED349335)

Mehana, M., & Reynolds, A. J. (1995). *The effects of school mobility on scholastic achievement*. (ERIC Document No. ED385381)

Montgomery County Public Schools. (1998). *Student and staff mobility in the Wheaton Cluster: Year 1 (1997–98) report*. Rockville, MD: Author. (Available at http://www.mcps.k12.md.us/departments/dea/PROJECTS/mobility)

Neuman, J. (1988). *What should we do about the highly mobile student?* Mt. Vernon, WA: The Research Center. (ERIC Document No. ED305545)

Reynolds, A. J. (1991). *Multiple influences on early school adjustment: Results from the longitudinal study of children at risk*. (ERIC Document No. ED334019)

Schachter, J. (2001, May). *Geographic mobility. March 1999 to March 2000.* Washington, DC: U.S. Census Bureau.

Sebring, et al. (1995). *Charting reform: Chicago teachers take stock.* Chicago, IL: Consortium on Chicago School Research.

Sewell, C. (1982). *The impact of pupil mobility on assessment of achievement and its implications for program planning.* (ERIC Document No. ED228322)

Temple, J. A., & Reynolds, A. J. (1999). School mobility and achievement: Longitudinal findings from an urban cohort. *Journal of School Psychology, 37*(4), 355–377.

U.S. Department of Education, National Center for Education Statistics. (1995). *The condition of education 1995.* National Education Longitudinal Study of 1988, Base Year (1988) and Second Follow-up (1992) Surveys. Washington, DC: Author.

Wasserman, D. (2001). *Moving targets: Student mobility and school and student achievement.* Paper presented at the annual meeting of the American Educational Research Association, Seattle, WA. (ERIC Document No. ED452267)

Waters, T. Z. (1996). *Mobility and reading achievement.* (ERIC Document No. ED394126)

CHAPTER TEN

Model-Based Mathematical Languages as Technological Literacy: Some Reflections on an Urban School Challenge

William F. Tate
Washington University in St. Louis

The *Standards for Technological Literacy: Content for the Study of Technology* describe technology as the modification of the natural environment to satisfy human needs and wants (International Technology Education Association, 2000). *Technological literacy* is defined as the ability to use, manage, assess, and understand technology. A technologically literate person comprehends technology in increasing nuanced ways that evolve over the course of a life span. Specifically, technological literacy includes understanding what technology is, how it is designed, how it influences social structures and interactions, and how it is in turn shaped by societal structures.

The International Society for Technology in Education (ISTE; 2002) initiated a set of technology standards that define technological literacy in six broad categories. The standards define specifically what teachers should know about technology. The six broad areas of technological literacy are:

- Understand technology operations and concepts;
- Design and plan effective learning environments supported by technology;
- Implement curriculum plans that include methods and strategies for applying technology to maximize student learning;
- Apply technology to facilitate a variety of effective assessment and evaluation strategies;

- Use technology to enhance productivity and professional practice; and

- Understand the social, ethical, legal, and human issues surrounding the use of technology in preK to 12 schools.

The purpose of this chapter is twofold. The main intent is to discuss the coaction of mathematics and technology as a model-based language. Model-based languages are an important kind of technological literacy. The second purpose is to describe one effort to implement a model-based approach to algebra in a large urban school district. In particular, I examine the capacity of the Dallas Independent School District (DISD) to develop a technologically literate teacher workforce in the area of school mathematics. Rather than examine the professional development model or other teacher-related activities in the district, my focus is on the technological infrastructure of the DISD.

Three particular ISTE standards relevant to the content domain of mathematics are central to this analysis.[1] The first ISTE standard is the ability to select and apply technology tools for research, information analysis, problem solving, and decision making in mathematics learning. A second ISTE standard that is central to my analysis of institutional capacity is the ability of teachers to investigate and apply expert systems, intelligent agents, and simulations in real-world settings that involve mathematics and its applications. A third and final ISTE standard is the willingness and ability of teachers to collaborate with peers, experts, and others to contribute to the mathematics knowledge base by using technology to compile, synthesize, produce, and disseminate information, models, and other creative works.

These three specific skill areas are part of what Skovsmose and Valero (2002) termed *technological action*. They stated:

> Mathematics does not exist as independent knowledge in society. Social actors, not only mathematicians, use mathematics as a descriptive and prescriptive tool. Mathematics, including its applied forms such as engineering mathematics and mathematical economics, is part of the available resources

---

[1]My discussion is in part based on my service in the school district from 1999 to 2001, where I served as scholar in residence and eventually assistant superintendent—mathematics and science. During this period, I also served as project director of the National Science Foundation funded Urban Systemic Program. Many of my remarks related to capacity are drawn from my experience and documents prepared by internal and external evaluators and review teams. This chapter is based on work supported by the National Science Foundation under award No. ESI-0227619. Any opinions, findings, and conclusions or recommendations expressed in this publication are those of the author and do not necessarily reflect the views of the National Science Foundation.

for technological action, involving planning and decision making. We use the term *technological action* (their emphasis) in the broadest possible sense, including making decisions about, for example, how to manage the economy of the family, establishing a new security system for electronic communications, investigating traffic regulations, organizing insurance policies, instituting quality control of mechanical constructions, providing a booking system for airlines, testing algorithms and computer programs. . . . To express this rapidly growing multitude of "actions through mathematics," we highlight three characteristics of the way in which society operates with and through mathematics in technological enterprises. First, using of mathematics, it is possible to establish a space of (technological) alternatives to a situation. Mathematics also provides a limitation of this space of alternatives. . . . In this sense, mathematics serves as a source of technological imagination. . . . Second, mathematics allows us to investigate particular details of a not-yet-realized plan. However, hypothetical reasoning about details of imagined constructions, supported by mathematics, also lays a trap because mathematics imposes a limitation of perspectives from which hypothetical situations are investigated. In particular, risks can emerge from the gaps in hypothetical reasoning, which might overlook whole sets of consequences of certain technological implementations. Finally, as a resource for technological action and decision making, mathematics becomes an inseparable part of our present reality and of other aspects of society. . . . In particular, the development of informational society is closely linked to the spread of mathematical based technologies. (pp. 395–396)

Skovsmose and Valero provided a way to think about mathematics as a building block for technological literacy. It should be obvious to the causal observer that the coaction of mathematics/engineering as foundational to a technological literacy is an indicator of not only what teachers and students should know, but also what school systems must support vis-à-vis policy, institutional priorities, and capacity-building activities.[2]

This chapter is organized into four sections. The first section provides some insights into the sociopolitical context of the Dallas Metroplex. This discussion focuses on supply and demand considerations related to technological literacy and urban education. The second section describes the systemic reform effort in the DISD and the technological mission associated with this initiative. The systemic reform program was a significant force in the district's efforts to develop a technologically ready teacher workforce. The third section is a discussion of the challenges of implementing a curriculum built on precepts of mathematics as a model-based language in the DISD. The final section consists of recommendations for

---

[2]The term *technological literacy* is broad and varies dramatically. I use the term as part of a coaction between mathematics and engineering. This is only one of many ways the term might be used.

improving the capacity of a school district to implement a technology-rich, model-based language approach to mathematics.

THE METROPLEX: A SOCIOPOLITICAL CONTEXT

Urban schools in the United States educate between 40% and 50% of the limited English-proficient students, about 50% of the minority students, and 40% of the low-income students (Lipman, Burns, & McArthur, 1996). Recent projections suggest that the nation's schools will have to replace over two thirds of the current teacher workforce (National Commission on Mathematics and Science Teaching for the 21st Century, 2000). This situation is most acute in our nation's urban centers. A survey conducted by the Council of Great City Schools (2000) of its member district indicated that over 95% of respondents had an immediate demand for middle- and high school science and mathematics teachers. Further, over two thirds of the respondents indicated a need for technology teachers. This same survey examined the subject areas of greatest interest to prospective teachers in Great City Schools of Education. The majority of future educators expressed an interest in elementary education, social studies/history, early childhood education, and special education. There was far less interest in mathematics and science. Thus, the demand for science, mathematics, engineering, and technology (SMET) teachers far exceeds the potential supply of teacher candidates being educated in urban settings (see also Darling-Hammond, 1995).

Teaching as a profession has generated little interest among Texas youth. Of the more than 68,000 Texans in the Class of 2000 who took the ACT college entrance examination, only 5.8% expressed an interest in teaching as a professional option. Yet the Dallas–Fort Worth Metroplex faces a critical shortage of mathematics, science, and technology teachers. For example, the DISD reported in August 2000 that 25.7% and 18% of their secondary mathematics and science teachers, respectively, would be eligible for retirement in 2004 (Payton, 2000). Further, similar to national trends, the vast majority of science and mathematics teachers leave the profession in the first 5 years of service. The inadequate supply of science and mathematics teachers is only part of the problem.

The shortage of competent science and mathematics teachers must be understood in the context of rising expectations and standards for students. The state of Texas has instituted a high school exit examination that requires all secondary students to demonstrate a level of proficiency in algebra, geometry, biology, and physical science. The state assessment is not only a signal for what students must know, but also establishes a clear benchmark for teacher knowledge. The learning expectations for students provide a framework for developing model teacher development experiences. It is imperative that universities respond with exemplary models of teacher development to support the state standards. The state mathematics and science standards are not the only indicators of rising expectations.

The state has established a teacher certification for engineering educators, thus signaling to the public, and more specifically colleges and universities, that engineering should be part of teacher education and the school curriculum. This recent policy development reflects a serious emphasis on mathematics and engineering education by state officials. Further, the policy change places new demands on teacher education—both pre- and inservice.

The demand for greater student proficiency in mathematics, science, and engineering education occurs during a period of unprecedented population expansion in the region. The Dallas–Fort Worth Metroplex experienced rapid population growth in the 1990s. Dallas is currently the eighth largest city in the United States. The population of Dallas grew 18% during the 1990s. Similar population growth occurred in Fort Worth (19.5%) and the technoburbs of Plano and Garland. Recent census data indicate the latter two Metroplex cities are among the fastest growing cities in the United States. This growth has intensified the demand for technologically proficient teachers and increased the competition across the metropolitan area for these professionals.

The Metroplex population growth coupled with the retirement eligibility status of SMET teachers, relatively low teacher preparation enrollments in mathematics and science teacher education programs, and a local technology-driven economy that offers mathematics and science graduates numerous options captures the essence of a real crisis that has significant implications for the technological literacy of teachers and students in this urban setting.

SYSTEMIC REFORM AND STANDARDS: A TECHNOLOGICAL VISION

With the 1989 release of the *Curriculum and Evaluation of Standards for School Mathematics* by the National Council of Teachers of Mathematics (NCTM), the standards movement in K to 12 education was born. Since that time, NCTM (2000) has released a series of standards documents, most recently the *Principles and Standard for School Mathematics*. The standards developed by NCTM have been embraced by local and state mathematics organizations, state departments of education, and federal policymakers. For example, the Texas Education Agency used the draft version of the Curriculum and Evaluation Standards for School Mathematics as a guide to develop their state textbook proclamation and curriculum objectives.

To support the advancement and implementation of standards-based curriculum and assessment, the National Science Foundation initiated a large-scale reform project entitled the Urban Systemic Initiative (USI). The DISD was awarded an USI in 1994. The Dallas USI represented a shared vision and cooperation of the District, the City of Dallas, the Chambers of Commerce, local colleges, and area business and industry for the improvement of mathematics, science and technology education (Payton, 2000).[3] One of the major goals of the Dallas USI program included restructuring K to 12 mathematics, science, and technology (MST) programs into a coordinated, unified curricular MST strand that maintains NCTM standards and appropriate professional development.

One key feature of the NCTM standards documents (1989, 1991) is the defining role of technology in school mathematics, particularly algebra. There is a problematic myth associated with school algebra. Many educators view algebra as a subject that is only part of the secondary curriculum. In reality, algebra is an integral part of the elementary school curriculum. This is more visible if a working definition of algebra is available for teachers and administrators. School algebra—and the origins of all algebra—is about the following:

- The basic number systems—integers and real numbers and those derived from them, such as the rational and complex numbers.
- The arithmetic operations (+, −, ×, ÷) on these number systems.
- The linear order and resulting geometric structure defined on the real line. For example, notions of size (whether one number is larger or smaller than another) and distance between numbers.
- The study of algebraic equations that arise naturally in these systems.[4]

This working definition of *algebra* reflects traditional notions about the subject. Curriculum writers often implement this definition of algebra or other similar interpretations of the domain with a central focus on the following topics:

---

[3]In 1999, the DISD was awarded a second five-year grant from the National Science Foundation–Urban System Program (USP). The USP represented an opportunity to continue and build on the work of the USI. For purposes of clarity in this paper, USI and USP can be used interchangeably to describe the DISD's systemic efforts in mathematics, science, and technology.

[4]This definition is taken from Bass (1998).

- Algebra is viewed as generalized arithmetic, where variables represent pattern generalizations.
- Algebra is viewed as the study of solving equations (at this level linear equations) and translating well defined problems into equations (with the intent to solve the equations). Here variables are either unknowns or constants.
- Algebra is viewed as the study of functional relationships. Under this view, a variable is an argument representing the domain value of a function or parameter representing a number on which other numbers depend.
- Algebra is viewed as the study of structure or properties of numbers and operations.[5]

In their chapter, "Flux in School Algebra: Curricular Change, Graphing Technology, and Research on Student Learning and Teaching," Yerushalmy and Chazan (2002) stated: "School algebra is a complicated curricular arena to describe, one that is undergoing change. Yet our capacity to track curricular change, to study the knowledge teachers use in implementing such change, and to understand what students learn as a result of such change all hinge on descriptions of this curricular arena" (p. 725). This is an excellent insight into curriculum development in the area of algebra. Absent from our working definition of algebra (derived from traditional notions of algebra) or the aforementioned views of algebra is a more recent perspective on algebraic thinking and reasoning that is linked to a dynamic viewpoint of the subject.

The dynamic view is part of the historical evolution of school algebra. The dynamic view of algebra is linked to important shifts in the syntax and problem context of mathematical representations. Confrey (1998) noted:

Most textbooks still begin algebra with solving for unknowns. Treating algebra as a "generalized arithmetic," teachers expect students to learn to decode complex syntax, and, typically, to solve for x. In these settings "x" is just an unknown, and its solution is either right (matches the teacher's or solves the equation), or it is wrong. A great deal of research show (sic) that even when students learn to carry out these sequences faultlessly, seldom can they adequately explain or justify their solutions. Implicit grammatical rules trip them up, and algebraic manipulation is only learned by those who, through diligence, repetition, and practice, are willing to gain familiarity and fluency in the rules and procedures . . . Research on a functional approach (to algebra, my addition) has shown that students tend to prefer this approach. They find the use of "real-world" problems to be highly motivating,

---

[5]These views of algebra are more fully articulated in Usiskin (1988).

and they show evidence of deeper thought at younger ages. Instead of focusing exclusively on the manipulation of symbols, they can move from problem context to problem context, often using these as the comparative structure rather than the symbolic algebraic form. The challenge becomes how to order the context so as to be assured that the students are gaining progressive conceptual development and also that their use of such powerful tools as graphing calculators and computer software is accompanied by a flexible and deep level of understanding. (pp. 37–38)

Confrey's remarks are consistent with curriculum standards calling for a dynamic view of algebra. The organizing themes of the dynamic view of algebra follow:

• Language and Representation. Algebra is viewed as the study of language with "dialects" of literal symbols, graphs, tables, words, and other visual displays. Different representations express and reconfigure quantities in a wide variety of situations.

• Structure. The study of algebraic structure implies thinking how systems operate; for example, what enabling characteristics of a system allow for operations on fractions or equations to be solved. The key aspect of the study is to build on generalized arithmetic to formulate and manipulate general statements about numbers.

• Functions and Relations. Functions can be expressed in virtually all the representational systems of algebra. Change and variation are important ideas within this theme.

• Modeling. Algebraic relations are viewed in terms of the phenomena they model. The goals for modeling include:

—representing quantity and relationships among quantities;

—predicting what happens in quantitative settings;

—controlling, where possible, the outcomes to quantitative processes;

—extending the applications and establishing the validity of new relationships in the structure of algebra.[6]

Modeling is the process of developing a language for describing patterns. These patterns can be tested internally with mathematics and observationally in the world with scientific methods. Modeling emphasizes the need for approaches to mathematical thinking that are traditionally limited in most curriculum frameworks. For example, the study of applied mathematics in high-tech engineering—like representing information bearing signals as discrete or continuous graphs and classifying signals as periodic or nonperiodic—is severely limited unless the student has access

---

[6]These goals for algebra are discussed in Dossey (1998).

to problem contexts that require an in-depth understanding of variability. Signals are patterns of variations that represent or encode information. They are important for measurement, evaluating other physical systems, telecommunications, medical instrumentation, and other areas.

The technological literacy skills developed in the modeling process include constructing a model, exploring the characteristics of the model, applying the model to resolve a question of interest, and assessing the appropriateness of the model throughout the process. The modeling process is particularly relevant because the knowledge base in mathematics, engineering, and science is expanding and changing rapidly, yet the time and opportunity to cover all newly developed ideas is relatively constant. Consequently, it is important that curriculum provide students an opportunity to develop skill sets that are generally applicable across the expanding scientific knowledge base. Model-based approaches to learning are central to this type of literacy.

To implement a model-based approach to mathematics means that a school district must have the infrastructure to support technology-rich learning environments. The remainder of this chapter is devoted to a closer look at some strengths and limitations of the DISD's technological infrastructure.

A CHALLENGE TO CHANGE

This section is a case history of the DISD's USP effort to implement a technologically focused, model-based mathematics learning environment—the Cognitive Tutor. This initiative was designed for Grades 9 to 12. The purpose of the case history is to provide important lessons learned about planning for technological literacy. Prior to discussing any specifics about the implementation process for this program, additional background information about the technological infrastructure of the district is important.

Access to computers is not uniform for all students across the school district. The school district is divided into nine areas, labeled Areas 1 to 9. Table 10.1 shows disparities in the student–computer ratio by area at the secondary level.

Overall students attending schools in Area 9 have an advantage in the availability of computer resources compared with all other areas of the school district. This disparity can be attributed in large part to the fact that Area 9 is composed of magnet schools (e.g., School Science and Engineering, Talented and Gifted, Communications, Business and Management, Health Professions, and Visual Arts). These schools are in general newer facilities as compared with other district buildings or they have un-

TABLE 10.1
Secondary Student–Computer Ratio by Area (2000)

Area	Student (in thousands)	Computer (in thousands)	Ratio
1	4.5	.7	6.3
2	2.9	.8	3.6
3	3.1	.5	5.8
4	3.4	.4	7.8
5	3.1	.6	5.1
6	5.2	1.0	5.1
7	3.5	.5	7.5
8	3.8	.5	7.3
9	8.1	3.1	2.7
Overall	37.6	8.2	4.6

Source. Texas School Performance Review—Dallas Independent School District, 2001.
Note. Ratio calculation is based on actual not rounded numbers.

dergone major remodeling. Thus, not only do they have more computers, but my personal inspections suggest the computer labs present in these buildings are more up to date compared with other areas. The data in Fig. 10.1 are somewhat incomplete in that it is not possible to get a sense of the age and capabilities of the technology across the areas. These data were not available to senior management of the district in a central location. This was a major infrastructure limitation for program managers seeking to implement technology-driven initiatives.

In response to this limitation, the leadership of the Dallas USP worked closely with school-level teacher technologists. The district's Teacher Technologist program was designed to provide a link between each school and the Instructional Technology Department. The purpose of the program was to promote the efficient integration of technology throughout the curriculum.

The teacher technologists were experienced certified teachers who, in a majority of the schools, were performing the duties of the full-time teacher in addition to the scope of work associated with technology support. The teacher technologists were paid the salary of a teacher plus a $2,000 supplemental stipend. An audit of the school district stated what most administrators knew about the work life of a teacher technologist— overwhelmed (Texas School Performance Review, 2001). Table 10.2 provides a comparison of the original scope of responsibilities for teacher technologists and the actual demands placed on them by colleagues and administrators.

The decision by the leadership of the Dallas USP to work closely with building-level teacher technologists added more stress to a support system that was operating beyond its stated duty and intended function. It is

TABLE 10.2
Teacher Technologists' Challenge

Initial Scope of Work	Expectations Beyond Initial Scope of Work
• Promote classroom technology integration. • Account for local school technology hardware and software. • Serve as liaison with the Technical Assistance Center for hardware repair and software support. • Distribute, install, and secure instructional technology software site license utilization.	• Serve as primary technology support for principals. • Provide informal instruction to individuals who have not attended formal training opportunities. • Set up and configure hardware. • Assist with nontechnical or minor problems, such as supporting word processing tasks, creating graphic figures, and assisting with e-mail messages. • Viewed as first line of support for all technical problems on campus.

Source. Texas Performance Review—Dallas Independent School District (June 2001).

important to note that the Teacher Technologist program was designed for program managers in the Instructional Technology Department, rather than subject matter specialists charged with curriculum design and implementation. This tension was never completely resolved during my tenure. The remainder of my discussion focuses directly on the Cognitive Tutor initiative.

Cognitive Tutor

Since the inception of the USI program, the school district has had a major push toward Algebra I for all students by Grade 9. Other tracks with lower mathematics course-taking standards were eliminated by policy. The achievement results as measured by the state's end-of-course algebra examination have improved, yet the scores remain below the state average and the district leaderships' expectations for all students. Table 10.3 provides a comparison of state pass rates and Dallas pass rates on the end-of-course examination beginning in 1996.

One response to address student performance in Algebra was to implement a curriculum program more consistent with the dynamic view of Algebra being assessed by the state. After careful review, the USP team chose the Cognitive Tutor as a possible intervention. Carnegie Learning's Cognitive Tutor Algebra program was listed as exemplary by the U.S. Department of Education's Mathematics and Science Expert Panel commissioned to evaluate educational programs. The Cognitive Tutor is a full-year, first-year Algebra course that integrates technology in its instructional design. It is consistent with the dynamic view of Algebra, which builds on the

TABLE 10.3
Passing Rates for State End-of-Year Algebra Exam

Year	State Average Pass Rate (%)	Dallas Average Pass Rate (%)
1996	17.8	18.3
1997	18.3	21.3
1998	35.9	10.8
1999	43.4	16.4
2000	43.9	24.8
2001	49.2	27.6

Source. Texas Education Agency, Accountability Rating System, 1996–2001.

model-based approach to mathematics (Koedinger, 1998). The following is a description of the Cognitive Tutor concept:

> To build a Cognitive Tutor, we create a cognitive model of student problem solving in that domain by writing production rules that capture students' multiple strategies and their common misconceptions. These productions are written in a modular fashion so that they can apply to a goal or context independent of how that goal was arrived at. For simplicity of illustration, I provide an example from the domain of equation solving:
>
> Correct: IF the goal is to solve $a(bx+c) = d$
> THEN rewrite this as $bx + c = d/a$
> Correct: IF the goal is to solve $a(bx+c) = d$
> THEN rewrite this as $abx + ac = d$
> Buggy: IF the goal is to solve $a(bx+c) = d$
> THEN rewrite this as $abx + c = d$

The first two productions illustrate alternative strategies for the same problem-solving goal. This allows the Cognitive Tutor to follow students down problem-solving paths of their own choosing. The third Buggy production represents a common misconception. Such rules allow the cognitive tutor to recognize such misconceptions and provide appropriate assistance. The Cognitive Tutor makes use of the cognitive model to follow students through their individual approaches to a problem. It does so using a technique called *model tracing*. Model tracing allows the Cognitive Tutor to provide students individualized assistance that is just in time and sensitive to the students' particular approach to a problem (Koedinger, 1998).

The Cognitive Tutor is a product of cognitive theory, empirical testing, and a focus on mathematics as a modeling language. In my opinion and that of my colleagues, this program represented a real opportunity to positively influence student learning of Algebra. Ultimately, in my capacity as assistant superintendent—mathematics and science—I investigated the fiscal conditions associated with the implementation of the Cognitive Tutor. The Cognitive Tutor is produced as a software package that is purchased at a rate of $25,000 per site license. A site license is issued to a specific school building. In the case of Dallas, there were 35 high schools. To outfit each high school with a site license would cost the school district $875,000. The student books were $5 a piece. The books are disposable and must be purchased yearly for each student. Carnegie Learning's School Care program provides initial teacher preparation (a 4- to 5-day centralized training course), ongoing updates and upgrades to the software and printed curriculum materials, and help-desk telephone and e-mail weekday support (another expense if it does not exist). The annual cost of this program is approximately $2,500 per site. To operate efficiently, the Cognitive Tutor requires up-to-date computers and specific networking capabilities. Tables 10.4 and 10.5 provide a summary of the computer and networking requirements for the Cognitive Tutor.

A classroom setting supporting the Cognitive Tutor should have a computer for every student in the class and the computers networked. Most secondary schools did not have the lab space available during school hours. Thus, there were two options. The first option was to eliminate other technology programs—school to career initiatives and other technology-related curricular opportunities. This option was not politically or academically viable. The second option was to purchase sufficient technology to support the Cognitive Tutor requirements. Moreover, there was a need to add portables to some schools to house any additional technology. This was not a good alternative for reasons related to security. However, assume this was a viable option and the fiscal support was possible. Now assume further you have the ability to secure the funding for the site

TABLE 10.4
Hardware Requirements to Support Cognitive Tutor

Requirement	Minimum	Recommended
Operating system	Windows 95, 98, ME, 2000 or NT 4.0 Workstation	Windows XP
Processor	200 MHz Pentium	450 MHz Pentium III
RAM	64 MB	128 MB 256 for Windows XP
Disk space	200 MB free	300 MB free
Monitor	800 × 600 resolution; 16-bit High Color	1024 × 768; 16-bit High Color
Network	10 MB Ethernet	100 MB Ethernet
Other	CD-ROM drive; TCP/IP	CD-ROM drive; TCP/IP

Source. Carnegie Learning.

TABLE 10.5
Networking Requirements to Support Cognitive Tutor

Requirement	Minimum	Recommended
Operating system	Windows NT Server 4.0 / Windows 2000 or Novell Netware 4.11	Windows 2000 or Novell Netware 5.11
Processor	300 MHz Pentium II	450 MHz Pentium III
RAM	64 MB	128 MB
Disk space	250 MB free	500 MB free
Other	CD-ROM drive; TCP/IP	CD-ROM drive; TCP/IP

Source. Carnegie Learning.

license, technical support, books, professional development (that often includes teacher pay), additional computers, networking, and portables; there is another possible hidden cost—wiring. I found that most of our middle and high schools did not have the electrical infrastructure to support this exemplary technology-driven program. As a result of this infrastructure problem, many of the schools could only implement the Cognitive Tutor with a limited number of students. However, the cost to the district is almost identical to full implementation cost (minus the cost of upgrading the electrical infrastructure). This is a type of hidden cost. Upgrading the electrical infrastructure would require a tax increase and/or be included in bond vote.

An additional structural barrier was onsite technical support. The teacher technologists were supportive, but ultimately they reported to another department with its own initiatives. Further, these colleagues were overworked and lacked the kind of support needed to complete their assigned duties.

The school sites that successfully implemented the Cognitive Tutor had one common feature—an innovative principal. These principals carved out the space and computers to support the implementation process. Their teacher technologists worked for the school, rather than for the central administration. Thus, onsite support for the initiative in these buildings was consistently high. It is not surprising that these successful principals took the time to attend the Cognitive Tutor Leadership program, rather than send a subordinate. In the zero-sum game often associated with curriculum implementation, mathematics was a priority in the buildings that implemented the Cognitive Tutor.

A strategy for gaining traction in reform is to communicate the successful implementation of the reform strategy to other sites. This is often accomplished in workshops and meetings. The USP staff also considered sharing best practices related to the implementation of the Cognitive Tutor vis-à-vis Internet communication. This was difficult to accomplish in the high school settings because of access challenges and our failure to develop a supportive culture for communicating with technology. The use of e-mail and Web-based structures requires central administration and on-site support systems. This was an area that needed improvement.

FINAL THOUGHTS AND RECOMMENDATIONS

Real opportunities for urban school students to learn important mathematical ideas and specifically model-based approaches to the subject depend on the development of appropriate technological infrastructure. The potential for the use of computer technology by secondary students is enormous. The constraints to the use of technology-rich mathematics environments rest not with the learner, but often with adults failing to organize appropriate infrastructure systems.

My experience in Dallas suggests that a few changes could drastically improve the potential of the system to realize the goal of providing all students an opportunity to learn using a model-based approach to mathematics. I offer a few suggestions for educators interested in supporting the implementation of a technology-rich algebraic modeling language in an urban school context. My recommendations are focused specifically on matters of infrastructure.

My first recommendation is that school districts should produce a profile that serves as a technology inventory and statistics report for system managers that provides data in the following areas:

- Quantity and types of computer and peripherals in schools;
- Types of software being used for instruction;
- Purpose and type of student computers used in schools;
- Technology programs being offered;
- Technology skill level of teachers; and
- Technology skill level of administrators.

My second recommendation is that the school district should establish a definition of technology proficient based on national standards for teachers and administrators. This would allow for system administrators to document the technology skill levels of teachers and principals. More important, professional development could be tailored to specific groups based on skill, rather than the "one size fits all" learning opportunities that permeate the culture of the school district.

My third recommendation is that the school district should allocate the funding and support learning opportunities to create a cadre to teacher technologists who work full time onsite in secondary schools. The part-time technologists lacked the time to truly support the implementation of the USP initiative and many other projects. Moreover, a full-time technologist could assist with the development a culture where communicating with colleagues off-site using technology was part of normal practice.

My final recommendation is to design a broad-based technology plan that includes organizational and space considerations. During my tenure, the mode of operation was a product of organizational tensions among departments including the Instructional Technology Department. Specifically, many departments and schools operated on a kind of technological island, with each group creating in real time their own technology program. The plans often did not take into consideration how best to effectively use space. A technology-driven Algebra program that is consistent with the dynamic view of algebra in many cases requires school districts to (a) adopt a set of mathematics standards, (b) identify the resources including the space necessary for achieving these standards, (c) formulate a long-term plan for developing an instructional program that incorporates the standards and allocating the aligned resources, (d) have an implementation plan in place before money is spent, and (e) adopt the necessary structural changes to maximize cost-effectiveness.

The future of urban school students to understand and appreciate the power of model-based languages in mathematics depends on many variables. An important start is to design and develop the appropriate technological infrastructure.

REFERENCES

Bass, H. (1998). Algebra with integrity and reality. In *The nature and role of Algebra in the K-14 curriculum: Proceedings of a national symposium* (pp. 9–15). Washington, DC: National Academy Press.

Confrey, J. (1998). What do we know about K-14 students' learning of algebra? In *The nature and role of Algebra in the K-14 curriculum: Proceedings of a national symposium* (pp. 37–40). Washington, DC: National Academy Press.

Council of Great City Schools. (2000). *The urban teacher challenge: Teacher demand and supply in the great city schools.* Washington, DC: Author. (Retrieved June 13, 2002, from the World Wide Web: http://www.cgcs.org/pdfs/utc.pdf.)

Darling-Hammond, L. (1995). Inequality and access to knowledge. In J. A. Banks & C. A. McGee Banks (Eds.), *Handbook of research in multicultural education* (pp. 465–483). New York: Macmillan.

Dossey, J. (1998). Making algebra dynamic and motivating: A national challenge. In *The nature and role of Algebra in the K-14 curriculum: Proceedings of a national symposium* (pp. 17–22). Washington, DC: National Academy Press.

International Society for Technology in Education. (2002). *National Educational Technology Standards for Teachers.* Eugene, OR: Author.

International Technology Education Association. (2000). *Standards for technological literacy*. Reston VA: Author.

Koedinger, K. (1998). *Intelligent cognitive tutors as modeling tools and instructional model*. Invited paper for the National Council of Teachers of Mathematics Standards 2000 Technology Conference.

Lipman, L., Burns, S., & McArthur, E. (1996). *Urban schools: The challenge of location and poverty*. Washington, DC: U.S. Department of Education, National Center for Education Statistics.

National Commission on Mathematics and Science Teaching for the 21st Century: *Before its too late*. (2000). Washington, DC: U.S. Department of Education. (Retrieved June 13, 2002, from the World Wide Web: http://www.ed.gov/americacounts/glenn/)

National Council of Teachers of Mathematics. (1989). *Curriculum and evaluation standards for school mathematics*. Reston, VA: Author.

National Council of Teachers of Mathematics. (1991). *Professional standards for teaching mathematics*. Reston, VA: Author.

National Council of Teachers of Mathematics. (2000). *Principles and standards for school mathematics*. Reston, VA: Author.

Payton, R. (2000). *Dallas Urban System Initiative: 1994–1999 summary report*. Dallas, TX: Dallas Public Schools.

Skovsmose, O., & Valero, P. (2002). Democratic access to powerful mathematical ideas. In L. English (Ed.), *Handbook of international research in mathematics education* (pp. 383–407). Mahwah, NJ: Lawrence Erlbaum Associates.

Texas School Performance Review. (2001). *Dallas Independent School District*. Austin, TX: Texas Comptroller of Public Accounts.

Usiskin, Z. (1988). Conceptions of school algebra and uses of variables. In A. F. Coxford (Ed.), *The ideas of Algebra, K–12* (pp. 8–19). Reston, VA: National Council of Teachers of Mathematics.

Yerushalmy, M., & Chazan, D. (2002). Flux in school algebra: Curricular change, graphing technology, and research on student learning and teacher knowledge. In L. English (Ed.), *Handbook of international research in mathematics education* (pp. 725–756). Mahwah, NJ: Lawrence Erlbaum Associates.

PART THREE

SAINTS AND THEIR RESCUE EFFORTS

CHAPTER ELEVEN

Logistics of Systemic Change: The Reading Academy

Georgia J. Thompson
Dallas Independent School District

Teacher training, education, and professional development are paramount as educators acknowledge the monumental challenges that face classroom teachers in a large urban school district. Our teachers must be skilled and *tooled* to make ongoing literacy decisions, adjust instruction to meet the needs of all students, have a cognitive foundation in reading and writing, and utilize pedagogical techniques to be effective implementers. With this premise in mind, the Reading Academy evolved as the major training component of the systemic *Dallas Reading Plan*. My responsibility in this chapter is not to review the literature on staff development models, but to reflect and give my perspective on this innovative initiative of which I have been a part since its inception in the fall of 1996.

I began my literacy crusade in Dallas as a Lead Reading Teacher (LRT) or literacy coach after almost 20 years as a classroom teacher. Two years ago, I crossed over to the administrative side of training and became the director of the Reading Academy. I have seen all perspectives now: working in the trenches with the teachers and students as a coach, directing the training through the Reading Academy, and serving as an adjunct for our partnering university.

The history of the Reading Academy began with the conception of the *Dallas Reading Plan* in 1996. It was constructed around a management system with five major components serving as a framework for providing students the literacy skills necessary for life in the 21st century (see Fishbone in Appendixes). The Delivery System or Training Model was one of those components.

To deliver training in the most efficient and effective manner the first year, the *Dallas Reading Plan* utilized a trainer-of-trainers model. Extensive training of a Vertical Team (principal and one teacher from kindergarten, first, second, and third grades) on key instructional strategies identified in the Dallas Plan was delivered by LRTs and national reading experts at a central site three times during the 1996 to 1997 school year. The intent of the Vertical Team training was to help one teacher at each grade level become an expert at teaching reading so that each grade level would have a model and coach. By including the principal as part of the Vertical Team, the desire was to develop instructional leaders at the campus level who would provide support for teachers while making reading instruction a school priority.

The content of the whole-day training sessions included research-based best practices such as: instruction in phonemic awareness, spelling stages, developmental writing, oral reading, comprehension strategies, assessment, benchmarks, language development, second language acquisition, and classroom management. This initial attempt by the Reading Department at controlling the delivery of the reading curriculum was designed to change the way reading was being taught in the district and to improve the quality of the instruction. The primary purpose of the training was to impact student achievement.

This whole-day, one-shot training model proved to be flawed for several reasons:

1. The one-size-fits-all sessions did not account for the differing levels of expertise and needs among teachers.
2. The sessions tended to overload the teachers with too much information and too many handouts.
3. The Vertical Team members had to plan for substitute teachers because they were away from their classes for the entire day.
4. There was an insufficient pool of substitute teachers; therefore, some classes were combined or taught by an aide or paraprofessional.
5. The building principal was away, sometimes leaving the management of the campus in the hands of a teacher or an office manager if there was no assistant principal or dean.
6. Some grade-level teachers did not work together as a cohesive team, making the dissemination of the reading information difficult.
7. Many times the Vertical Team members lacked the coaching and presentation skills to be effective experts, and the message often became misconstrued.
8. The time constraints at grade-level meetings limited the amount of information that could be passed on.

9. Many times the principals were unable to or did not set aside training times because of the unavailability of substitutes or personnel to cover classes.

In the 1997 to 1998 school year, Year 2 of the *Dallas Reading Plan*, the same Vertical Team model continued. There was a slight modification to the concept in an attempt to correct some of the problems found in the Year 1 implementation model. The training plan still pulled the Vertical Team members from all 144 elementary schools to a central location three times per year for the professional development sessions. This time the job of the Vertical Team members was to go back to their campuses and set up their class as a model classroom for the other staff members to visit and observe expert teaching. A condensed half-day version of the Vertical Team training was provided later by the Lead Reading Teachers (LRTs) for all the K to 3 teachers who were not Vertical Team members. This was done at grade-level meetings, in after-school sessions at neighboring campuses, on Saturdays, or during the day on each campus if classes could be covered. This training plan was devised because many teachers said they wanted to experience the training firsthand, not from their Vertical Team members. The response to this change was overwhelmingly positive, but expensive. The Reading Department not only paid for the Vertical Team training, but picked up the expense for the substitutes and supplemental pay for the masses of teachers if their training sessions were after school or on Saturday.

The content was divided into three modules—Modules A, B, and C—making it easier for the LRTs to replicate the training. The research-based best practices were expanded to include a coaching model for the Vertical Team members to help them coach their peers with the reading implementation. The idea was for the LRTs to coach the Vertical Team members and for the Vertical Team members to coach their peers. In addition to coaching techniques, the training included: skills instruction, direct comprehension instruction, reading benchmarks, Texas Assessment of Academic Skills (TAAS) strategies, graphic organizers, higher order thinking, teacher read alouds, guided reading, running records, oral language development, shared reading, independent reading, classroom design and management, assessment and profiling, grouping for instruction, lesson planning, and evaluation. Scripts were prepared to provide consistent training throughout the district.

This second-year model overcame the problems of inconsistency of message and lack of coaching expertise. Still seemingly insurmountable were the problems of training teachers without pulling them from their classrooms, obtaining adequate numbers of substitutes, or the cost of supplemental pay for after-school or Saturday trainings. During this training year, the instructional delivery system was expanded to include video training modules on specific instructional methods aligned to current research on best practice instruction, tools and resources for authentic assessment, connections to lesson content, classroom management strategies to increase organizational effectiveness, and access to national speakers. During this second year, the Research and Evaluation Department was asked to provide accountability quantitatively through the Iowa Tests of Basic Skills (ITBS) scores and qualitatively with program observations in the classrooms of Vertical Team and non-Vertical Team teachers. Fifty observers were trained on a program observation tool and sent out to code teacher and student behaviors, higher order questions, grouping configurations, and implementation of the training components. I was part of this observation team and remember the excitement of seeing evidence of change in the now print-rich classrooms filled with student work, small flexible groups, teacher and student ownership of new instructional strategies, and an observable change in attitude.

Thus, we arrived at our third calendar year of the *Dallas Reading Plan*, a pivotal year in terms of being halfway through a 5-year financial commitment from the business community to help fund the reading initiative. It was also pivotal in the sense of showing growth—student growth, with an increase in student achievement (test scores) and teacher growth, with a paradigm shift for many teachers from the old ways of teaching to the new. We were seeing some change in the classrooms of the Vertical Team members because they were receiving most of the coaching by the LRTs. However, we were not seeing much carryover with the other teachers in the building (Shapley, 1998). The ITBS scores had gone up a little, but certainly there was no big bump in test scores.

What had we learned from those initial 2 years?

1. We learned that a trainer-of-trainers model with whole-day training sessions did not work.
2. We learned that our training needed to be delivered to everyone thoroughly, consistently, articulately, and in ongoing increments.
3. We learned that with a lack of follow-up support, unsupervised training could result in wasted time and money, as well as wasted instructional time for students.
4. We learned that a coaching model dependent on perceived needs of the teacher did not work.

Still motivated to improve student reading ability districtwide and to have an enduring impact on teachers' literacy instruction, we revised and redesigned the Reading Academy model in the fall of 1998. This new model was to be systemic deep training provided over time coupled with an implementation expectation in combination with immediate coaching in the classroom by LRTs. In creating a climate for lasting change at the building level, it was critical to offer administrator training in effective literacy methods. So a Southwestern Bell-sponsored Principals' Fellowship was established. This graduate-level course offered administrators an overview of the basic tenets of balanced literacy and outlined how to establish an effective building-wide literacy program.

The Reading Academy was created, offering teachers a two-semester graduate course to develop capacity for consistently delivering balanced literacy instruction. With the help of academic deans and professors of reading from a number of area universities, the Reading Department designed a two-semester course entitled "Literacy, Assessment and Instruction I and II" to serve as the cognitive foundation of the Reading Academy. The K to 3 balanced literacy curriculum was designed around a backbone of five instructional methodologies: skills instruction and practice, oral reading/writing, instructional level reading/writing, independent reading/writing, and developmental writing (see Literacy Backbone in Appendixes). The content of the Reading Academy was in agreement with current research literature and meta-analyses of effective reading instructional practices. The theories, strategies, and techniques elaborated on the Texas ExCET Language Arts competencies for Elementary Education and the Texas State Master Reading Teacher competencies. Katy Denson, the evaluator of K to 12 reading in DISD, concluded that the curriculum of the Reading Academy was research based and relevant to DISD educators (Denson, 2001).

The Reading Academy was voluntary, held after school from 4:00 p.m. to 6:40 p.m., and included 450 K to 3 teachers (one teacher each from K, 1, 2, 3) for the 1998 to 1999 school year. As compensation for taking the course, the teachers received a $500 stipend and graduate-level credit for 6 hours in Reading. In addition, the Reading Department paid for their books and tuition. Teams consisting of LRTs, university professors, and credentialed DISD administrators taught the course. The geographic proximity of the course locations was another key to teacher involvement. The course was taught at 20 local DISD school campuses to provide easy accessibility for the teachers. The syllabus was comprehensive, and each class session was scripted to prevent fragmentation of information and encourage consistency in course delivery. The idea was to develop a common language, vocabulary, and toolbox for all teachers. Our goal was to make "every classroom teacher as good as our best."

Professional development should not be conceived as something that ends with graduation from college, nor as something that happens primarily during inservice activities or a day spent at a conference with an outside consultant. Rather ongoing weekly training, ongoing weekly support and coaching from master reading teachers, and regular opportunities for reading and reflection are critical components of the development of excellent teachers. The importance of an effectively trained teacher can never be underestimated. Dr. William Webster, Special Assistant to the Superintendent—Evaluation and Accountability for DISD, stated that, "Teacher-proof programs cannot be designed. Competent teachers can make almost anything work, while incompetent ones can ruin even the most brilliant instructional design" (*Dallas Reading Plan*, 1998). The DISD teacher workforce is not unique to a large urban school district. We have 10,385 teachers: veterans with 20 to 50 years experience, teachers with master's and doctorate degrees, teachers with under 5 years experience, anywhere from 500 to 800 alternative certified teachers (ACs) each year, and permanent substitutes. The experience and ability range is extremely diverse, so the academy was a vehicle to even the playing field.

In redefining our staff development model to achieve true systemic reform, we considered the quality of design and consistency in delivery to be of foremost importance. Our academy design needed to be long term so teachers would have time to learn together, collaborate, and form a supportive community. The teachers needed time to read, reflect, and discuss, and students needed time to practice the strategies learned in class. Their learning was to be a process, during which they would reinvent, reorganize, and construct knowledge through active learning and by linking new information to what they already knew (Robb, 2000). The academy design was not to follow the model of a traditional college course, but was an implementation-based course designed to bring about noticeable change in classrooms. Relatedly, there was a weekly Implementation Goal or Classroom Action Plan (CAP) to be implemented in developmentally appropriate ways by each participant. Weekly visits by the LRT assigned to their building helped coach theory into practice. The LRT's primary role was to offer the level of coaching each participant needed to be comfortable with each new practice.

The required textbooks for the Reading Academy were provided to participants at no charge. Each week a journal entry or written response to the required readings was expected to be submitted to their instructor. As the focus of the academy changed over the last 4 years with each new administration, so have the textbooks. A writing committee comprised of LRTs and DISD reading experts was in charge of writing the course syllabus and weekly sessions for the participants and adjuncts. The writing committee has remained constant and provided stability as we have rewritten and refined the course content each year based on evaluations, focus, and administrations. The LRTs were the primary conduits of training, serving as adjuncts for our partnering universities and teaching the academy course. As adjuncts, they were provided with weekly scripts, handouts for participants, transparencies, and all resources necessary for each session. The partnership agreement with the area universities included the district's payment of the full graduate tuition for each participant.

To augment the weekly Reading Academy sessions and to count as two class meetings, the Reading Department held a Reading Conference on a Saturday each semester. Nationally known reading experts provided numerous workshops for the teachers. This allowed participants to feel confirmation in what they were already doing, hear about national research and hot topics, and learn new strategies. The Reading Conferences have been overwhelmingly successful, increasing in attendance each year. The Fall 2001 Reading Summit involved 1,500 pre-K to 12 teachers and administrators and 35 presenters. Many teachers were turned away due to budget constraints.

Expertise is not conferred in a 6-hour graduate course, but quality, competence, and a motivation to continue learning effective practices in literacy certainly are. For this reason, the 450 teachers who completed the Reading Academy in 1999 were designated not as graduates, but as Laureates and honored with a plaque at the Spring Laureate Banquet.

Challenged to bring all teachers to Laureate status, the Reading Academy continued in 1999 to 2000. Without an administrative mandate, the academy remained an invitational model, but enrollment increased twofold. There is no precise blueprint for designing a professional development system that works. A good design equals success, whereas a bad design equals failure (Lyons & Pinnell, 2001). We were successful. The academy was serving as both a staff development opportunity and an opportunity for teachers interested in furthering their education to apply the course toward a graduate degree. The academy became infectious with visible and substantive changes in instructional practices occurring in Laureate classrooms. It was no longer possible to walk through the halls of an elementary campus and distinguish a Laureate classroom from a non-Laureate classroom. There was carryover to the other teachers in the building. Of course the most important benefit of the academy must be improvement in children's reading. Because of the implementation design of the Reading Academy, teacher growth translated immediately into literacy growth for children. Teacher and student development are reciprocally related and intertwined (Fullan & Hargreaves, 1996). We were beginning to see a rise in test scores for children being taught by a Laureate teacher (Denson, 2000). For the 1999 to 2000 school year, the enrollment in the Academy was 725 teachers at 53 campuses across the city. Four sites were designated as bilingual and taught in Spanish. That meant adding a bilingual writer to the writing team to translate the sessions into Spanish and supplementing our textbooks with an additional ESL/bilingual resource.

With each year came a change in administration and, with that, a change in direction and focus for the Reading Department and Reading Academy. Each year we have had to fight for the Reading Plan and the continuation of the academy. In 2000 to 2001, the assistant superintendent for reading, Dr. Robert B. Cooter, was able to negotiate a true partnership with our participating universities where DISD paid one half of the teachers' tuition and the universities provided scholarship money for the other half of the tuition. This lowered our costs, and we are now able to pay the teachers a $1,000 stipend for successful completion of the year-long course. Due to increased pressure from teachers and principals, we opened the academy to include fourth-, fifth-, and sixth-grade and special education teachers. We hired more writers and revised and rewrote the course to reflect the needs of older learners. We kept the sites separate because of the developmental differences between the K to 3 and 4 to 6 content.

The arrival of the 2001 to 2002 school year brought a whole new set of challenges. For the first time, we had a DISD general superintendent who was willing to take a stand and mandate the use of a research-based reading program—*SRA-Open Court*. This program has helped stabilize instruction for new and veteran teachers alike and for our highly mobile student population. The Reading Academy content was again refined and aligned with *SRA-Open Court*. We changed our textbooks and implementation goals. The role of the LRT became one of coaching the implementation of *SRA-Open Court* and less coaching of the Reading Academy. The spring semester of 2002 expanded to include 2 *Success for All* sites (DISD has 7 Edison schools), 3 bilingual sites, 16 Grade 4 to 6 sites, and 20 pre-K to 3 sites. Next year the proposal includes incorporating a deaf-education class with the teachers learning visual phonics. This semester was also different because more than half of the academy participants were AC teachers. It was a positive move for the AC Department to require the Reading Academy as part of their certification program.

For the first time in the better part of a century, the national focus is on the quality of teaching as a key element in the improvement of education (Darling-Hammond, 1999). Teachers are being asked to educate the most diverse student body in our history to higher academic standards than ever before. This enormous task is one that cannot be teacher-proofed through testing mandates, management systems, or curriculum packages (Darling-Hammond, 1998). The National Assessment of Educational Progress (NAEP) has shown that the qualifications and training of teachers affect reading achievement. The 1996 report of the National Commission on Teaching and America's Future found that investments in teacher knowledge and skills net greater increases in student achievement than other uses of the education dollar (Darling-Hammond, 1999). With this in mind, school districts must radically rethink how professional development should occur. There is a growing consensus that professional development should be sustained, ongoing, and connected to teachers' daily activities with students. We know that teachers learn best by studying, doing, reflecting, collaborating, looking closely at students and their work, and sharing what they see. This kind of teacher learning cannot occur in college classrooms without practice or in school classrooms without knowledge about how to interpret practice.

For the last 6 years, the DISD has been creating a new model of professional development for teachers and principals. Teacher academies that provide ongoing courses of study tied to practice, observations, demonstrations, and coaching by LRTs and a district–university partnership are featured. This approach has shifted from the old model of teacher training or inservicing that was done *to* teachers to a newer model that is done *with* and *by* teachers. The new model is a three-pronged approach: (a) a programmatic remedy of mandating a basal series for districtwide implementation, (b) a training vehicle for offering ongoing teacher development, and (c) the university partnership. A knowledgeable teacher is always more effective in implementing a reading program. Growing evidence suggests that this kind of professional development not only makes teachers feel better about their practice, but also reaps learning gains for students, especially those for whom education is the only road to survival and success. We are working to revive the urban classroom in the DISD.

REFERENCES

Dallas Reading Plan. (1998). Dallas, TX: Dallas Public Schools.

Darling-Hammond, L. (1998). Strengthening the teaching profession: Teacher learning that supports student learning. *Educational Leadership, 55*(5).

Darling-Hammond, L. (1999). Target time toward teachers. *Journal of Staff Development, 20*(2).

Denson, K. (2000). *Final report—Reading and language arts grades K–6: 1999–2000* (REIS00-147-2). Dallas, TX: Dallas Public Schools.

Denson, K. (2001). *Final report. Reading and language arts grades K–6: 2000–2001* (REIS01-147-2). Dallas, TX: Dallas Independent School District, Division of Evaluation, Assessment, and Information Systems.

Fullan, M., & Hargreaves, A. (1996). *What's worth fighting for in your school?* New York: Teachers College Press.

Lyons, C. A., & Pinnell, G. S. (2001). *Systems for change in literacy education*. Portsmouth, NH: Heinemann.

Robb, L. (2000). *Redefining staff development*. Portsmouth, NH: Heinemann.

Shapley, K. (1998). *Final report of the 1997–98 Dallas Reading Plan* (REIS98-300-2). Dallas, TX: Dallas Public Schools.

CHAPTER TWELVE

Mentoring Teacher Change:
Even Cinderella Had a Coach

Jane Moore
Dallas Independent School District

So much of what we know pedagogically, socially, contextually, and culturally has not made its way into the urban classroom. The effects of teacher knowledge of pedagogy, content, and practice appear across curriculum fields and at every level of education (Darling-Hammond, 1999). The National Assessment of Educational Progress (NAEP) has shown that the qualifications and training of teachers can directly affect student performance and reading achievement (National Center for Education Statistics, 1994, n.d.). Moreover, teachers have the lead role in advancing the cutting edge of research-based practices.

Informed teachers make a difference. Teachers who have had more professional staff development in literature-based approaches to reading and writing are more likely to use a wide variety of texts (National Center for Education Statistics, 1994, n.d.). They also seem to be more likely to integrate content areas across the school day, make connections from one content area to another, model learning processes, carefully guide their students to independence, and encourage a life-long desire to read and write. They are more likely to value their students' learning approximations, and they encourage their students to view themselves as readers and writers. This can lead students to higher reading achievement and produces a sense of self-efficacy (Darling-Hammond, 1998, 2000). A characteristic of the profession is that each classroom becomes a community of learners. These minicommunities are isolated by the nature of job duty and becomes driven by what the teacher knows. It is what the teacher *does* when the classroom door is closed that makes the ultimate difference.

With this philosophy in mind, an effort to curricularize, strengthen, and provide consistent instruction of research-based best practices into every K to 3 classroom was undertaken in the Dallas Independent School District (DISD). Its Board of Trustees adopted a set of end-of-year reading benchmarks for baseline measures of student achievement as part of a Dallas Reading Plan. Together with the support of the business community, the Curriculum and Instruction Department developed an implementation plan that included the hiring of literacy coaches, called *Lead Reading Teachers* (LRTs), who would mentor and coach well-researched teaching practices into place. The term *teacher* in the job title was a philosophically important one. It was meant to convey the notion of collegial *teaching* as opposed to a supervising or evaluating role.

Staff development was the main focus of the Dallas Reading Plan. The phrase *staff development*, at least in our context, implied a change process having a carefully planned desired outcome (Meister, 1998). Before the Dallas Reading Plan, staff development in Dallas consisted of district-wide training at the beginning of the year focusing on curriculum changes and perceived needs on individual campuses, supplemented by occasional attendance at national, state, regional, and local conferences. The new model recognized that, when given a choice, staff development is influenced by belief systems. Moreover, the Dallas Reading Plan recognized that staff development should not only improve instruction, but also create conditions that allow for change.

Teachers bring their personal values, beliefs, professional readings and learnings, as well as life knowledge into their classroom (Delpit, 1995). They construct understandings of what students *can do* based on their students' performance on tasks given to them. Dependence on short-answer bubble sheets, reading kits, basal readers, and workbooks is associated with lower levels of reading achievement and produce students who can do little more than fill in blanks (National Center for Education Statistics, 1994, n.d.). These activities produce a product rather than a process-driven orientation to instructional understandings.

This chapter provides a review of relevant research, ideas, and theories on teacher and school change that affected the newly created reading department's actions; provides a historical glimpse of the evolving roles of an LRT; and offers personal reflections on that process.

OUR URBAN SCHOOLS TODAY

Conflicting Mandates

Dallas schools are committed to accountability and student achievement. Much agreement exists in the literature and the district that collegial dialogue focused on improving instruction and student performance promotes professional growth (Costa & Garmston, 1994; Darling-Hammond, 1998; Fullan & Hargreaves, 1996). To stay current with the converging research that governs classroom curriculum reform, teachers must be committed to being life-long learners. This cannot be mere rhetoric, but professional practice. Ironically, teachers and schools nationwide are faced with top–down mandates from national, state, and district sources during a time when many teachers are focused on bottom–up school-based empowerment. Additionally, pressure for increased accountability comes from parents, community, media, and politicians. The societal issues of high student mobility rates, generational poverty, multilingualism, inadequate health care, and home instability are reflected in classrooms regardless of the average income of the school population (Fullan & Hargreaves, 1996), but these issues seem to be most acute in urban schools. Teachers may have little control over what is going on outside the school, but they have a great deal of control concerning what happens inside.

Teacher Shortages, Uneven Knowledge, and Inconsistent Practices

Teacher shortages have brought a new kind of teacher to the school. In large urban school districts, there is a wide variety of qualified teachers per school. Students are being instructed by novice and veteran certified teachers or teachers who are certified, but teaching outside their certifications. Many classrooms have emergency permit teachers who hold college degrees in other fields of study, but hold no teacher certifications. Still other classrooms have permanent substitutes who may only hold high school diplomas. Individuals seeking alternative certification by attending education classes and being concurrently assigned to a classroom guide many other classrooms. State and national efforts have brought a number of retired military personnel to the classrooms and into alternative certification programs. Thus, the lack of depth in understanding basic school curriculum and expectations, the social nature of the school culture, and the needs of diverse learners and child development leads to a plethora of gaps in common professional language and understandings (Denson, 2001; Fuller, 1999).

Ineffective practices and incompetence are evident in many schools, but it is important to recognize excellence and allow effective teachers continuous opportunities to grow professionally and mentor others. Those teachers dragging their feet or failing to change their practices need to face individual consequences. Without strong school leadership, the complex and weak appraisal systems, coupled with union and contract issues, may allow the unethical practices of those not competent to remain in the classroom. The weakest link(s) can control a school's advancement, but, most important, they jeopardize the educational success and futures of those in their tutorage.

Rosenholtz (1989) described schools as being *stuck* or *moving*. Schools that are *stuck* are typically learning impoverished workplaces for students and teachers. Students perform poorly on standardized tests. Teachers work in isolation with little or no collaboration. They are not usually supportive of change and are content with the status quo. Teachers remain uncertain and disconnected without means of positive feedback, and this corresponds negatively to student gains. In contrast, schools that are *moving* are learning enriched and constantly strive toward student improvement and teacher collaboration. They focus on continuous growth and support, and their evidence of success can be tracked on standardized tests. Teachers work collaboratively to ensure school and student success.

Cognitive Coaching

Staff development is often disconnected from school realities and the needs of its teachers. There is no accountability for implementation, and this perpetuates the chasm between practice and research. To combat this, Costa and Garmston (1994) advocated a cognitive coaching model where teachers are assigned coaches who have similar roles, backgrounds, and experiences. Coaches are in nonjudgmental positions about classroom practices and are not responsible for teacher evaluation. The focus of the teacher and coach is centered on setting goals in a planning preconference, an observation of lesson delivery, and a postreflective dialogue.

Three principles govern the relationship between the coach and teacher: establishment and maintenance of trust, facilitated mutual learning and understanding, and enhanced growth toward holonomy. *Holonomy* is defined by Costa and Garmston (1994) as "individuals acting *autonomously* while simultaneously acting *interdependently* with the group" (p. 3; italics original). Teacher and coach have a shared understanding of the theory, they determine what part of teaching is to be improved, the teacher demonstrates or watches the coach, and then feedback is offered relative to a particular lesson dimension.

Effective classroom practice cannot develop and school reform will not move forward unless teachers adopt effective practices as part of daily teaching. The focus of training must shift from the one-shot staff development experience to capacity building of teachers through continuous learning. They not only must know *what* to do, they must have a clear understanding of *why* they are doing it. A colleague called this "knowing the why behind the what." When teachers understand this basic principle, they can critically evaluate their own teaching and the practices presented to them by the coach.

There are several change theories used by organizations. Most important, examining how individuals respond to change is critical to deep and enduring change. A knowledgeable trainer must first persuade the individual that there is a need for change. The individual responds to that persuasion, either discarding or accepting the idea. Once a decision is made to accept, the individual takes action or implements suggested tasks.

It is at this point that the degrees of resistance or acceptance become evident. Teacher behavior is not dissimilar to the general work environment. One individual may take on new information and implement effectively and admirably. Another may balk at any suggestions made by another, feeling the way he or she does it is just fine. Other individuals seek to make changes and implement suggestions, but may need nudging and modeling to feel it is a worthy endeavor. After the suggestion/task has been tried, the individual confirms the worthiness of the task. Balkers, naysayers, and doubters are often willing to give up on new ideas after one try or a series of weak attempts. Only those ideas given time to take hold become firmly entrenched.

THE EVOLVING ROLE OF LEAD READING TEACHERS

One way to combat the inherent isolation felt by classroom teachers is to empower school communities and districts to share a common vision and language and professional practice. It often takes an outsider with insight and expertise to help a school build a shared direction. In this section, I offer a kind of chronology of how LRTs in Dallas evolved as peer coaches.

Year 1: 1996–1997

LRTs Are Selected. The first year of implementation of the Dallas Reading Plan included the hiring of 15 LRTs. They were recruited from suburban and urban classrooms and had wide repertoires and master track records in teaching reading, particularly in Kindergarten through Grade 3 classrooms. In addition, each had extensive experience in staff development, content delivery, and mentoring. Working with a new school board document outlining end-of-year reading benchmarks for each grade, the LRTs were assigned 10 to 12 schools each and given the task of mentoring four teachers at each school. They were in the schools 4 days per week, sometimes two schools per day. The classroom teachers were vertically aligned (i.e., one teacher representative for each grade level [K–3]). Participating classroom teachers became know as *vertical team members*. They had no specific qualification other than they were teachers of reading. Veteran, novice, and uncertified teachers filled these positions with the administrators' confidence that they could deliver information back to their team. Some were assigned the duty and some volunteered.

The idea was to have those teachers attend large-group focused staff development sessions tied to the benchmarks, and then they were to train their grade-level partners. Authentic, research-based practices that could be quickly implemented were presented. These staff development sessions were taught by the LRTs and held during the school day. Teachers were paid a stipend for their school-based efforts.

The LRTs followed up with visits to participating teachers' classrooms and met with them during their planning times at least once every other week. Together they clarified understandings of content, scheduled the delivery of demonstration lessons by the LRT, and problem solved both perceived and real barriers. LRTs knew it was critically important to treat each teacher individually, valuing their knowledge, experience, and expertise. Trust, rapport, and credibility with each school administration and teacher was key to successful establishment.

Early Challenges.   One barrier to implementation became room arrangement and management of classroom routines. The majority of classrooms were designed to accommodate the teacher lecturing from the front of the room using an overhead projector or chalkboard. These were obviously not learner-centered, but teacher-centered communities. Small areas for student exploration and practice of skills were not prevalent, and large-group areas for read-alouds and up-close activities rarely existed. Furniture needed to be physically rearranged, materials needed gathering, and management systems and class routines needed to be established. LRTs came to a school early and stayed late, rolling up their sleeves to help teachers redefine their classroom operating philosophy. LRTs worked closely with teachers at each school, setting up vertical team members' classrooms to serve as models for their peers. Teachers and administrators slowly became comfortable with the seemingly chaotic, sometimes noisy environments by watching students take some responsibility for their learning and practice skills independently in literacy centers. Literacy centers freed the teacher to begin small-group instructional lessons where students could be assessed and monitored for individual growth.

Consistent administrator and teacher training was continuously planned and delivered. Each Friday, LRTs gathered together to problem solve, attend training, share successes and failures, and plan for the next wave of instructional foci. A large-scale effort was made to create videos demonstrating best practices to assist in the vertical and horizontal training of teachers. The videos featured LRTs demonstrating strategies in real classrooms with real students and were made available at the school level.

Trust was being established with the staff in the schools. LRTs were really teachers. Unlike overly stretched curriculum specialists in the district, they could be counted on and were present in the schools on a routine basis. They logged in thousands of hours mentoring, training, and physically demonstrating in classrooms with students, dispelling the notion that "my kids can't (or won't) do that."

It was critical in the first year to help teachers understand the depth of the commitment by the district to improving reading instruction and allay fears of failure. The attitude that "this too shall pass" undermined strong implementation and buy-in from some teachers and administrators. Veteran teachers especially doubted the longevity of the classroom expectations because they had been around long enough to see several district initiatives come and go.

LRTs also had to turn around the thinking that the skill lessons taught were not something done *to* students. Skills were to be adequately modeled to students, demonstrated with students actively participating, and ample time was to be allocated for each student to be guided to independent proficiency. Teachers were led to become critical consumers of expert advice and helped connect with their own understandings of research-based practices. Meeting individual student needs was paramount when planning for instruction.

Year 2: 1997–1998

The second year brought additional staff: 15 additional LRT positions and a new nationally recruited *reading czar* who reported directly to the superintendent. School assignments per LRT were reduced. A typical LRT load consisted of approximately eight schools still operating under the vertical team model. Teacher turnover challenged the LRTs, and they backtracked and repeated previously trained content, instructional foci, and content and strategy demonstration lessons.

Problems With the Vertical Team Concept.   Inadequacies associated with the vertical team concept became increasingly evident. Classroom teachers simply did not have time to mentor their teammates. District, school, classroom, and personal barriers encroached on time for reflective conversations, peer demonstrations, and observations. Staff members of small schools were overburdened with extraneous responsibilities such as serving on multiple committees and school operating tasks. Attempts to coach teachers at large schools were often impinged on due to constraints concerning overlapping planning times and poor classroom proximity. Some small schools had as few as eight K to 3 teachers,

whereas some larger schools had 50 or more K to 3 teachers. This latter scenario did not permit time for the trained vertical team member to collaborate or inform colleagues.

The role of the LRT expanded to convey information to more staff members. Approximately 450 vertical team members were trained districtwide; however, this did not translate to competent execution of the board initiative by all 3,000 K to 3 teachers. In response, the reading department planned larger, more inclusive districtwide training sessions and began efforts to write performance-based assessment for each benchmark.

Providing Teaching Materials: Literacy Resource Libraries. Another real barrier to implementation rapidly became evident—the availability of materials. Historically, schools with large Title I allocations had special Title I reading teachers who ordered and received books and materials to use with their small-group instruction. Yet with the shift to school-based funding, those materials were difficult to round up and use efficiently. It became apparent that literacy resource libraries would alleviate this problem by centrally locating materials for general short-term checkout by teachers. Housing these materials together provided a wider range of instructional materials for all classrooms. This involved convincing administrators of the efficiency of a literacy resource library and the need to allocate space for one. Teachers had to understand that giving up underutilized sets of books from their shelves, closets, and hiding places would benefit all students within the school and would make accessible by all teachers.

LRTs were the driving force behind these libraries and were instrumental in getting the materials organized into instructionally leveled collections of reading materials, literature read-alouds, big books, chapter books, and charts. This involved an incredible amount of man hours locating, cataloging, leveling, and systemizing the wide range of materials. In addition, district and school funds were routed so that materials could be ordered to fill in gaps. To provide start-up materials, materials stored centrally for Title I summer school programs were redistributed to schools. To assist and speed the process, LRTs were issued heavy-duty moving carts and physically hauled materials into the schools. Materials were introduced routinely and added to the literacy resource libraries' central collection, and thus the possibilities flourished.

At first many teachers feared that materials would not be available and were reluctant to relinquish the materials they had garnered through the years. Veteran teachers know how this works. Materials bought with school funds stay in the school, but as teachers vacate their positions materials are routed to those who ask for or get to it first. This often leaves newer teachers with little or unequal access to desired instructional materials. As the literacy resource libraries took shape, staff development and ribbon-cutting ceremonies were held to celebrate the accomplishment. The value of sharing resources became evident, and the trust that they would be there when needed was established. Small- and whole-group skill instruction designed to meet the needs of the students could now be accomplished. As the majority of schools put these libraries into place, the teachers became confident that even if they changed schools or grade levels appropriate materials would be available.

LRTs as Staff Development Trainers.   Training also began to focus instruction around the *Dallas Literacy Profile (DLP)*, a performance-based assessment written to address the board-approved benchmarks. Vertical team teachers piloted these assessments. The Research and Evaluation Department collected the data and calculated student progress. The *DLP* information allowed for continuous monitoring of skill-based teaching, an awareness of classroom instruction needs, collegial brainstorming of strategy development, and systematic monitoring of individual student progress.

Realizing the handiness of having an LRT, principals requested that their LRTs provide school-based staff development sessions for their faculties. Campus LRTs addressed needs campus by campus through school-based staff development. Unfortunately, this created a hit or miss delivery across the district and somewhat fragmented information dissemination.

A weakness noted from the year's previous observations was a lack of consistent implementation of phonics instruction (Shapley, 1998). Due to the changes at top administration levels, mandating consistency was difficult. At the school level, LRTs focused staff development training in alphabetic principle and phonological knowledge and instructional strategies that supported them. If a school had a phonics program firmly or sporadically in place, the LRT encouraged consistent implementation of that program. For example, one LRT might find her various schools using *Saxon Phonics*, Visual Auditory Kinesthetic (VAK), *Spelling Through Phonics* (McCracken), Modern Curriculum's *Plaid Phonics*, or no program at all. Blackline masters might be a predominant student practice in these essential skills. Variety and inconsistency prevailed.

Teachers also needed training on how to put children into instructional-level reading groups and how to orchestrate flexible skill groupings. More large- and small-scale staff development was planned both large scale and small scale. LRTs observed, mentored, and demonstrated in the classrooms 4 days a week, struggling to fill the gaps in teacher knowledge and understandings.

Year 3: 1998–1999

Amazingly enough all 30 LRTs returned despite the ups and downs associated with large-scale change. Adjustments in school assignments were
made according to school size. LRTs received in-depth cognitive coaching
training to shore up mentoring skills. The department found funds to dis-
tribute take-home backpacks filled with books, parent training videos, and
tips for parents cards. Often LRTs used heavy-duty moving carts to personally deliver materials. Literacy resource libraries grew. LRTs scheduled and
led material labeling and distribution as well as staff and parent training
sessions. The responsibility for maintaining the literacy library collections
shifted to the teachers as they became knowledgeable caretakers of the
self-running collections.

In Year 3, the *Dallas Literacy Profile* was streamlined and became an
important assessment tool. Schools had the option of using the *Texas Primary Reading Inventory* (a state informal assessment instrument) or the
Dallas Literacy Profile. LRTs were versatile in their knowledge and
guided teachers through either assessment. Teacher training focused on
using assessment to guide instruction and test-wiseness strategies for standardized tests.

The Dallas Reading Academy.   Year 3 also marked the beginning of
the Dallas Reading Academy. Four teachers from each school were asked
to attend, and LRTs were assigned as their coaches. Day-to-day LRT operations focused on classroom demonstrations, observations, and assisting
teachers with the academy's implementation goals. LRTs and university
professors taught the Reading Academy courses, but were not, except in
rare instances, the instructors for their coaching charges. It was established that the Reading Academy was graduate coursework and not a typical staff development session. Teachers actively read the research and put
research into practice in their classrooms.

Envious of the rapid changes taking place in the classroom next door,
administrators and teachers prevailed on the LRTs to lead book discussions and inservices for nonacademy teachers too. As time permitted, the
LRTs complied with the requests, which resulted in consistency in language and direction throughout the district. LRTs no longer gave campus
staff development unless the content was related to the academy. This energized the initiative. The reputations of the LRTs were firmly established
and schools increasingly depended on them for information, guidance,
and training. Completing the 6 graduate hours earned teachers the distinguished title of *Dallas Reading Academy Laureate*.

The state regional service center recruited LRTs to train teachers in
Texas State Kindergarten Reading Academies during off-contract time. As

Dallas teachers participated in their state-mandated training, this added another layer of understanding that these initiatives were not going away. It also gave confidence to the teachers that the reading department was in line with the state initiative.

Year 4: 1999–2000

Several new LRT positions were filled, leading to school assignments based on the number of Reading Academy participants needing coaching support. Now schools could send multiple teachers to enroll in the Dallas Reading Academy. Most Laureates in residence encouraged their team members to take the classes. With the expansion of the opportunity to enroll in the academy, LRT services were stretched to coach and mentor more K to 3 teachers. School-based Reading Academies accommodated whole faculty staffs. Anyone assigned to K to 3 classrooms was enrolled as space permitted. LRTs, serving as university adjuncts, were given the choice to teach and coach the same participants. In most cases, this facilitated the training and established more school-based consistency. The heavy-duty carts continuously delivered materials developed to support implementation of district and state initiatives.

First-grade teachers were now required to attend the state's Reading Academy sessions during summer months. Once again LRTs were trained to support this initiative as well. This informed them of the state direction and allowed the district to stay well within the state focus for student instruction.

Year 5: 2000–2001

Despite the roller coaster of administrative changes, LRTs and their service to schools and teachers remained constant. Few changes in school assignments were made. Laureates routinely sought out LRTs to clarify understandings and request demonstrations. New Reading Academy participants included teachers in Grade 4 to 6 configurations on a limited basis, adding to the coaching diversity.

Informal assessment shifted districtwide to the state *Texas Primary Reading Inventory*, and school-based staff development sessions supported a clear, consistent district implementation. The district implemented new state-adopted reading textbooks (basals). This adoption moved the state and district from literature-based reading instruction (mandated in the last adoption) to the dominance of decodable texts in the early grades.

Low-performing schools received additional service with the inception of Success With a Team (SWAT). LRTs served on these teams and delivered intensive school-based support to students who needed assistance. LRTs wrote curriculum and model lessons and ordered materials to accelerate the progress of students. The lessons were carefully scripted so that the most novice teacher could be successful in instructional delivery. State reading academies were mandated for second-grade teachers, and state-trained LRTs delivered this training locally. As before, teachers who were Dallas Reading Academy Laureates saw many similarities to the Dallas Reading Academy content.

Year 6: 2001–2002

Year 6 brought with it a top–down mandate to implement yet another new basal reading program. Supporting the new superintendent's mandate, LRTs took on the responsibility of ensuring the thorough implementation of *SRA-Open Court* in the majority of K to 6 classrooms. The basal overview given teachers by publishing company representatives did not begin to cover the complex understanding and implementation of the new basal routines. Attention was paid to the instructional delivery of all components, and, for the first time, a consistent phonics focus and language was districtwide. Teachers requested demonstration lessons and focused training to deliver appropriate and accurate instruction. Clarifying *Open Court* implementation for all K to 6 teachers became the LRT job focus. Little time was devoted to coaching Reading Academy content, which now included pre-K teachers.

Even Cinderella Had a Coach

I cannot resist a Cinderella fairy tale analogy here. *Cinder-teachers* are in the trenches. Burdened with mandates from multiple sources, they struggle to achieve the ultimate goal of student success. Five superintendents and their accompanying leadership teams in just 6 years had schools jockeying to meet new initiatives, demands, and mandates. The goal of all students reading on grade level is hard to argue against, but can seem unattainable for even the most hard-working, conscientious teacher. Administrators dust interfering cobwebs away and address school issues with initiatives that superficially dress. All this prepares for the testing dance that determines their state ranking. Isolated and weary from her daily toil, the Cinder-teacher despairs.

Along comes an LRT fairy godmother. She hovers close by, serving as a mentor/coach, and is available for all teachers. When time permits or when Cinder-teacher requests, the LRT fairy godmother waves her magic best practices wand and conjures up from her repertoire appropriate research-based practices to demonstrate with real students. Together they take the time to analyze and look at the converging research and put into place effective strategies. Cinder-teacher understands (a) the reciprocal processes of reading and writing, (b) the differences in the text structures of narrative and expository text, (c) the importance of oral language and vocabulary development, (d) the relationship between comprehension and fluency, and (e) the value of ongoing assessment that informs teaching. She carefully balances her lessons with direct explicit instruction of skills leaving no learning to chance. With the accoutrements in place, Cinder-teacher transforms the classroom into energized possibilities that exude teacher and student confidence and control as she instructs in small flexible groups and whole groups. Students move forward with skillfully arranged minilessons that serve to accelerate student performance. Students are provided a conveyance through developing, emerging, and strategic avenues of learning. Powerful strategies are employed, metacognition takes place, and students are ready for the big testing day. Stakeholders hold their collective breaths as students transform their learning into testing bytes until the clock runs out.

The state and district rank schools according to their pass rate on the high-stakes test. If the slipper of student achievement is a perfect fit, Cinder-teachers at their school celebrate with monetary rewards, plaques, banners, and congratulations.

The story does not end here. If your school's slipper does *not* fit, teams of district personnel, the media, parents, and community members turn your efforts into ashes. Cinder-teachers must then rise and, with their fairy godmothers, start the cycle again.

Observations of a Coach (or LRT Fairy Godmother)

Since Day 1, I have seen firsthand examples of stuck and moving schools and teachers. Sometimes the stuck teachers are in moving schools or, conversely, moving teachers are found in stuck schools. Exemplary teaching exists and does not always depend on certification levels. Some of the most intellectual, well-thought-out instruction is from the most rudimentarily trained individual. Yet not just anyone can be a good teacher. One must come by way of the profession with honest desire and integrity. It is difficult to watch teachers waste the precious little time they have with their students. What is most rewarding is to find that the majority of teachers try to do their best. They are not found on their cell phones, sitting at their desks, or blame placing when their ineptness is a major underlying cause of student failure.

Excuses and blame placing are the talk of some in the teachers' lounge (e.g., there is not enough time, the students come ill equipped, parents do not help, last year's teacher did not teach them anything, and the administration does not support us are common justifications for the lack of student success). Real teachers are mobile, child-watching, compassionate individuals who want real achievement for those they tutor and seek it regardless of influences over which they have no control. They control what they can influence.

There are several saboteurs to teachers' best efforts. Many of these are presented for you in other chapters, but the most insidious ones are the teachers. Teachers get stuck in what they perceive works for them. Habit and inertia are comfortable. Teachers who feel they are helpless tend to abdicate their responsibility to teach. It takes a consistent prod to take someone from where they are to a carefully planned desired outcome. Vygotsky defined this aspect of learning as the *zone of proximal development* (Bodrova & Leong, 1996). Coaching, to quote Costa and Garmston (1994), is to "convey a valued colleague from where he or she is to where he or she wants to be" (p. 2). These two key elements persist in my thinking to (a) value my colleagues, and (b) help them get where they want to be. Teachers must want to work to be the best they can be for their students and our profession.

Anyone stepping through a classroom threshold on a regular basis sees the real teacher. A good coach must know what, when, and why an alternative needs to be offered (if at all). All the aspects concerning change theory comes to play with each and every action made or considered. The coach must firmly establish trust to really make a difference. When trust is firmly established, open minds may consider change if they understand why it might make a positive difference for their students. This comes easily in some relationships and is hard earned with others. Trust is multidimensional. Teachers must trust their administrators to provide them with all the proper curriculum tools. District and upper administrative changes aside, good classroom instruction and student performance boils down to the competent teacher. Enduring change needs to be self-generated rather than outwardly imposed.

Teachers have a lot to consider and juggle every moment of their day. Someone always wants something from them, whether it is routine attendance and lunch counts, student referrals, or other accountability paperwork; therefore, there is little concentrated time to plan effective instruction. There are many daily interruptions: parents, untimely loud speaker announcements, covering class for another teacher's absence or tardiness, assembly programs, scheduled restroom breaks, and so on.

In the aggressive staff development model of the Dallas Reading Academy, each participant had a coach to assist in the understanding of content. It took time for teachers to realize that we were there to do something *for* them, not *to* them. Our intent was never to stop instruction, but to be a partner in the classroom and assist in the mutual endeavor of student achievement.

It is when a coaching partnership works optimally that you know you are making a difference. Each Reading Academy participant had several semester-long goals that included a Classroom Action Plan (CAP). If, for whatever reason, the participant was unsure of the action or desired additional information, the coach provided it. This led to hundreds of demonstration lessons over the 6 years I have served as a mentor/coach. Many of these lessons were on the spot, with little or no preparation for delivery in the requested classroom. At times we were able to schedule demonstrations when we returned the following week. Needless to say, those of us who served in this capacity were sure of our content and ready to do what was needed to support the teacher and her students.

Each day LRTs filled out accountability sheets that were signed by the principal or other school personnel. LRTs categorically checked the grade levels and type of interactions they had that day. One statistical accounting by the district's Research and Evaluation team in 2001 indicated that 35 LRTs spent time serving the districts K to 3 classrooms making 6,306 classroom observations; led 4,689 classroom demonstrations; held 16,743 planning and debriefing sessions; and attended and/or led 1,701 grade-level meetings. They spent 20,493 hours working in schools (Denson, 2001). All of this was only done in an average of 4 days per week because Fridays were devoted to their training, district projects, and planning.

The vehicle that drove classroom instructional focus and changes the fastest was the Dallas Reading Academy. The rigorous coursework informed teaching—the delivery of instruction. The strategies we coached through the Academy had the strongest and longest lasting impact on phonics, comprehension, and vocabulary development. When the teachers were given action plans that held them accountable for implementation, we saw a marked difference. A weekly encounter with the participant teacher who orchestrated his or her own deep understanding was an art form in action. The conditions they set up for learning to take place create masterpieces of cognitive levels that can leave you in gaping awe. To watch their students grasp understanding, well, I doubt I can articulate the breadth of the effect. It is what teaching is about regardless of the student's age.

Teachers who are Laureates of the Dallas Reading Academy remark with considerable frequency how what they learned in that class has opened them to really look at individual student performance and their teaching. Most Laureates proudly display their graduation plaques inside their classrooms or just outside their classroom doors. Teachers who are Laureates and have been through the Texas State Reading Academy have additional confidence when it comes to analyzing instruction and knowing what to do, especially when the student is not making progress. They are able to determine where each student's weaknesses are and fill in the gaps with instruction that meets their needs.

Year 6 was probably the most difficult. When the new administration made the top–down decision to implement *SRA-Open Court* in every K to 6 classroom, teachers were armed with questions about every lesson and were reluctant to dig in. However, they readily admitted that the phonics component would offer stability and strength to unlocking the alphabetic code. They also understood that districtwide consistency was a vision that would assist students, especially those who were likely to change schools in their early educational years. It was our charge to demonstrate and lead them to make connections with their prior learning.

Reading mandates were not the only changes going on during Year 6. The teachers were on their second year of a new inquiry-based science curriculum implementation. In addition, they were beginning their first year of *SRA-Everyday Mathematics* instruction, which took them from their traditional comfort zone of math computational skills taught in isolation. Combined with this were the shifts in focus for bilingual education and English language learning; the teachers were overwhelmed with attempting to balance it all. Evidence that our coaching efforts paid off are in the consistency, deep understanding, and instructional delivery of the *Open Court* adoption rather than the other district mandates. The ways of the past have and will continue to have value. To move forward, we must take the best from the past and the best from the present to construct the way into the best future. This may create turbulence and uncertainty, but even when given many resources, only some teachers can do it effectively without assistance. Every step of the way, LRTs have coached, mentored, supported, and demonstrated for teachers, changing the direction to be in line with state and district initiatives. That is not to say that they would not have come to the realization or practice on their own, but it has become the job of an LRT coach to hurry the process along. There is not a moment to lose in the education of a single child.

I celebrate and take great satisfaction in our mission when teachers get excited over their students' performance. I am eager to get to some schools each week to hear the teachers talk knowledgeably about the changes their students are making. They understand that tests are not the end-all-be-all, but they know and can appreciate how far their students come in a year. Collegial dialogue, problem solving, diagnosing, and being extra eyes and hands are what isolated teachers need to affirm their students' progress. Even when our school assignments have shifted, most of us have retained some of our original schools. In those schools, Laureates depend on us for answers and articles that will inform them. We support and encourage many of them as they continue to gain higher education degrees. In reflective conferences, it can humble you when they verbalize about where they were and contrast to their difference now. Connecting with the students: I love the interactions I have had and cherish the title "The Reading Lady" that many have dubbed me.

CONCLUSIONS

Regardless of the outside influences that affect our students, they are our charges for instruction. We must have a wide repertoire of knowledge to counteract the influences over which we have no control. Teachers can easily lose sight of the changing student population and fail to keep up with their own professional growth. Providing a strong mentor/coach coupled with qualitative and quantitative research-based practices can close the gap and provide a common vision and district language. Cognitive coaches can support diverse professionals to work together in support of common change goals.

Providing for or mandating team meetings during planning times do not sufficiently define collaborative planning. Clearly articulate direct explanation that clarifies strategic implementation of instruction must be the scholarly discourse of teachers. Time and resources must be allocated to accomplish this. A shared density of knowledge moves schools and students. Mentoring of novice instructors, regardless of their level of preparation, must be given adequate time and focus. All teachers need to feel they can ask instructional leaders/mentors/coaches direct and explicit questions when and where needed without feeling like failures. When teachers are considered individually and given on-the-spot guidance, they can better consider options for their students. Print-rich environments, quality reading time and instruction, cross-curricular use of reading and writing strategies, and best practices are infusing our classrooms. Sometimes when we are involved in personal growth and change, we cannot accurately recall where we have been, but a fairy godmother/coach can.

REFERENCES

Bodrova, E., & Leong, D. J. (1996). *Tools of the mind: The Vygotskian approach to early childhood education*. Columbus, OH: Merrill.

Costa, A. L., & Garmston, R. J. (1994). *Cognitive coaching: A foundation for renaissance schools*. Norwood, MA: Christopher-Gordon.

Darling-Hammond, L. (1998). Teacher learning that supports student learning [electronic version]. *Educational Leadership, 55*(5).

Darling-Hammond, L. (1999). Target time toward teachers. *Journal of Staff Development, 20*(2), 31–36.

Darling-Hammond, L. (2000, January 1). Teacher quality and student achievement: A review of state policy evidence. *Education Policy Analysis Archives*. (Retrieved April 10, 2002, from http://olam.ed.asu/epaa/v8nl/)

Delpit, L. (1995). *Other people's children: Cultural conflict in the classroom*. New York: New Press.

Denson, K. (2001). *Final report. Reading and language arts grades K–6: 2000–01* (REIS01-147-2). Dallas, TX: Dallas Independent School District-Division of Evaluation, Assessment, and Information Systems.

Fullan, M., & Hargreaves, A. (1996). *What's worth fighting for in your school*. New York: Teachers College Press.

Fuller, E. J. (1999). *Does teacher certification matter? A comparison of TAAS performance in 1997 between schools with low and high percentages of certified teachers*. Austin: Charles A. Dana Center, University of Texas–Austin.

Meister, J. C. (1998). *Corporate universities: Lessons in building a world-class work force*. New York: McGraw-Hill.

National Center for Education Statistics. (1994). *Data compendium for the NAEP 1992 reading assessment of the nation and the states: 1992 NAEP trial state assessment*. Washington, DC: U.S. Department of Education.

National Center for Education Statistics. (n.d.). *NAEP 1992, 1994 national reading assessments—Data almanac—Grade 4: Teacher questionnaire weighted percentages and composite proficiency means*. (Retrieved March 3, 2002, from http://nces.ed.gov/nationsreportcard/reading/results)

Rosenholtz, S. (1989). *Teachers' workplace: The social organization of schools*. New York: Longman.

Shapley, K. (1998). *Final report of the 1997–98 Dallas Reading Plan* (REIS98-300-2). Dallas, TX: Dallas Independent School District.

CHAPTER THIRTEEN

Coaching the Coaches: Challenges of Implementing the Lead Teacher Concept

Barbara Mathews
Dallas Independent School District

Two good eggs do not a cake make. The key ingredient (or one of the key ingredients) to improving reading instruction, particularly in a large urban school district, is campus-level support for teachers. However, much like cake making, creating an exemplary reading program depends on the availability of a number of other ingredients, the quality and quantity of those ingredients, the method of their assembly, and their interaction. Professional mentors or coaches are one of the non-negotiable ingredients. Much of their success, however, depends on how well the coaches are focused, supported, and coordinated with other elements. In Dallas, we learned much about coaching by trial and error. Three of the essential ingredients—teacher training, classroom assistance, and support for the coaches—are addressed in this chapter chronologically in a year-by-year description of our trials and errors and the adjustments we made during the first 3 years of implementation of a massive training effort known as the *Dallas Reading Plan.*

Although the Dallas Reading Plan was carefully planned with wide input from stakeholders in the community, business leaders, district personnel, and national experts in the field of reading, there was no kitchen-tested recipe for effecting change in a district with some 3,000 kindergarten through third-grade teachers, 144 schools, and over 60,000 K to 3 students. Fortunately, a part of the plan allowed for monitoring and adjusting based on efforts and assessment of the effectiveness of those efforts.

It was recognized from the beginning of the Dallas Reading Plan that classroom assistance for teachers implementing new strategies was essential. In prior years, our department had consisted of a director and three or four specialists who helped produce curriculum documents, conducted teacher training, and provided troubleshooting on campus request—across all grade levels (K–12). Thus, much of the teacher training was necessarily delegated to consultants mainly sponsored by the basal reading series publishers (Note: There were no campus reading teachers in the primary grades.) The Dallas Reading Plan called for establishing an initial cadre of 14 master reading teachers (called *Lead Reading Teachers* [LRTs]) to provide classroom assistance; to have 14 reading experts to assist K to 3 teachers was unprecedented in our district. To impact all 3,000 teachers with just 14 LRTs, a trainer-of trainers model was utilized. The 14 LRTs were to train a Vertical Team of five professionals (i.e., the principal and a teacher from kindergarten through third grade) in effective strategies of balanced literacy instruction. The Vertical Team members were to then take this new information being disseminated back to their schools and train their grade-level colleagues on what they had learned—hence, the trainer-of-trainers concept. In addition to training the Vertical Team members, the LRTs also provided classroom support to these Vertical Team members and conducted study groups with other interested teachers after school.

As we assessed our mission to ensure that *all* students read on level by the end of third grade, we decided that the major focus of the reading department should center on building capacity in our teaching force. Thus, teacher training is addressed first in each section. Classroom assistance describes both support to individual teachers as well as support to schools. Support for and direction to the coaches is loosely described as *coaching the coaches*. My responsibility for focusing the efforts of the coaches as well as reflections, cautions, and recommendations based on our experiences are included in the final section.

ASSESSMENT OF YEAR 1

Teacher Training

During the first year of the plan, 3 full days of staff development spaced throughout the year were provided for the Vertical Teams. Because of the large numbers of teachers and principals to be trained, each session was delivered twice—half of the schools coming to a central location on one day and the other half receiving the training on the following day. About 350 persons attended on each of these training days. The sessions took on the feel of a major reading conference such as those hosted by the national teacher associations. The LRTs, as our in-house master teachers, were largely responsible for designing and preparing the training. These preparations took significant time—as much as 2 weeks for each of the 3 training days. Thus, the preparation and delivery of the 3 days for all Vertical Teams consumed 9 weeks of LRT time during the year.

A high standard for this and all training to come was soon established. Training was held on a vacant floor of a large corporate complex we rented for that purpose. The all-glass showrooms in that building enabled participants to see into every session, adding to the visual effect of the training environment. Sessions were filled with displays of the latest children's books, magnetic letters on boards, beautifully illustrated Language to Literacy charts, large illustrated plans to help teachers see ways to organize their learning centers, decorations of the season, and so on.

LRTs delivered the training from a script to ensure consistency for all participants. In addition to launching specifics of the Dallas Reading Plan to the district, the training showcased the competence of the LRTs and helped establish their reputation as a cadre of true experts. One of the behind the scenes decisions was to ensure that teachers attended sessions conducted by LRTs other than the one who served their school to help increase their exposure as classroom mentors. These initial sessions were impressive and well received.

Classroom Assistance

In our first year, each LRT served approximately 42 Vertical Team members at 10 schools during a 4-day week. (Fridays were reserved for LRT training and preparation.) Time was lost, of course, as LRTs traveled from one school to another. Similarly, the 9 weeks of preparation time for our Vertical Team training conferences mentioned earlier cut into our service to schools. Typically, LRTs would go into a teacher's room and ask how things were going, whether they could clarify or demonstrate a strategy covered in the training sessions, or help them with any other teaching issues (e.g., classroom management, assessing student development, etc.). The role was definitely one of helping; the teacher was the customer and determined the service to be rendered.

Success was mixed. LRTs were warmly received, and teachers frequently requested demonstration lessons. For example, the Language to Literacy (Roser, 1990) strategy alluded to earlier, which involves reading aloud to students and constructing a supportive graphic organizer, was requested and demonstrated time and again. Although teachers seemingly enjoyed the demonstrations, LRTs would often come back the following week only to find the teacher had not implemented the strategy and yet wanted another demonstration of the Language to Literacy method. Thus, classroom support that first year was heavily weighted toward demonstrations. In addition, other teachers in the building complained that the Vertical Team did not share the strategies as required—the Vertical Team trainers did not train.

Coaching the Coaches

LRTs' own professional growth was supported with training by national leaders (e.g., Marilyn Adams, Jerry Treadway, Jeanne Osborne, Kathy Escamillia, John Shefelbine, Orlando Taylor, Andrea Butler, Josefina Tinajero, and Richard Gentry) who were brought to Dallas. Although the work of Joyce and Showers (1988), entitled *Student Achievement through Staff Development*, was part of a laser disc library used in LRT professional development, no training was offered to LRTs on how to actually work with adult learners. The Assistant Superintendent of Curriculum and other central administrators offered guidance to the LRTs, many of whom were new to the district, in understanding chains of command, protocol, and lines of communication. Other mentoring helped LRTs avoid problems that can be encountered when a stranger goes into a building or classroom. Because of the myriad other responsibilities of the program managers, the LRTs were often left on their own on Fridays to prepare for demonstrations and to *figure out the job* cooperatively.

As might be expected, LRT stress was high. Expectations were high, the workload was enormous, and administrative guidance was limited. Fortunately, the LRTs were natural leaders, selected because they were some of the best teachers in the profession. When left alone with no designated leader, tremendous responsibilities, and little direction, this group of leaders (and no followers) frequently had trouble agreeing. Dedication to the mission of significantly improving reading instruction, the excitement of the challenge, and the stimulation of the quality of content training provided helped keep frustration from overwhelming the operation. Although the friction never affected productivity or was apparent to teachers in the field, it did cause some angst within the group; some in the central office staff came to regard the LRTs as opinionated *prima donnas*.

ASSESSMENT OF YEAR 2

Teacher Training

I came to work with the LRTs during the second year of the Dallas Reading Plan. We were able to add an additional 15 LRTs to bring the total to 29—a 50% increase in our work force. The addition of these LRTs reduced the weekly load for each LRT to five schools. We continued to implement our trainer-of-trainers model—3 full days of training for all five members of the Vertical Team from every campus. We thought we could hasten the classroom implementation and satisfy the non-Vertical Team teachers' request to hear the training firsthand if we were to offer an abbreviated version of the 3 Vertical Team training days to the masses (2,424 teachers). It truly seemed like masses as we trained these teachers in three 3-hour sessions after school in groups of 35.

That year, Dr. Robert Cooter joined us to serve as our Reading Czar. (His actual title was Assistant Superintendent for Reading.) His knowledge and charisma helped rally the entire district around the Reading Plan. Teachers and administrators began to believe the Reading Plan held answers for our children's reading needs and was going to last. Our teachers were likewise becoming familiar with balanced literacy strategies.

Classroom Assistance

Although we reminded ourselves that change takes time, we were not pleased with our progress. I had mid- and final year reviews with each LRT that second year. We talked about each Vertical Team teacher's progress (teachers were not identified by name). A form was given to each LRT in advance of the conference so that she could have time to reflect on each person's progress (see Fig. 13.1). When asked whether they could see evidence of positive change, the answer was positive in almost every instance. Teachers were trying some of the new strategies, but it appeared that our full days of training were more than teachers could digest at one time; they were picking and choosing random strategies to try. When asked whether the changes they were seeing were enough to significantly impact student achievement, the answer was almost always negative. It seemed that many of our teachers did not understand the reading process, the purpose of the strategies, and how to design and implement balanced literacy experiences for their class.

Other problems surfaced in these conferences. Although the Vertical Team members were supposed to be chosen because of their expertise, not all fit this criterion. Some of the Vertical Team members were first-year teachers, some were new alternatively certified teachers, and a number were having problems with classroom management. One Vertical Team member was a permanent substitute; one was new to first grade from sixth grade. This was discouraging news because we had provided what seemed like state-of-the-art training, and our LRTs, whose knowledge and work ethic was unparalleled, had worked so hard. How could the LRTs be so knowledgeable and such effective practitioners and not be able to impart that knowledge?

During the second year, we began to face that schools did not have the books and materials to support some of the key strategies we were teach-

In preparation for our mid-year review conference, please use this form to reflect on the progress of your teachers and schools. (This form is to be used to structure our conversation and will not be turned in.)

School _____

Vertical Team Member	How do you assess this teacher's degree of Implementation of the Vertical Team Training and the DRP?	What are your goals for the second half of the year with this teacher?
	low *medium* *high*	
Kindergarten		
First Grade		
Second Grade		
Third Grade		

Has this school set up a central resource room for materials?

Do you have any specific goals for the whole school?

FIG. 13.1.   Mid-year review planning guide.

ing, particularly shared and guided reading. Schools did not have big books or leveled texts with which to teach. We provided some money to each campus with which to purchase books ($10,000 per school), and schools began to likewise spend their own funds to enhance their resources. Based on the model of one school in our district, which had developed on its own a professional library of materials to support balanced literacy instruction, we developed a prototype Literacy Materials Center. We found sources for appropriate shelves, containers for leveled text, and tubs for big books. We provided lists of books according to reading level from various companies so books could be appropriately marked. LRTs spent many after-school hours setting up these materials centers. This *rolling up of the sleeves* and pitching in to do the hard physical work further cemented the relationship between LRTs and teachers.

Coaching the Coaches

We began Year 2 with 5 days of training for LRTs, much of which focused on Peggy Sharp's (1993) book, *Sharing Your Good Ideas*. Other nationally known reading professionals (e.g., Ray Reutzel, Timothy Rasinski, John Jacobson, Richard Gentry) came to work with the group in professional de-

velopment. The good deal of LRT training time this year was spent participating in the New Jersey Writing Project.

ASSESSMENT OF YEAR 3

Teacher Training

Based on the 2 prior years of experience, we made significant modifications in our training and teacher support design. I realized that most of
the LRTs had become successful as classroom teachers, and now as
coaches, because they had had Reading Recovery™ (DeFord et al., 1991)
training. This had involved deep training over the course of a year, with
time to practice their new learning with guidance from a coach (called a
teacher leader). Further support during Reading Recovery had continued
after their initial training year.

Our model of teacher training and support was to be loosely based on
the Reading Recovery™ training model—primarily deep training over
time. Dr. Cooter worked extensively with representatives from five area
universities to develop a syllabus for a two-semester graduate reading
course, which would be delivered consistently in all sections through the
use of an instructor's script. We named the new training effort *The Dallas
Reading Academy*. Our director of training planned recruitment strategies
and university registration. Four LRTs and a consultant were commissioned to write detailed scripts for each session.

We saw a need for structured expectations for our teachers to ensure
that new learning translated into practice. We considered the behind the
glass experience of Reading Recovery™ training, where teachers are asked
to perform in front of other teachers who then critique their work. We
also looked at the work of Kussy (1997) in *Learning Network Schools*,
with particular interest in the use of action plans to ensure application of
the strategies learned and provide a vehicle for teacher reflection. Our solution, worked out mostly by LRTs, was a Classroom Action Plan (CAP)
that identified an implementation goal for the week following training on
new strategies (see Fig. 13.2). The CAP required teachers to work on the
goal and reflect on their efforts. LRTs were to sign the teacher's CAP,
which became part of the course requirement.

It was a massive effort for a school district to undertake the design and
implementation of this project. Our director of training set up the equivalent of a college registrar's office, formed sections, arranged for learning
sites, assigned students to sites based on which quadrant of the city they
preferred, and assigned adjuncts. LRTs worked to get teachers' applications and transcripts turned in. LRTs who were writing the course worked

```
┌─────────────────────────────────────────────────────────────────┐
│                                              The Change Process   │
│   Classroom Action Plan        FYI                                │
│                                                                   │
│   Name_____School_____   │
│   Grade_____Date: Week of Sept. 7-10  Semester I  Session 2    │
│   IMPLEMENTATION GOAL #2:                                         │
│   Create five simple literacy centers in collaboration with your LRT. │
│   Date due: Week of Sept. 20-24                                   │
│   ─────────────────────────────────────────────────────────────  │
│                                                                   │
│   REFLECTIONS (Include the following: materials used, how the goal impacted you as a teacher, │
│   changes that occurred, assistance from your LRT, how the goal appeared to affect your students │
│   including attitudes and response, whether you will continue with this goal, why or why not, etc.) │
│                                                                   │
│                                                                   │
│                                                                   │
│                                                                   │
│                                                                   │
│                                                                   │
│                                                                   │
│                                                                   │
│                                                                   │
│                                                                   │
│   Adapted from Herzog (1997)   LRT_____Date_____    │
└─────────────────────────────────────────────────────────────────┘
```

FIG. 13.2.   Classroom action plan.

nights and weekends to get the sessions written. Often the copies of the sessions were still warm from the duplicator when distributed to course instructors.

Classroom Assistance

With Dr. Cooter's strong leadership, we declared that our two priorities were to be the training and coaching of participants in the Reading Academy. Participation in the Reading Academy was to be voluntary, although we wondered whether we would have enough participants. We were somewhat surprised and pleased when 450 teachers registered. However, participation was not uniformly spread across the district. Some building principals encouraged their teachers to participate. Some did not. Some area superintendents (there are nine subdistricts in the Dallas system each having their own superintendent) were much more supportive of the effort than others.

The decision to focus our efforts almost exclusively on academy participants was not universally appreciated. Some wanted LRTs to serve all teachers. Some principals wanted the services of the LRT, but wanted to dictate how they would be used. Many principals were frustrated with weak teachers (many had lost control of their classes) and wanted LRTs to work with the least successful of the district's work force. Others wanted LRTs to also serve teachers in Grades 4 to 6 where the need was great.

Dr. Cooter maintained that the Reading Department offered a service. In the professional judgment of the reading experts and based on our 2 years of experience, the Reading Academy represented the best training model. Thus, if schools felt they needed assistance with their reading program, they could encourage their teachers to participate in the Reading Academy and receive an LRT's coaching services. If they were satisfied with their reading program or if they wanted to go a different direction, they were on their own. We held firm and concentrated our efforts on the Reading Academy and its participants, although we did try to honor other requests as time permitted.

The Reading Academy classes significantly impacted LRTs' ability to assist teachers. Content was taught in the academy classes so LRTs did not have to teach content on their classroom visits. Their coaching centered on implementing the specific strategy/practice teachers had learned in the academy and/or read about in reading assignments the previous week. They were at the teacher's elbow to assist when the focus was setting up the classroom, planning instruction, implementing a strategy, grouping students for instruction, and making sense of diagnostic data. Coaching the Reading Academy participants was time-intensive, and LRT time was spent more effectively. LRTs continued to do classroom demonstrations, but not to the degree as during the first 2 years. Although LRTs were not supervisors, the fact that they signed the action plans added a dimension of accountability for the teacher–coach relationship. It was during this year that our LRTs truly became coaches—significantly more than the helpers or mentors they had previously been.

Coaching the Coaches

This year we had a series of training sessions for LRTs on the cognitive coaching model of Costa and Garmston (2002). One of the key under-standings gained from this training was the importance of building trust before attempting change. A second important impact of their training on coaching occurred when we broke into groups of three to coach one an-other. One LRT presented a problem she wanted to solve, another served as the coach to question and help her come to understandings and solu-tions. A third LRT served as an observer. We were problem solving cooper-atively, much as LRTs had done informally during the first year. Probably the most important problem solving and planning occurred informally at lunch as the LRTs discussed their work with their colleagues, sharing frus-trations and successes.

An important thing happened this year: We could literally see the prog-ress of our teachers—the fruits of our labors. Others in the district also noted the progress. One area superintendent remarked that he did not need a list of teachers from his schools studying in the academy because he could readily identify classrooms of Reading Academy participants. Not only did the classrooms look different, but teachers and students were more actively involved in reading tasks. The students were more moti-vated and successful. Principals and teachers also noted the change. One board member reported that she had never had a teacher comment posi-tively about staff training before the Reading Academy. We could see change and feel the momentum. This progress was indeed rewarding to the LRTs and spurred us on.

Teachers often complained about how hard they were working both in the academy and with their classroom implementations. I would some-times meet teachers in the grocery store who would tell me how hard they were working and that they had to hurry home to read for the academy and prepare for their class. They complained in the lounge and principal's office, but the complaints of hard work were tempered by feelings that the work was worth it. The teachers were working very hard. The course of study and implementation was rigorous. We tried to reward their work and reinforce the pride they felt by providing a banquet for the Reading Academy participants at the end of the year, proclaiming them to be Reading Academy Laureates and giving them a bronze plaque to display outside their rooms. A standard of quality had been established. We were absolutely ecstatic when more than 700 teachers signed up to participate in the academy for the following year.

The Dallas Reading Plan was fortunate to have an evaluator from the department of Research and Evaluation. As part of the evaluation, evaluators asked teachers to anonymously rate their LRT on four of the key elements of their service twice per year (see Fig. 13.3). The data were reported to each LRT with information on how she ranked individually as well as how she compared to other LRTs. The ratings, on a four-point scale, were always exceedingly high—between 3 and 4. However, this evaluation was always traumatic. Highly motivated and very competitive, every LRT wanted to be perceived as a 4 by every teacher. Painful as it was to get less than a

LRT: Susie Smart

K-6 Students' Ratings of Usefulness of Weekly Visits from the Lead Reading Teacher*

<3.0	3.0	3.1	3.2	3.3	3.4	3.5	3.6	3.7	3.8	3.9	4.0
		LRT	LRT		LRT	LRT	Susie	LRT	LRT	LRT	LRT
			LRT			LRT	LRT	LRT	LRT	LRT	LRT
						LRT	LRT	LRT	LRT		LRT
						LRT	LRT	LRT	LRT		LRT
						LRT		LRT	LRT		LRT
								LRT	LRT		
									LRT		
									LRT		
									LRT		
									LRT		
									LRT		

*Note. Students rated each item on a 4-point scale (1 = *Not Useful*; 4 = *Very Useful*).

K-6 Students' Ratings of Usefulness of Discussion of Classroom Action Plans with the Lead Reading Teacher*

<3.0	3.0	3.1	3.2	3.3	3.4	3.5	3.6	3.7	3.8	3.9	4.0
			LRT	LRT	LRT	LRT	LRT	LRT	Susie	LRT	LRT
			LRT	LRT	LRT	LRT	LRT	LRT	LRT	LRT	LRT
						LRT	LRT	LRT	LRT	LRT	LRT
						LRT	LRT	LRT	LRT	LRT	
						LRT	LRT	LRT	LRT		
								LRT	LRT		
								LRT	LRT		
								LRT			

*Note. Students rated each item on a 4-point scale (1 = *Not Useful*; 4 = *Very Useful*).

FIG. 13.3. Evaluation report: Lead reading teachers.

LRT: **Susie Smart**

*K-6 Students' Ratings of Usefulness of Demonstration Lessons with
Their Students from the Lead Reading Teacher**

<3.0	3.0	3.1	3.2	3.3	3.4	3.5	3.6	3.7	3.8	3.9	4.0
				LRT	LRT	LRT	LRT	Susie	LRT	LRT	LRT
					LRT	LRT	LRT	LRT	LRT	LRT	LRT
						LRT	LRT	LRT	LRT	LRT	LRT
						LRT	LRT	LRT	LRT	LRT	LRT
					LRT	LRT	LRT	LRT	LRT	LRT	LRT
						LRT	LRT	LRT	LRT	LRT	
						LRT	LRT	LRT			
						LRT					

*Note. Students rated each item on a 4-point scale (1 = *Not Useful*; 4 = *Very Useful*).

K-6 Students' Ratings of LRT's Feedback After Observing Teacher Presenting a Lesson*

<3.0	3.0	3.1	3.2	3.3	3.4	3.5	3.6	3.7	3.8	3.9	4.0
					LRT	LRT	LRT	LRT	Susie	LRT	LRT
					LRT	LRT	LRT	LRT	LRT	LRT	LRT
					LRT	LRT	LRT	LRT	LRT	LRT	LRT
						LRT	LRT	LRT	LRT	LRT	LRT
							LRT	LRT	LRT	LRT	LRT
							LRT	LRT			
							LRT	LRT			
							LRT				
									LRT		
									LRT		
									LRT		

*Note. Students rated each item on a 4-point scale (1 = *Not Useful*; 4 = *Very Useful*).

FIG. 13.3.   *(Continued)*

perfect score, each LRTs used these data to help work on parts of her service that were not at the top of the scale. For example, an LRT might have scored a 4.0 on three of the elements of service, but scored only 3.2 on the value of demonstrations. This enabled her to assess her own work to determine whether she needed to provide more demonstrations, improve the quality of the demonstrations, and so on. One of our efforts to help LRTs improve was a group session where we brainstormed what behaviors contributed to the quality of LRT service. Then using a Total Quality Management (TQM) tool, we ranked the behaviors to come up with the groups' view of the most significant factors (see Table 13.1).

TABLE 13.1
Lead Reading Teacher Brainstorming

My Teachers Find It Helpful When I:	*I Have Learned to Be Effective I Must or Must Not:*
1. Demonstrate	*Must:*
2. Coach	1. Get to know teachers
3. Problem solve	2. Listen
4. Tell them what to do	3. Respect
5. Give suggestions	4. Build relationships
6. Listen (to them vent)	5. Build trust
7. Answer questions	6. Value what they do
8. Share resources	7. Accept approximations
9. Give alternatives	8. Have high expectations
10. Show up	9. Show it's "do-able"
11. Give feedback	10. Model gradual-release
12. Assist with assessment	11. Follow through
13. Order materials	12. Become part of school
14. Assist in LMC	*Must Not:*
15. Sit in meeting w/ principal	1. Talk down to
16. Document students	2. Do the work for them
17. Attend grade level mtgs.	3. Accept excuses
18. Staff development	4. Assume anything
19. Assist with room arrangement	5. Compare teachers against each other
	6. Go too fast

ASSESSMENT OF YEARS 4, 5, AND 6

Years 4, 5, and 6 are not described in detail because by the end of Year 3 we felt we had discovered the best model for impacting our district's reading problems through teacher capacity building. Furthermore, as noted in Table 13.2, summarizing the highlights of these subsequent years, we adopted the *Open Court* reading program as our basal reading series in Year 6. Our training and coaching efforts were necessarily refocused on the effective implementation of the new materials. (*Editor's Note:* This move in Years 4–6 effectively shifted the school district's emphasis away from teacher capacity building in comprehensive reading instruction to the effective use of a basal reading program. Programmatic approaches versus teacher capacity building are discussed more thoroughly in chap. 2, this volume.)

DIRECTING THE COACHING FOCUS

Dr. Cooter urged us to adopt as our motto, "Every classroom as good as our best." It was not a challenge we took lightly. The LRTs, who were in classrooms every day, all day, 4 days a week, were keenly aware of the

TABLE 13.2
Dallas Reading Plan

	Year 1	Year 2	Year 3	Year 4	Year 5	Year 6
Training	Three 7-hour days at Apparel Mart for Vertical Team = 21 hours	Three 7-hour days at Apparel Mart for Vertical Team = 21 hours	Two 3-hour college courses for Vertical Team = 90 hours	Two 3-hour college courses for Vertical Team = 90 hours	Two 3-hour college courses for Vertical Team = 90 hours	Two 3-hour college courses for Vertical Team = 90 hours
LRT Support	16 (1 bilingual) 10–11 schools	29 (3 bilingual) 5–6 schools	37 (12 bilingual) 4–5 schools	41 (13 bilingual) Assignment based on # in Reading Academy and # of Laureates	41 (13 bilingual) Assignment based on # in Reading Academy and # of Laureates	41 (13 bilingual) Some supported the implementation of Open Court
Reading Academy Participants			446	728	585	600
"Masses"		Abbreviated training after each Vertical Team meeting = 9 hours	14-hour waiver training on Saturday = 14 hours			All teachers trained in Open Court

enormity of the task. It was my job to help focus their efforts and support their work. Because of their competence and commitment, sometimes this was an easy task. Because of their tenacity, it was sometimes challenging. It was always exciting.

Perfecting the Interview Process

As a coach to the coaches, one of my major responsibilities was to continue to recruit and hire talented LRTs. The Dallas Reading Plan was fortunate to begin with a stable of grade AAA coaches. A grant from a Dallas foundation, which provided a $10,000 per year stipend for each LRT to supplement their district-provided salary, enabled the department to recruit top-of-the-line practitioners. That stipend, along with recruitment efforts in neighboring districts and from within the district, produced a large pool of qualified applicants. The hiring of the original 14 LRTs, as well as the second group of 15 LRTs, was conducted in cooperation with the foundation. A foundation representative who had been a former assistant superintendent helped us recruit from his previous district and other districts in the area. His experience in interviewing and his tenacious dedication to this project resulted in a rigorous interview process: Interviews for hiring the second group of 15 LRTs took four interviewers 3 weeks time to complete. Although the foundation representative died shortly after the second-year interviews were completed, we continued to make the hiring of competent LRTs a high priority. By this time, we clearly understood the maxim "you win on talent."

Screening New LRTs.   Initially, we relied on questions used during the first rounds of interviews. Because the position was so lucrative and because LRTs became more and more respected, our applicant pool grew. We realized some of our interview questions were no longer secure when several applicants answered "Readers' Digest" when asked what professional journal they read on a regular basis. We developed a performance task and a number of new questions to help us screen applicants. The performance task involved giving applicants a copy of a leveled text (a passage on a certain level of difficulty) and asking him or her to plan a guided reading lesson as he or she waited for the interview to begin, then demonstrate how to teach that book to the interview panel. Because applicants could not know what text they might receive, they could not prepare for the question. The effectiveness of applicants' performances on this task differed significantly. We came to view this task as our *acid test* (see Fig. 13.4).

We also developed several other questions that helped us identify knowledgeable candidates. For instance, we asked the following: "Teachers often

Welcome, we appreciate your application. The interview panel will want to talk to you about your experiences and training to enable us to get to know you as a reading teacher.

As a practical part of this interview, we would like for you to demonstrate how you would teach the attached book. As you are waiting, please preview this book. Assume that you are teaching a group of second graders and you have selected this book as appropriate for their instructional level. Plan a Guided Reading lesson. Think about how you will introduce the book, what you expect the challenges to be, what you will do to help students meet those challenges, the steps of your lesson, and possible extension activities. You may use this paper to make notes, however you will not be asked to turn your notes in to us.

We will call you as soon as we are ready to begin your interview.

FIG. 13.4.

assess comprehension by asking questions. In ADDITION to questioning, what strategies do you utilize to teach comprehension?" Some applicants seemed not to understand the question. Although we specifically asked for strategies in addition to questioning, many applicants described how they questioned students during and after reading. They seemed to feel that comprehension was to be assessed, but did not know how to teach comprehension. The most competent applicants described building background knowledge, using graphic organizers, and mentioned authorities on comprehension they had read.

Another telling question we asked, borrowed from *Classrooms that Work* (Cunningham & Allington, 1994), was this: "What strategies or programs do you feel are worth fighting for?" Again some applicants seemed not to understand the question. They would describe a reading program they had previously taught, but did not seem to understand the need to describe the program's value. Many said they would "fight for reading." Stronger candidates said they would fight for bilingual education, Reading Recovery™, teacher training, and quality literature.

We also looked for teachers who had had significant advanced training in reading education. Many had master's degrees in reading education, and most (in subsequent years) had taken our Reading Academy. A number of teachers were Reading Recovery™ trained. Many had participated in the New Jersey Writing Project training, which our department had sponsored. We looked for extensive experience in teaching reading in the primary grades and, because our population included many second language learners, we valued and actively recruited teachers with bilingual or English as a Second Language (ESL) certification. In the latter instances, we

TABLE 13.3
LRT Training
($n = 41$)

Master's Degree	Doctoral Degree	Reading Recovery Trained	Reading Recovery Teacher Leader	Bilingual Certified	ESL/ESOL Certified	New Jersey Writing Project Trained	New Jersey Writing Project Trainers
26	3	25	3	14	21	30	5

conducted part of the interview of bilingual candidates in Spanish. More subjectively, we tried to determine whether the applicant would be well received by other teachers and was dynamic and articulate enough to provide quality staff training. We knew our interview process was effective when the original group of 29 found the new hires to be exemplary (see Table 13.3).

Coaching the New Coaches

Although our new hires were competent, we had the problem of bringing them up to the knowledge level of the veteran LRT group. Time for training was always a problem, and our Fridays were hectic. There was no way to replicate the training provided to previous groups and, with the academy in full force, new hires were needed immediately to coach academy participants.

Perhaps our best training decision came during the second year of the academy. That year we were able to work with the universities to permit LRTs to serve as adjunct college faculty working in the Reading Academy. We began what we called *Friday Previews*. On Fridays, the LRT who had written the next academy session would actually explain and demonstrate the content. This preview helped shorten LRT/adjunct preparation time. It also helped LRTs who were not serving as adjunct Reading Academy faculty to better understand the content for coaching purposes. Reading Academy sessions represented the latest research on comprehensive reading instruction, and the writers of the academy scripts were genuine scholars who constantly read around each topic included.

The sessions always included some new learning for LRTs. Thus, Friday previews virtually served as postgraduate training for the LRTs. This new learning was immediately internalized because, as adjuncts, they had to teach the session the following week. Each year of the academy, the sessions were updated and rewritten for state-of-the-art knowledge. Thus, LRT growth continued.

A RECIPE FOR CHANGE

Ingredient 1: Remember That You Win on Talent

The LRTs came to the job as experts. They were highly intelligent, motivated, and, to a person, had an exceptional work ethic. It made sense to give them much responsibility and latitude. LRTs naturally took charge of the instructional direction. When Dr. Cooter first came to Dallas, he stated that he expected to be actively involved in training the LRTs and making curriculum decisions. Because of the extraordinary competence of the group, he was able to devote much of his time to strategic planning, working with the business community and administration and acting as a spokesman for our efforts. I had a similar revelation. Previously I had been personally involved in teacher training, determining strategies, and curriculum writing. Like Dr. Cooter, I could relinquish these activities (which I enjoyed) because the LRTs were so competent. They wrote the academy content, selected the implementation goals, selected learning materials for the academy participants, helped schools stock their professional libraries and Literacy Materials Centers, determined their own schedules, and had much input into their own training opportunities.

Ingredient 2: Maximize Your Team's Time on Task

Because the LRTs were so talented and because our needs were so great, it became an important part of my responsibility to ensure that we maximized LRT time in the schools. Because they were hired to serve campuses, I made it a rule to never let extraneous projects, however pressing, interfere with service to schools. In the past, reading department staff had been frequently pulled from campus service by central office superiors to help produce curriculum documents, participate with testing task forces, and serve on monitoring teams. Reading departmental staff now took responsibility for these extra projects as much as possible to shield the LRTs so the work could go forward.

Ingredient 3: Make Strategic Assignments

At the beginning of each year, much of my time was spent in making school assignments. It was important that LRTs were matched to schools where they would be most effective. It was difficult distributing the workload evenly, ensuring that we had coaches to serve every Reading Academy participant each week at each school, ensuring that bilingual LRTs were assigned to schools with the greatest number of second language learners, and that travel time was minimized. With 144 schools varying in size from 250 to 1,200 students, strategic assignment of the talent was often challenging. Some schools had as many as 20 teachers in the academy and some had only a few. On a more positive note, in the second year of the academy, participants began coming from across the district in significant numbers; virtually every school was represented.

It was difficult to change an LRT's school assignment. Before the end of each year, principals, teachers, and district superintendents began to call and request, implore, or demand that their LRT be reassigned to their campus the following year. As we hired additional LRTs, I would ask the current group to list its schools by preference. I wanted to maintain established relationships, yet not assign all of the most difficult schools to new LRTs. LRTs were always able to keep their favorite school and were invariably sad when they lost a school even if the school had been their last preference.

LRTs were responsible for determining their own schedule, although we did request that they have a permanent schedule for each week. Service Logs helped us account for LRT service to schools and served as a communication device when the LRT debriefed with the principal after each day of campus service (see Fig. 13.5).

Ingredient 4: Create Innovative Tools to Meet Your Specialized Needs

LRTs created a number of significant instructional tools/products. One of the most useful was the construction of continuums (i.e., rubrics) for implementation of various teaching strategies. Each strategy was broken down into its critical attributes (e.g., running records was divided into conventions, frequency, scoring, and analysis). Descriptions of teacher behavior moving along the continuum from *ineffective* to *most effective* were written. These continuums helped LRTs and principals know where help was needed and also enabled teachers to self-assess (see Table 13.4). LRTs, under a special external grant, also wrote a series of lessons used to accelerate the learning of students experiencing difficulty. The most significant product of the department was the scripted Reading Academy sessions. Finding time to produce these ambitious products during our busy Fridays was a challenge. However, the quality and usefulness of the products outweighed the considerable time and effort required.

In Retrospect

There are a number of things we could have done better, most having to do with time. I wish we had found a way, for instance, to provide more ongoing support for our Reading Academy graduates (Laureates). After a year of participation in the Reading Academy, our Laureates had made sig-

WHITE-Principal
GREEN-Research & Evaluation
YELLOW-Dallas Reading Plan
PINK-LRT

Lead Reading Teacher Service Record
Reading/Language Arts Department
Dallas Reading Plan
2001-2002

Date (mm:dd:yy): ____________________

Time In (hh:mm): ____________________ **Time Out** (hh:mm): ____________

School: ____________________ **TEA:** ______ **Area:** ____________

LRT/Specialist Name: ____________________ **LRT's ID#:** ____________

SERVICES RENDERED :	Kinder	Grade 1	Grade 2	Grade 3	Grade 4	Grade 5	Grade 6	Other
Classroom Observation(s)/Debriefing								
Classroom Demonstration(s)								
Coaching/ Monitoring Needs								
Grade Level Meeting								
Open Court Focus for Discussion/Training								

LRT met and/or debriefed with principal, assistant principal, or dean.

Yes ☐ **No** ☐ **Not available** ☐

Other Services:

____

____

____

Comments:

____

____

____

Administrator Signature: ______________________________

FIG. 13.5. Lead reading teacher service record.

nificant progress. However, they still needed and wanted coaching and continuous training. We planned early on for this kind of support, but it never became a reality because we were all stretched for time. Although LRTs did try to stop by Laureates' rooms and touch base, and Laureates were invited to our fall and spring conferences, more was needed to continue their capacity development.

TABLE 13.4
Self-Assessment/Goal Continuum

Running Records

Conventions	I have never received training on a universal marking system.	I created my own marking system.	I use markings that can be interpreted by my grade level.	I use markings that can be interpreted by my school. Some markings can be universally read.	I use markings that can be interpreted by district teachers. Most markings can be universally read.	I use markings that can be interpreted universally by teachers.
Scoring • Accuracy rate • Error rate • Self-correction	I do not score Running Records.	I score for accuracy rate percent.	I use the conversion chart to score for accuracy rate percent to group my students.	I use the conversion chart to score for accuracy rate percent and error rate to group my students.	I use the conversion chart to calculate accuracy rate percent, error rate, and self-correction rate for grouping.	I use the conversion chart to calculate accuracy, error rate, and self-correction rates daily to inform my instruction.

(Continued)

TABLE 13.4
(Continued)

Running Records

Analysis • Meaning • Structure • Visual	I do not analyze my Running Records.	I sometimes analyze errors on Running Records.	I analyze all errors on each Running Record.	I analyze all errors and self-corrections on each Running Record.	I analyze all errors and self-corrections for meaning, structure, and visual on each Running Record to guide and inform instruction.	I analyze all errors and self-corrections for meaning, structure, and visual on each Running Record. In addition, I look for patterns over time to further guide instruction.
Frequency	I do not use Running Records.	I use Running Records two times a year, at the beginning and end of school.	I do Running Records occasionally throughout the year.	I do one Running Record on my struggling students once per six weeks.	I do one Running Record on all my students once per six weeks.	I perform Running Records daily so that each student is assessed each six weeks. My struggling students are done twice each six weeks.

Note. Using a red marker, draw a vertical line after the description on each row that best describes your current implementation of each aspect of Running Records. Using a yellow marker, indicate your end-of-the-year goal for each aspect.

Although we knew what a demanding job—both physically and mentally—the LRTs had serving so many teachers and schools, they continued to work with the same intensity. To address some of the stress these professionals faced, we provided an in-house retreat on team building. However, the group should have had more training on the change process in addition to content training. We could have discussed the books we provided the LRTs—*Who Moved my Cheese?* (Johnson, 1998) and *Dance of Change* (Senge, 1999)—to better help us all understand how people react to and cope with change. On one occasion, when we did take time out for this type of dialogue, we had a change management consultant talk to the group about the change process. The LRTs were rather surprised to learn that scholars had studied change processes and described our own experiences so accurately. More training on change management would have helped us better know what to expect in the field and lessened our stress level.

It was often difficult to harness the energies of such a talented group. We never approached any project with less than full commitment. Although we only paid lip service to the slogan "do a few things well" (coined to help us manage our tendency to overplan), we did many things very well—probably too many things, too well.

In addition to coaching the coaches, I was responsible for the elementary reading division. This meant responding to many district requirements, where I often fell victim to the *tyranny of the urgent*. I responded to requests for memos, requests for products, and expectations to attend numerous meetings. Many things that had to be done had little to do with focusing and supporting LRT efforts in the schools and the mission of our department.

Our progress was not as steady as it could have been. The top administration—the general superintendent's office—changed five times during the course of our initiative. Beginning with Year 2, we had limited support from the superintendent. Most of the progress we made was based on our persuasiveness. Although we never would have wanted to mandate the initiative, had we had the strong support of the superintendent, our task would have been much easier. During the sixth year of the plan, Dr. Mike Moses became the general superintendent and made clear that reading was a priority and that he expected the schools to implement the somewhat modified plan with fidelity. Had he been present earlier, our progress would surely have been accelerated.

Although it was recognized from the beginning that change would take time, it would have been optimal if a kitchen-tested recipe existed to guide our efforts. Our first 2 years of the trainer-of-trainers model were not wasted—they served to introduce the Reading Plan and establish the credibility of the Reading Department staff. However, had we not had to spend those years figuring out an effective model of teacher training and classroom support for our urban teachers, we might have had an easier time reaching our goal. When students' futures are at stake, district personnel are understandably anxious for results, and that sort of pressure increases stress on those charged with improving student performance. We knew much about how children learn and came to understand that the context of teacher education must have the same characteristics as any other learning context (Lyons & Pinnell, 2001). The Reading Academy we developed using deep training over time, combined with specific teacher expectations and support of an expert coach, was a meaningful translation of what we know about student learning to adult learning.

In closing, I offer the following suggestions and caution to those undertaking change in an urban reading program. Although these suggestions may be applicable to any school district because they embody sound learning theory, they are particularly applicable to large, urban districts where systemic change is needed. These final suggestions are written using cryptic, recipelike language for easy consumption.

1. *Avoid the temptation to do too much.* Change takes time. Remember that, despite the urgency, there is no quick fix.

2. *Make quality teacher training a first priority.* Trainer-of-trainers models do not work. Training must include both the why and how of teaching and should be divided into digestible chunks and presented over time.

3. *Build in campus coaching to accompany training.* Change is difficult. Support is essential.

4. *Build in accountability for teachers.* Teacher training must translate into classroom practice.

5. *Avoid spreading resources too thin.* Effecting change takes resources, both human and monetary.

6. *Avoid responding to other people's agendas/crises/responsibilities.* Reading decisions must be made by reading experts based on student data.

7. *Recruit knowledgeable coaches who subscribe to the philosophy of the initiative.* Win on talent. There is no substitute for knowledgeable coaches who are also excellent practitioners.

8. *Allocate resources for the purchase of books.* Effective reading instruction requires quality and plentiful materials. Teachers must have access to materials appropriate to students' instructional levels.

9. *Remember the affective needs of teachers.* Efforts of teachers participating in rigorous courses of study should be rewarded for their

efforts. Banquets, plaques, and materials for the classroom worked well for us.

10. *Support coaches with quality training and time for reflection.* It is true that you win on talent. To keep mentor/coaches at the forefront of the profession, remember that they too will require ongoing capacity development.

REFERENCES

Costa, A. L., & Garmston, R. J. (2002). *Cognitive coaching: A foundation for renaissance schools*. Norwood, MA: Christopher-Gordon Publishers.
Cunningham, P. M., & Allington, R. L. (1994). *Classrooms that work: They all can read and write*. New York: HarperCollins.
DeFord, D. E., Lyons, C. A., & Pinnell, G. S. (1991). *Bridges to literacy: Learnings from Reading Recovery™*. Portsmouth, NH: Heinemann.
Johnson, S. (1998). *Who moved my cheese?* New York: G.P. Putnam's Sons.
Kussy, K. (1997). The change process. In M. Herzog (Ed.), *Inside learning network schools* (pp. 14–16). Katonah, NY: Richard C. Owen Publishers.
Lyons, C. A., & Pinnell, G. S. (2001). *Systems for change in literacy education*. Portsmouth, NH: Heinemann.
Senge, P. (1999). *The dance of change: The challenges to sustaining momentum in learning organizations*. New York: Doubleday.

CHAPTER FOURTEEN

Teaching the Teacher: Reflections of a Reading Academy Laureate

Leigh Walker
Dallas Independent School District

The Reading Academy changed my life. That is a powerful and passionate statement—one that could sound exaggerated, brash, and melodramatic. Yet it is true, and let me tell you why: I went from a novice teacher to a state-certified Master Reading Teacher in 3 years; I love my job; and, most important, I am confident that I effectively teach the students with whom I interact. The Reading Academy enabled me to be the teacher I am today. In this chapter, I share my background, my experience in the Reading Academy, and my reflections on that experience.

BACKGROUND KNOWLEDGE

As with our students, understanding a teacher's background experience is relevant to her education. I graduated from college with a degree in English and history, with one education class under my belt. After substituting in two suburban districts, I had the epiphany that elementary education was for me. DISD was the only institution to offer alternative certification in elementary education, and I jumped at the chance to get into the classroom immediately. Throughout my year as a first-year teacher and Alternative Certification intern, I completed 12 hours of graduate-level classes in reading instruction, assessment, and early childhood education. After completing 1 year of teaching and receiving my certification, I enrolled in the Dallas Reading Academy in its second year.

As a first-year teacher, I had completed 75 hours of staff development. These staff development sessions were mainly campus and district based. However, I did have the opportunity to attend a 2-day workshop on literacy centers, which I thoroughly enjoyed. Unfortunately, when I returned to school, the everyday tasks of teaching distracted me from implementing much of what I had heard, and the workshop packet collected dust in my file cabinet.

The Reading Academy piqued my interest, but I have to admit I approached the year-long training with a sigh. I had already been in classes and staff development that wasted my time, and I was mentally and physically exhausted from surviving my first year. At the same time, I yearned to channel my raw enthusiasm from my first year into more effective teaching.

MY READING ACADEMY EXPERIENCE

I realized during my first session in the Reading Academy that this was not a typical workshop. First, the Reading Academy outlined high expectations. Not only was there the commitment of 3 hours a week for the entire school year, but we would receive grades and graduate credit. This instantly set my purpose for learning. To reinforce this, you had to receive at least a C in the class or you would be responsible for buying your textbooks and paying tuition at the end of the year—a $400 to $600 expense. Moreover, we would have a midterm and a final just like a real college class. From the onset, the message was clear: Slackers need not apply. The high expectations of the Reading Academy set the tone for the rest of the year and, for the most part, motivated the teachers to pay attention in class. (How many workshops have you attended with teachers talking the entire time, balancing their checkbooks, etc.?) I walked to my car after that initial class with mixed emotions: I was tired, worried about what I had gotten myself into, but excited about the opportunity to learn and shine.

The framework of the Reading Academy classes engaged me: read and reflect before class; discuss, learn, and practice in class; and implement after class. The reading and reflection on that reading challenged me throughout the year. My class was on Monday night, and, just like one of my third-grade students, I dreaded doing my homework. There were usually several assignments in different textbooks, and I often skimmed the assignment instead of reading it thoroughly. However, in retrospect, the reading and reflection accomplished its purpose, forcing me to create background knowledge and context for that week's lesson.

Once in class, I was delighted to find that the Reading Academy practiced what it preached. Our instructor did not lecture to us for 3 hours about research-proved best practices—she modeled them. We discussed, made things, practiced lessons, broke up into small groups, complained, presented to the group, laughed, learned, and bonded. I saw my fellow classmates (the majority of whom taught at my school) in a new light. Laughing, learning, and creating as a group fostered a "we're all in this together" sense of camaraderie, and the collegial dialogue in class also developed an intellectual feel. I enjoyed feeling like a true professional honing my craft. This sense of camaraderie spilled over into my daily interactions with my colleagues: We discussed and griped and shared our trials and tribulations during lunch or in the hall. As one of the newer teachers on staff, this camaraderie was an unexpected and welcome side effect of the academy.

However, without a doubt, the most powerful part of the Reading Academy was what we did out of class: implement. Each week we had a classroom action plan (CAP) that focused on one of the activities discussed in class. The Lead Reading Teacher (LRT),who was also my professor, came in weekly to observe and discuss the CAP. Having one implementation goal a week was perfect because it broke down what we were required to do into small, manageable baby steps. I was amazed at the end of each semester at how much I had accomplished in the preceding 10 weeks. The CAP *made* me implement. Knowing my professor was going to walk in and expect me to show made me implement what we discussed in class. The CAPs took it from class discussion to real-world application. I could not let the packet from the previous week gather dust on the shelf—I had to use it immediately. I could not wait for the perfect time to try what I had learned. (By the way, is there ever a perfect time?) Therefore, I struggled, made mistakes, and learned. After my first CAP observation and follow-up discussion with my LRT, I was relieved to discover that she did not mind whether the lesson was a disaster. She wanted me to learn from my mistakes. Which I did: I learned what strategies I liked, which ones my students liked, which ones I should do small group, and so on. As the weeks progressed, my favorite day of the week became Tuesday—my LRT day.

THE IMPORTANCE OF MY LRT

My next point is the role of the professor/LRT. Those weekly CAPs created face-to-face accountability. (Because my professor and LRT were the same, I had to make sure that if I talked the talk in class, I had better walk the walk in my classroom.) Most important, meeting with my LRT weekly made me realize that I was not alone. During my first year of teaching, I had felt so isolated. Although I had a mentor and was a third-grade team member, when I shut my classroom door it was just me. Seeing my LRT weekly changed all that. Just like a child with a teacher, I had someone to show off for, to guide me, someone's opinion I trusted, a role model, and someone to give me feedback, positive and constructive. The CAPS made me implement; meeting with the LRT weekly is what made me excited about doing it.

READING ACADEMY REFLECTIONS

So the Reading Academy changed my life. It was the reason I stayed in DISD despite many other negative factors (revolving high administration, safety, students' challenges). After taking the Reading Academy, I could not fathom teaching any other way so I could not leave. I felt like I was part of something bigger than my classroom and my school. I was part of a community of learners inspired by a common vision that would lead the district to greatness. The Reading Academy empowered me as a teacher because it made me think and problem solve consistently for a year. I felt like the Reading Academy recognized and valued creative teachers, and it allowed me to create, analyze, synthesize, and evaluate my own teaching. The Reading Academy gave me knowledge and confidence. When I finished that year, I knew I could go anywhere with nothing but a set of leveled books and teach reading. In conclusion, teaching is an art and a science, and the Reading Academy enabled me to learn one and define the other.

CHAPTER FIFTEEN

Creating a Balanced Literacy Curriculum: One Elementary School Principal's Perspective

Judy Zimny
Dallas Independent School District

WHAT DOES IT TAKE?

People often ask me for a formula for successful school change. Despite our disdain as educators for generalized, one-size-fits-all kinds of answers, I do believe there are backbone processes from which successful school change can take place more easily and effectively. The steps described here are strategies that L.L. Hotchkiss Elementary School used (and continues to use) to move from a limited basal-based reading curriculum to a comprehensive balanced literacy curriculum.

Templates are important. Templates provide the structure from which creativity and individualization can evolve. Templates provide the routines that free up the time and energy to work with the unexpected.

Our template molds the work and ideas of others into our own school's creation. Deming's Quality Principles (Deming, 1986; Walton, 1986), along with David Langford's (see online reference for Langford) work in this area, support the entire framework. Years of priceless professional mentoring provided by Texas Instruments' vice president, Shaunna Sowell, enabled the hands-on implementation of Quality Processes in the school (vs. business) setting. Decades of reading research (Clay, 1972; Cunningham & Allington, 1994; Dewey, 1976; Goodman, 1986; Reutzel & Cooter, 2003; Routman, 1991; Thorndike, 1977; Vygotsky, 1962, 1978) provided substantive direction in the area of reading and writing curriculum, as well as best practices. Perhaps most important, for the last 8 years, key staff in my building assumed tremendous leadership roles in staff development—training themselves, colleagues, and their administrator (me). It must be acknowledged that the humble steps presented here emerged only as the result of the genius and the passion of many before me.

STEP 1: BELIEFS—CREATE A SHARED SCHOOL BELIEF STATEMENT

Organizations need published, shared belief statements. Personal and organizational beliefs must be in alignment. Beliefs, although pretty much taken for granted, truly do drive our daily decisions and behavior and are thus monumentally important. Our belief statement, for example, included the following points:

1. All children can and want to learn to read and write.
2. A balanced literacy program orchestrating the use of several strategies is the most effective and joyful means for creating life-long readers.
3. Learning to read and write is learned both implicitly and explicitly.

STEP 2: THE VISION—CREATE A SHARED SCHOOL VISION

Both informal and formal leaders in the school (representing all of the various subgroups) must collectively create and document a vision statement explaining what they want their school to be like in 5 years. This vision statement must answer such questions as:

- What do teachers expect to see in their balanced literacy school?
- How compatible is this picture with what is expressed in the belief statement?
- What are the children doing?
- What is the staff doing?
- What do the classrooms look like?
- What does the school smell like? Taste like? Sound like? Feel like?
- What kinds of staff development activities are taking place?
- What are teachers discussing in the lounge?
- What kinds of resources are available?
- What kinds of test scores is the school achieving?

- What is going on with underachieving students?
- What is going on with non-English-speaking youngsters?

Too often overlooked or minimized, this vision is truly what drives the change. The goal is for the vision to be so compelling, so vivid—so consuming—that it serves as a positive force pulling the staff forward. The vision must be able to serve as a source of motivation, enthusiasm, and energy. Time invested here is time well spent.

Assistance from outside consultants enables all involved to more fully participate (vs. some assuming the roles of facilitators) in this collaborative, visioning process. Many large corporations have leaders trained in quality management who are willing to donate their time to schools for this purpose.

STEP 3: IDENTIFY THE GAP BETWEEN WHERE THE SCHOOL IS VERSUS WHERE YOU WANT THE SCHOOL TO BE

Do some prioritizing within your vision. What are the most important components? What are the musts? Shoulds? Coulds? Ranking of priorities are also helpful later when you develop timelines and make judgments regarding your investments of time and energy. Multigroup voting methods, sometimes referred to as *nominal group technique* (Langford, 1995), work well to achieve consensus when establishing priorities with a large group of people.

Second, articulate the gaps among your description of your future, an ideal school, and where you are now. Do classrooms currently have 20 or fewer books in their classroom libraries? Are basal readers the only consistent material in the school for providing literacy instruction? Use both quantitative (test scores, attendance, budgets) and qualitative (surveys, observation, interviews) information to inform your decisions. Accurate knowledge of the real and perceived gaps provides for a more accurate sense of direction for staff and community. Gap analysis articulates a fairly clear description of what is. It provides your baseline.

STEP 4: BACKWARD MAPPING

Using your prioritized vision components, along with any district or state mandates, it is ultimately the school principal's responsibility to establish three to seven (absolutely no more than seven) measurable goals for Year 1. State, district, building, grade-level (or team), as well as individual staff and student goals should ultimately cascade within each other. Educators often must discipline themselves to maintain a focus on measurable student achievement—*results* versus *means* for achieving those results. Include goals measured by high-stakes testing if your district or state holds you accountable for achieving certain results. Note how the goals for my school changed from 1996–1997 to 2000–2001.

Exercise caution to refrain from listing strategies as goals. *Strategies* are those things you do to make goals happen. All of the strategies in the world are worthless if the goal is not met. For example, the goal may be for 80% of students in all subgroups to pass a state reading exam. Strategies might include daily read-alouds, expanding classroom libraries, and staff development related to implementing guided reading groups. The goal, however, is for these strategies to result in higher reading achievement as measured by a state-mandated exam. Strategies must be put in place under the goals as needed to enable the goals to be satisfied—they are not the same as the goal.

A projected, tentative timeline can also be established for Years 2 through 5. At this point in your timeline, you are only dealing with goal statements (student achievement) that support your vision, not how you are going to reach the goal. That comes later in the form of a 3W Chart (i.e., Who, What, When).

STEP 5: THE LEADER MUST DEVELOP A SENSE OF URGENCY

Change is difficult. It is rarely fun—and almost always uncomfortable—even when it is for an individual's or group's benefit. The principal and staff leaders must be able to create a sense of urgency that eventually lights a fire (or at least a spark) under a good portion of the staff. Many times comparing one's own student achievement scores to similar but higher achieving schools helps serve this purpose. Many times visits to other schools that illustrate your vision for your own campus help staff to feel excited about what is possible. Many times a consultant or outside speaker is perceived as a greater expert and is more readily received. I found I needed all of this to continually nurture a sense of need for change among my own staff. It is simply too easy to continue doing what one has always done—even when it is not working.

It is not essential (although it would be nice) that you have majority staff support to initiate a successful change effort. I believe it can be done with as little as 20% of staff initially supporting reform. Teachers want to be successful. The success of others is eventually contagious, even by the most reluctant. School change is one of those areas where the power of one is continually demonstrated.

Truth does exist in the adage that people tend to support what they help create. That is one of the main reasons for developing the school's belief statement, vision, and strategies through a collective, collaborative process. All learners perform better when a leader can build from and maintain previously existing strengths. All schools have points of pride and success. It is important to acknowledge and build from these, thus the significance of the drivers within the next section.

STEP 6: FORCE FIELD ANALYSIS: PRIORITIZE DRIVERS AND BARRIERS TO YEAR 1'S GOALS

Again it is best to recruit help from outside of your school to lead your team through the completion of a force field analysis. Administrators need to be equal contributors to this process and are, therefore, unable to serve as facilitator.

Begin by formally brainstorming current processes or procedures that drive or enable acquisition of your current school goals. Prioritize through multivoting. Recognize, celebrate, and be sure to maintain those processes (as well as the funding and personnel needed to enable them) that are driving student achievement. Starting with drivers provides the group the sense of success needed to sustain them during the next, more difficult phase. List current processes or procedures that are preventing acquisition of current school goals. It is helpful to sometimes cluster ideas if they appropriately fit together (e.g., ideas related to materials, discipline, parents, staff development, monitoring). Care must be taken, however, to capture the details of the individual idea within the cluster. Discussion related to span of control versus span of interest (what barriers we can more directly vs. less directly influence) is often useful to people prior to brainstorming barriers.

Although teachers readily acknowledge classroom difficulties stemming from poverty, student mobility, and language needs, there is little in their immediate control that they can do to significantly influence these variables. Simply being aware of and accepting these kinds of items as limits, versus allowing them to be used as excuses or distractions, is sometimes helpful. Again when formal brainstorming is fairly exhaustive (i.e., lists often contain 40 to 50 items), prioritize through multivoting (or nominal group technique; Langford, 1995) factors that are preventing the school from reaching its first year's goals.

Results from the force field analysis provide you with a listing of most significant drivers to make sure you maintain while also helping the staff identify problem-solving strategies and funding to diminish one to three of the most significant barriers identified. For example, the first year we implemented this process (1995), we identified two major barriers to student achievement: off-task, disrespectful student behavior and poor literacy (reading). From this point forward, all new funding and professional energy was required to address the question, "How will doing this help improve student behavior or reading?"

Educators are bombarded with countless well-meaning opportunities for children—one of our biggest challenges is identifying the best practices. It is also important to recognize that there may be steps to solving the ultimate problem—poor reading—that really do not look like they have much to do with teaching reading (like working on improving student behavior). These root problems, however, must be addressed if the surface concern is to ever be resolved.

STEP 7: DEVELOP A WHO/WHAT/WHEN CHART. THEN, MONITOR/ADJUST, MONITOR/ADJUST

This is the really fun part . . . the strategy part. Here you begin researching best practices, discuss what others are doing, and decide which activities will give you the most student gains for your investment of staff time and energy. Reviews of the literature, visits to other schools, and onsite consultant visits can all be helpful here. Your decisions can only be as good as the information you gather. As obvious as it seems, it is critically important to choose the right strategies—and not just jump in with traditional or known interventions—especially if these have not previously gotten your school to where you want it to be.

Reading recovery-trained teachers or master reading teachers (a Texas certification) can be extremely helpful in this process. You want experts in the field presenting possible solutions and alternatives while also including classroom teachers in the dialogue and collaboration. Selected interventions must be doable and effective in the regular classroom.

Know that there will never be enough funding for all children to be served by specialists, such as reading recovery teachers. One of our schoolwide interventions was to ensure that the regular classroom teacher had access to the same materials and similar training to that of reading recovery-trained teachers. That was an action we could control, finance, and use to impact learning across the school.

Always include checkpoints (scheduled times to formally monitor student achievement and adjust your strategies accordingly) within this 3W (Who, What, When) chart. How often should the leadership team get back together to review student achievement and adjust classroom instruction or building strategies accordingly? Sometimes a particular classroom will not be doing as well as anticipated. Others times you may need to adjust for unexpected staff changes. Student achievement must be monitored for the school, each grade level, individual classrooms, and each child. Ongoing monitoring of student learning and related adjustments in instruction is fundamental for student success. Anticipating the need to make minor strategy changes and building this need into your overall plan definitely facilitates success.

When student success fails to meet expectations, focus on the processes that are impacting learning. Processes can be changed and thereby provide hope. Instructional leaders must enable colleagues to change their classroom or instructional processes when students do not meet achievement criteria. Some of the strategies we found most useful in successfully implementing a balanced literacy program are as follow:

1. *Using reading recovery-trained teachers to provide supported, in-classroom staff development for half of every school day.* This enabled extended learning over time for teachers after school and/or during the summer. Two years into our own staff development program, we were able to augment the coaching efforts of our building specialists with assistance from the lead reading teachers (LRTs) provided by the school district's Dallas Reading Plan (LRTs came 1 day per week).

Another tremendous boost to our building staff development effort was the addition of the Reading Academy established by our district's reading department. The Reading Academy systematically taught balanced literacy strategies and provided follow-up coaching in teachers' classrooms via the LRTs. Consistent with our building-level practice of monitoring student achievement and adjusting, our own reading recovery teachers simply adjusted their schedule to meet the staff development needs of teachers who had not been through the Reading Academy. Although unable to provide the comprehensive curriculum taught in the Reading Academy, these talented professionals at least responded immediately with quality, highly personalized balanced literacy staff development. These teachers clearly understood that their main job was to enable others to do what they already did so well—help all children become skilled readers.

2. *Creating and maintaining a reading resource room.* We provided our 50 homeroom teachers with countless leveled books, big books, novel sets, and other critical teaching materials in both English and Spanish. These materials were available to teachers for checkout throughout the year for classroom instruction.

3. *Team monitoring of student performance on a regular basis and adjusting the use of resources (including personnel) in an ongoing kind of way.* Learning to work together as teams and collectively viewing stu-

dents' formative assessment results—versus working as isolated class-rooms or teachers—presented its own growth opportunities.

4. *Providing increased time for teachers to collaborate and plan together.* Teachers were paid every third Monday for an extra 1.5 hours to stay after school and attend grade-level meetings. Additionally, substitute teachers were provided a half day for teachers four to five times during the school year to provide more in-depth planning and coordination.

5. *Implementing Project Achieve* (Knoff & Barsche, 1995), a school-wide behavior management/violence prevention program, reduced discipline referrals to administrators from more than 500 cases in 1994 to 1995 to fewer than 30 per year from 1998 to 2002.

6. *Partnering with and fully welcoming the support of a corporate partner (Texas Instruments) greatly contributed to our school's achievement.* Mentoring, coaching, volunteer tutors, extensive grant funding, and increased accountability all significantly impacted the training and materials required to establish, maintain, and continually nurture a balanced literacy curriculum. Coaching in the use of quality management tools and strategies further strengthened our ability to work effectively as a team toward common goals.

7. *Enabling different levels of ongoing staff development for different levels of staff.* Training in literacy and classroom organization and management is provided for all new staff. Training in communication, leadership, and cutting-edge research is provided for more experienced personnel.

CHALLENGES

Change

There are challenges inherent in any change process. Research in the area of change has identified phases of change that most individuals normally go through. Principals attempting to change reading instruction in their school can expect staff members to go through phases of denial ("I won't really have to do this . . ."), anger and resistance ("Who does she think she is?"), ambivalence and the messiness of growth ("Hmm . . . maybe there *is* some merit to this plan. . . . Where did I put that handout?"), and acceptance. Knowing that these behaviors are normal make it easier to deal with negative behavior when it does occur—it is simply normal and to be expected. The challenge for school leaders is to help faculty members move through each of the phases of change until they can embrace, advocate, and teach new teachers the new curriculum.

Standards and High-Stakes Testing

Standards and high-stakes testing are realities in the current public school classroom. As public school employees, we are hired by the state, as agents of the state, to reach state-mandated goals. Frame this reality in a way that supports best practices in literacy instruction. What the state and school district truly want out of schools are high achievement scores. They believe high achievement scores reflect high literacy levels, and we in the field must admit that this is at least somewhat accurate. At an even higher level, politicians and business leaders are looking for schools that can provide solutions and directions in solving national problems related to literacy. I do not believe they truly care whether we use phonics, whole language, basal programs, or a combination of strategies. Their interest is in *results*—and, quite frankly, that is where our interests need to be also.

We should work to allow high achievement scores to be a by-product of high-quality instruction. We in the trenches know that there is no one answer to illiteracy, and that is where the real challenge lies. When schools put into place balanced literacy programs that can differentiate instruction to the point where 90% of students (regardless of socioeconomics or ethnicity) demonstrate on-level reading, influential administrators and community members will be coming to learn from you (vs. pushing for unnecessary prescriptive policies or legislation).

Maintaining Sufficient Print

We finally came to accept that classroom libraries had to be renewed every year. It pains me when I look at classrooms with libraries of 100 to 150 varied books when I know my own children have more than that in their individual bedrooms. Hundreds of books representing all different genres, as well as many levels, must be available for students to read. A wide variety of resources must be available so that matches between children's interests and print can be made. Books are lost, books are stolen (a mixed blessing), and many books simply wear out. Securing funding and continuing to order high volumes of literature for classroom libraries (including periodicals) are ongoing challenges.

Retention Versus Social Promotion

The sad reality with this controversy is that neither intervention meets student needs. Hundreds of research studies done throughout the 20th century unsuccessfully called for the establishment of consistent, effective, just-on-time interventions for low-achieving youngsters. The current political climate has again assumed that one or the other of these interventions will increase student learning despite countless research debunking this

premise. Clearly there is much work left to be done in the areas of identifying and establishing early intervention, as well as implementing and monitoring best practices for students developing literacy.

Student Mobility

Student mobility is a national challenge. Mobility in my own building is
about 55%; most teachers end the school year with a little over half of the
students in their classroom having left (and replaced by other highly mobile students). Not only does this present tremendous challenges in the
important area of teacher–student relationships, but it presents obstacles in the areas of curriculum coordination, assessment, and instructional delivery.

The Bilingual Debate

English language learners (ELL) acquire literacy in much the same way as
native English speakers (Fitzgerald, 1995). Although educators continue
to debate the ethics and ideals of bilingual versus English as a Second Language (ESL) instruction, schools must deal with the reality of there being
few bilingual teachers for native Spanish speakers and virtually no bilingual teachers for the thousands of students with native languages other
than English or Spanish. Professionals need to unite their efforts to efficiently provide and monitor comprehensive, high-quality ESL instruction
for all non-English-speaking students regardless of a child's first language
or culture. A common need all of these students share is the need to be
fluent English speakers, readers, and writers. Refocused energy must be
placed on developing, implementing, and ensuring a systematic (vs. random), research-based ESL curriculum.

Incompetent Teachers

Ironically, at a time when the number of alternative and emergency certified
teachers is at its highest, there is also a renewed call in the education establishment for greater accountability and courageous leadership. Teaching is
more difficult and demanding than those who have not done it can ever
imagine. There are those for whom the teaching profession simply is not
appropriate. It is not the principal's role to ultimately determine whether
an employee is unwilling or unable to perform. After ample opportunities
have been provided to enable low-performing classroom teachers to increase their effectiveness, either student results must improve or the principal must do whatever is necessary to remove unsuccessful teachers from
the classroom. A personal responsibility matrix that my coach, Shaunna, has
reminded me of on several occasions has six levels:

6. Make it happen.
5. Take action.
4. Make a plan.
3. Wait and hope.
2. Blame.
1. Denial.

It is ultimately every school employee's responsibility to make student achievement happen.

Staff Development and Turnover

Reading recovery-trained and other highly competent teachers from my school have been promoted at a fast rate. As a result, we are always watching for new leadership to be developed. Three to six staff members can be expected to leave each year due to understandable family reasons. Maintaining a comprehensive training program is something we are continually working to achieve. Several times we thought we had the right program in place only to find ourselves adjusting it time and time again. What we have come to accept is that we will always have staff at different levels of professional development, and that comprehensive, ongoing training of all deserves as many resources as we can provide.

Principal as a Role Model

The power of the principal as model continues to amaze, perplex, and sometimes frighten me. Staff will talk about what the principal talks about. Staff will do what the principal does. Therefore, what principals say and do becomes extremely important, and we must be conscious of what our words and actions are saying. If we want out teachers to be talking about best practices in reading instruction, we must be talking about that every day. If we want our teachers to continually and visibly improve their professional expertise, then we too must model that practice. What messages do our school's weekly newsletters have? What messages do our daily announcements carry? What messages do our conversations with students send? The urgent demands in an administrator's schedule must be constantly balanced with the more important decisions and behavior related to improving reading instruction.

Fewer Resources Than Needs

Without a doubt, the biggest challenge remaining in the public schools is that needs *greatly* outnumber resources. Needs relative to classroom materials (teachers continue to personally fund many of their classroom supplies), time for planning and professional collaboration, time for professional training and feedback, and time and personnel to meet the tremendous and varied needs of thousands of families all are great concerns. Perhaps the most realistic way school leaders can begin to address this dilemma is through the acquisition of additional grant funding. Adequate funding is simply not going to be provided through regular school budgets, even with the additional resources provided through federal funds. For that matter, grant funding will not provide even a short-term answer to the shortage of resources. However, additional funding will enable some teaching strategies that would otherwise not take place. School leaders who are truly serious about lasting building-wide change will want to pursue grant funding to support staff development and time for teacher collaboration. These kinds of leadership efforts need to be allowed for extended professional learning over time.

Celebration

Dedicated public school employees continue to ache over unmet student needs, regardless of how many gains are made. There are still those special education students who could be receiving better services. There are still those new teachers who are struggling longer than their mentors want. What about those shadow children, such as slow learners, who never receive help in critical need areas?

Nevertheless, time must be made for play and celebration. Stephen Covey (1994) explained in his work *First Things First* that the root word of *recreation* is "re-create." Time must be built into the hectic, routinely overwhelming schedule of public school employees to rejoice, savor, and celebrate their countless successes. Time and permission for public school employees to re-create their spirits is essential. The motivation, energy, and even zeal to persist in the face of unrealistic demands, limited resources, and temporary setbacks all ultimately stem from one's heart. We must find ways to replenish their energies through celebration.

A CALL TO ACTION

Excellent public education and effective school change are each forms of missionary work. In fact, given the current budget restraints placed on schools (and the resulting 60- to 70-hour work weeks for truly effective educators), in addition to educators' salaries compared to other professions, many highly qualified people are avoiding or leaving the education profession. It frightens me to think that one of the fundamental institutions on which our country's principles are based is dependent on, more than anything else, work of the heart.

Transforming one school's curriculum is possible. Transforming America's schools to authentic, meaningful, integrated balanced literacy curriculums requires political, corporate, and administrative paradigm shifts. These paradigm shifts are dependent on changes in deep-rooted belief systems; beliefs about the value of teachers, the value of planning and collaboration, the value of literature, and the value of what the research tells us about how children learn best.

This message is not new. Practitioners and researchers since the beginning of the 20th century have essentially advocated for a balanced literacy reading curriculum. Now 100 years later, I wonder what it will take to make that happen.

REFERENCES

Clay, M. M. (1972). *Reading: The patterning of complex behaviour*. Portsmouth, NH: Heinemann.

Covey, S. (1994). *First things first*. New York: Simon & Schuster.

Cunningham, P., & Allington, R. (1994). *Classrooms that work: They can all read and write*. New York: HarperCollins.

Deming, W. E. (1986). *Out of the crisis*. Cambridge, MA: Massachusetts Institute of Technology, Center for Advanced Engineering Study.

Dewey, J. (1976). *The school and society*. Carbondale: Southern Illinois University Press.

Fitzgerald, J. (1995). English-as-a-second-language learner's cognitive reading processes: A review of research in the United States. *Review of Educational Research, 65*(2).

Goodman, K. (1986). *What's whole in whole language?* Toronto: Scholastic.

Knoff, H. M., & Barsche, G. M. (1995). Project ACHIEVE: Analyzing a school process for at-risk and underachieving students. *School Psychology Review, 24*, 579–603.

Langford, D. (1995). Information is available on the multi-voting process and other related information online at http://www.langfordlearning.com.

Reutzel, D. R., & Cooter, R. B., Jr. (2003). *Strategies for reading assessment and instruction*. Upper Saddle River, NJ: Merrill/Prentice-Hall.

Routman, R. (1991). *Invitations: Changing as teachers and learners*. Portsmouth, NH: Heinemann.

Thorndike, R. L. (1977). *Reading comprehension education in fifteen countries: An empirical study*. New York: Wiley.

Vygotsky, L. S. (1962). *Thought and language*. Cambridge, MA: MIT Press.

Vygotsky, L. S. (1978). *Mind in society*. Cambridge, MA: Harvard University Press.

Walton, M. (1986). *The Deming management method*. New York: Dodd, Mead.

CHAPTER SIXTEEN

Marry Well . . . Divorce Less: Helping Principals Choose Effective Literacy Programs

Kathleen S. Cooter
Texas Christian University

The campus has its third principal in 4 years. There are seven different literacy programs being implemented in some fashion. Children are labeled, unlabeled, tested, and placed in these programs with no discernible design except availability either in the child's schedule or in the reading class. This scenario repeats itself over and over in urban centers across the nation.

Leading an urban elementary school is by its nature hazardous duty. Little wonder, given the complexities of the job and the vagaries of being assigned to it, that principals are an endangered species. Gilman and Lanman-Givens (2001) reported that the school principal must be:

> the school's community relations director, disciplinarian, business manager, marketer, safety officer, facilities supervisor, fund-raiser, labor relations officer, medical supervisor, social service agent, facilitator and enforcer of the laws, policies, and regulations from various levels of government. Finding the time to wear the hat of instructional leader, which should be the principal's primary task, often becomes difficult. (p. 73)

Furthermore, with literacy deservedly being the hot topic politically, the campus leader must purchase materials and choose training formats that meet the campus goals and supply teachers with the expertise, training materials, and time to make the literacy program viable.

Here is some advice based on my many years as a principal and from my work as a consultant to urban schools having what might be termed as LPD—literacy program distress: *Marry well . . . divorce less.* (Actually, this adage is paraphrased from something my mother taught me many years ago.) As applied to the selection of reading programs for urban schools, *Marry well . . .* suggests that principals, as the curriculum leader, should take the necessary time required to select high-quality, research-based reading and writing programs for schoolwide implementation. *Divorce less* suggests that, once a decision is made, the principal should make sure that the program is implemented correctly and stay with it for at least a few years before considering another. In the remainder of this chapter, we take a closer look at ways principals can improve literacy development in their urban school by following this motto.

MARRY WELL . . .

Over the years, I have found that many principals (including myself) ask some of the same questions: Is reading available in a box? Can you as building leader *buy* higher reading scores using off-the-shelf commercial programs? Should you look for blue-light specials, or is a high-dollar Neiman Marcus program what your students should have?

First, you cannot simply buy good literacy instruction, otherwise we would all have purchased a six pack long ago and gotten on with life. Literacy can only be obtained through thoughtful leadership and study, as well as quality teaching skillfully delivered using well-designed, functional materials. So what are the most pertinent questions principals should ask on their odyssey to literacy improvement?

1. *What do you need to know as the point person of the literacy team on your campus?* Teacher and administrator quality is by far the most important factor in student achievement (Pogrow, 2001). In a qualitative study of elementary principals done by McCay (2001), six conditions were identified that assist principals in meeting their own learning needs:

- *Information that challenges their thinking and in a time frame that adjusts to their hectic schedules*—Leaders can find time to read research syntheses, quick data representations, and policy briefs. These are short info shots that help inform and maintain a knowledge base.
- *Feedback*—Trite as it sounds, it is lonely at the top and principals feel isolated. The politics of a school district often preclude objective feedback. The leader must find a professional friend or a network of

other principals with whom he or she can tell all safely and get collegial assistance and guidance without retribution.

- *Interactions with colleagues outside the district*—Principals have few opportunities to meet others in similar situations to discuss mutual concerns and brainstorm solutions. This is time well spent in reframing and rethinking school issues.
- *Time for reflection*—Principals are all too often forced by frantic scheduling to make hasty decisions with too little data—decisions that could be penny-wise and pound-foolish. Making time for thoughtful reflection should be a high-priority task. For many, it may take leaving the office for this to occur.
- *Access to resources*—Principals need flexibility in budgeting both time and money so that they can attend conferences, professional development opportunities, and special programs. The principal has to place a high priority on staying informed and active in educational change.
- *Hands-on learning*—Professional development time for teachers must also include campus leaders. This enables principals to have a common understanding of new information necessary for supporting their teachers as they implement new programs and strategies.
- *Opportunities to teach others*—Presenting literacy success stories at conferences and seminars, or engaging in college teaching as an adjunct faculty member renews one's knowledge and should be part of the professional growth of the campus leader.
- *Principals must be learned*—Literacy must be more than a fond memory of some obscure course taken long ago. The challenges of school reform require that principals be active learners (Erlandson, 1994). The term *principal* was historically coined in reference to the *lead-* or *principal teacher*—*principal* is not only a noun, it is also an adjective (Tell, 2001). A leader must know the paths, obstacles, and hallmarks of quality literacy programs both to introduce those features to her campus and to study their ongoing effectiveness.

2. *What is the current state of the school in terms of literacy learning? Are the current programs doing their part in the literacy program—that is, are teachers using the program as designed with the children for whom the program is designed?* Important factors to be addressed in considering these programmatic issues include the following:

- Access to program training for new teachers
- Benefits (or lack thereof) of the current literacy program for special populations

- Program cost per student per year
- Whether teacher training is provided by the vendor and how often
- Vendor availability for feedback or assistance after the initial purchase is made
- Vendor availability for additional training and program updates
- The extent to which your student population has changed (e.g., mobility, second language learners, etc.) since the current program was purchased, and the program's goodness of fit to your student population
- How teachers react to the existing program (i.e., whether they like it, complain about it, understand it, misuse it)
- How long the program has been in place (allow at least 3 years for a new program to make a difference in test scores and other indicators)
- Effectiveness of the program with poorer teachers (i.e., how their students perform)

This last factor, effectiveness of the program in helping students succeed even when placed with a weak teacher, must not be ignored. The top one third of teachers can produce as much as six times the improvement in student achievement as the bottom third (Haycock, 1998). It may be that you are looking at a problem that is not pedagogic in nature. The program already in use may meet your campus literacy needs well when strong teachers use it. Study your data carefully.

3. *Who should answer these questions?* Bring your teacher stakeholders to the table. Share the data you have assembled about the current program, as well as any data from like schools for programs you may be considering. Create a teacher research team charged with the task of meeting with vendors, interviewing current on-campus users, and other campuses like your own that use both the current and considered programs. Doing this early in the process helps eliminate sabotage, foot dragging, and eye rolling at the implementation stage.

Researchers have suggested that this team approach is the only pathway to substantive campus change. Pugach and Johnson (2002) suggested that campus-wide collaboration on key issues such as literacy requires extensive data study, information gathering, and discussion. It is the only logical and thoughtful way to identify programmatic successes or failures.

In an article entitled, "Building a Learning Organization," Mohr and Dichter (2001) suggested that a campus can and must develop teams comprised of teachers and administrators that ask the hard questions and promote rigor in teaching and learning. Neuman and Pelchat (2001), quoting former principal Gayle Griffin, labeled this *establishing a culture of competence*. Too often teachers are accountable for decisions made by others without any campus input. Small wonder they sometimes fail to feel responsible for proper implementation and programmatic success (Brandt, 2001).

4. *What does an effective program look like?* About 80% to 85% of school-age children learn to read at or near grade-level expectations when there is proper schoolwide implementation of leading basal programs. To judge program effectiveness in an urban school having a high mobility rate, study the data of youngsters with at least 3 years of continuous enrollment; otherwise you will be analyzing too many children having only cursory experience in the program to measure its effectiveness reliably.

DIVORCE LESS!

Let us assume your school-level research team has studied the data and concluded that the current literacy system is largely effective, but has some large leaks. This is not the time for program replacement, but rather for renovation and repair. The first course of action is to identify and prioritize the problematic program issues that are lowering literacy effectiveness. (There should be no more than three significant issues or this is not the program to keep.) In other words, where did the literacy program fail or stumble? With which groups, grade levels, and teachers? Is there a problem with material allocation or use?

Devise a step-by-step campus improvement plan (CIP) to get the program back on track with teachers and students. Schedule regular meetings with the school-level research team to monitor progress. Call in the vendor and get some (free) help. The vendor has a vested interest in keeping the literacy program sold on your campus, so now is the time to get her cooperation as you fine-tune and repair the system. Allow for a 2-year timeline for remediation; this will become the drop-dead date for satisfactory improvement. If student literacy is not markedly improved by that date, the program should be tossed.

Another possibility is that the teacher research team may conclude that a new reading program or supplemental teaching structure (e.g., comprehension workshop, fluency training, phonics program, writing workshop, etc.) is essential if you are to achieve your campus literacy goals. Further, the team may find alternative programs that appear to be effective in similar urban schools and seem affordable. Indeed, if it is time for a programmatic divorce, choosing a replacement should be a painstakingly and studious endeavor. Publishers make available technical manuals and data about program effectiveness. Insist that vendors provide these data to your faculty, and allot faculty time for explanation and questions. It is time for lengthy meetings between the teacher research team and vendors.

What questions should be addressed with the vendors? Here are a few I have found insightful:

- What is the teacher-training component?
- Is teacher training included in the purchase price?
- Will the vendor reliably reappear during the school year to fix problems, meet with staff, and check on progress?
- How will the vendor help with new staff training?
- What is the turnaround for purchase of needed materials? (Momentum can be stymied when teachers do not have necessary materials for program implementation.)
- Has the program been researched independently with children like those on your campus?
- Is the program more effective at certain grade levels?
- What are the short- and long-term gains that can be expected?
- What is the short- and long-term cost per child?
- Will the vendor provide in writing the cost of teacher training—not only initially, but ongoing with new staff?
- Will the vendor cost out each program component for 5 years—both pupil and teacher costs?

One more question your research team should study is: Can the daily schedule of the school accommodate this program? If the program requires 2 hours daily for maximum effectiveness, for example, will your campus be able to make that accommodation?

THE STARRY-EYED STAGE

The choice has been made and a new effort begins. What a grand time! The materials are fresh, the teachers are excited, parents are happy, and the training goes as planned. The year begins and all is well until . . .

Our First Fight

Conflict is inevitable. Indeed it is a healthy albeit uncomfortable part of the process. Some recommend that teachers be warned before conflict occurs so as to prepare them for its inevitable appearance (Mohr & Dichter, 2001). Too much compromise in using a new reading program can lead to mediocrity, whereas too little compromise can lead to rigidity. The research team may begin to question their choices.

It is far too early to dismiss program changes as inadequate. When people understand that change and conflict are common and can be weathered, they relax. It takes a calm, focused leader to assist school personnel in learning from research, their own experience, and the experiences of others and to analyze those experiences (Mohr & Dichter, 2001).

KEEP THE FIRE GOING

The work to date by the instructional leader and teacher research team has been prodigious; they have carefully studied their campus and its needs. As a team, they have chosen and implemented a programmatic and training backbone for their literacy program, and they have made the commitment of time and money to make the program viable and effective for their learners.

Yet their work is far from over. There are no quick and dirty fixes (Gough, 2001). Walsh, Sattes, and Wiman (2001) suggested a process called *Data in a Day*. This seven-step process strives to systematically collect and analyze data to provide a high-quality snapshot of school practices, affirming as well as identifying areas of needed change. Data in a Day is distinguished from other self-study formats by its focus on observations; inclusion of school children, parents, and community members; and well-defined tasks. This process makes Data in a Day relatively brief, but potent. A summary report is generated and becomes part of the ongoing continuous improvement plan. It might be likened to a yearly health check-up. The campus literacy program is certainly an area where this type of short but thorough study is needed at least biannually.

CONCLUSION

The campus leader, with the assistance of the teacher research team and community, has responsibility for many serious and difficult decisions—many that are indeed life-changing events for children. Truly, choosing a literacy path or *compass* for the campus is one of the most critical of those decisions. It requires that the campus leader be well educated pedagogically, capable of data analyses, organize the talents of staff to work on a common goal, utilize resources effectively, and steer the campus toward effective literacy instruction for all children. In a world of choices, she must be the wise guiding light to define directions for the good of the youngsters and play to the strengths of her staff. In the end, the principal can help teachers to *marry well*—that is, find an appropriate literacy program and augment its effectiveness through teacher training—and *divorce less*—that is, to stay with programs and trainings that work with refinement and continuous literacy improvement.

REFERENCES

Brandt, R. (2001). No best way: The case for differentiated schooling. *Phi Delta Kappan, 83*(2), 153–156.

Erlandson, D. A. (1994). *Building a career: Fulfilling the lifetime professional needs of principals*. Fairfax, VA: National Policy Board for Educational Administration.

Gilman, D. A., & Lanman-Givens, B. (2001). Where have all the principals gone? *Educational Leadership, 58*(8), 72–74.

Gough, P. B. (2001). No quick and dirty fixes. *Phi Delta Kappan, 83*(4), 278.

Haycock, K. (1998). Good teaching matters a lot. *Thinking K–16, 3*(2), 3–5.

McCay, E. (2001). The learning needs of principals. *Educational Leadership, 58*(8), 75–77.

Mohr, N., & Dichter, A. (2001). Building a learning organization. *Phi Delta Kappan, 82*(10), 744–747.

Neuman, M., & Pelchat, J. (2001). The challenge to leadership: Focusing on student achievement. *Phi Delta Kappan, 82*(10), 733–736.

Pogrow, S. (2001). Avoiding comprehensive reform models. *Educational Leadership, 58*(8), 82–83.

Pugach, M. C., & Johnson, L. J. (2002). *Collaborative practitioners: Collaborative schools* (2nd ed.). Denver, CO: Love.

Tell, C. (2001). Appreciating good teaching: A conversation with Lee Shulman. *Educational Leadership, 58*(5), 6–11.

Walsh, J., Sattes, B., & Wiman, E. (2001). A quickie checkup: Gauging continuous school improvement. *Phi Delta Kappan, 82*(7), 547–549.

CHAPTER SEVENTEEN

Addressing the Literacy Needs of African-American Students and Their Teachers

J. Helen Perkins
Southern Methodist University

Our schools can do a better job of educating all of their students, especially students of poverty and minority students. The ability and will of our country's African-American students to read has long been a concern of parents and educators. It seems that, although our knowledge has improved concerning the best methods to enhance literacy, we have most often failed especially those in the urban areas (Doughtery, 1997). Whether they lack the interest, opportunity, parental support, materials, or appropriate instruction, many of these students have failed to master the skills needed for success in literacy. At this point, the Matthew effect is established (Stanovich, 1986), and the students who can read, read more, build fluency, improve their ability to comprehend, and, consequently, learn more; those students who lack the needed literacy skills, read less, learn less, and may even lose the ability to perform any of the skills they had previously acquired.

Research on suspensions, expulsions, retention, and dropout rates indicate that many African-American students are being excluded from mainstream America (Allington & McGill-Franzen, 1991; Banks, 1994; Hill, 1989; Kuykendall, 1992). There is a disproportionately high failure and dropout rate among African-American students. Many youth who live in poverty are at high risk of becoming school dropouts, experiencing academic failure, and engaging in antisocial behavior (Banks, 1994). Strickland (1994) noted that many of the at-risk students are African American and live in poverty. Students labeled as *at risk* are described as not achieving reasonable literacy levels or who fall behind their peers in literacy development (Cunningham & Allington, 1994).

Allington and McGill-Franzen (1991) pointed out that many students are repeating grades because they are behind in reading. In many situations, ability tracking—grouping students according to their ability—often separates students according to their race, and African Americans are often placed in the lowest track (Comer & Poussaint, 1992). According to Dilworth (1992), African-American students are often disproportionately represented in the lower track programs. Irvine (1989) explained that there is overwhelming research that tracking students has no educational benefit, and the teachers for these students are often inexperienced, incompetent, or both. Obiakor (1992) also noted that these students are overrepresented in special education programs. The preponderance of these students in low-ability groups and White students in high-ability groups reinforces beliefs and stereotypes among adults and children that African Americans are intellectually inferior to Whites (Irvine). A problem identified by Obiakor is that poverty and the culture of African-American students are seen as deficits; because of this, students are misidentified, misassessed, misplaced, and misinstructed.

Billingsley (1992) noted that education is the opportunity through which African-American families find their position in life, and education has played a preeminent part among all sources of survival. These families endured hardship and danger to ensure that the Supreme Court decision to outlaw school segregation remained intact. Billingsley (1992) and Foster (1997) explained that African Americans have always had a deep-rooted commitment to attaining an education. Education has been a major focus for these families and has helped shape their lives. Banks (1991) stressed that African-American adults are deeply troubled about the erosion of their children's educational status because they believe that education is a primary means to support upward mobility. Because of these concerns, the author of this chapter conducted a study.

RESEARCH

Perkins (2001) conducted a study to identify effective literacy methods for African-American fourth-grade students. Their administrators identified teachers, and documented success of teaching these students was noted. A diverse group of experienced teachers met in four separate focus group interviews, naturalistic inquiry as qualitative research, and identified methods they believed enhanced their students' literacy. The methods they identified are:

- Independent reading and writing—Students practicing reading and writing (self-selected books and topics)
- Phonics and vocabulary—Understanding letter–sound relationship and building students' word banks
- Modeling—Teachers demonstrating literacy strategies and concepts
- Multicultural education—Materials/books representing all cultures
- Parental involvement—Parents reading and writing with their children. A partnership is established between parents and the school.
- Prior knowledge/schema—Students background, what they already know, their experiences
- Cooperative learning—Students working together to accomplish specific objectives/task

These methods are used daily by teachers and have proved to be successful and continue to enhance the literacy of the students. Strickland (1994) stressed the importance of effective strategies and methods in the teaching of students, such as initiating family programs, instruction in phonics, cooperative group activities, peer teaching methods to promote active learning, direct instruction, teacher modeling, and multicultural literature.

Gloria Ladson-Billings (1994) conducted research and identified several of the same methods as being useful with African-American students. She conducted ethnographic interviews with eight teachers. First, parents and principals identified the eight teachers whom they believed demonstrated effectiveness with these students. Then Ladson-Billings conducted her study with five African-American and three White teachers to examine effective teaching methods through teacher interviews and classroom observations. She used their comments and classroom observations to explain their culturally relevant practices. She identified some of the best practices of culturally relevant pedagogy, such as cooperative learning, multicultural materials, phonics, and teachers who care about their students and their culture. She described these practices in detail in her book.

Person, Amos, and Jenkins (1995) conducted a study assessing a series of four institutes at Mississippi State University on instructional methods for culturally diverse students. The institute was developed because of concerns about the quality of education available to African-American students. The study surveyed the 73 educators who had participated in the Strategies for Instructing Culturally Diverse Students (SICDS) Institute over the summers of 1989 to 1992. Thirty-nine (54%) returned surveys were determined to be usable.

This study found that teachers are important and play a vital role in improving the quality of life for African-American students. They also noted that teachers must implement behaviors that are appropriate for positive learning opportunities to occur. Person et al. believed that intensive staff development programs are needed for teachers during the summer months.

Many of the surveyed educators made an effort to involve the parents; the parents were included on various committees and contacted on a regular basis. They also found during the study that the participants appreciated and valued the diverse students in their classrooms. The teachers were aware of cultural differences that existed in their classrooms. The participants also used multicultural education principles in their instructional activities.

Baumann, Hoffman, Moon, and Duffy-Hester (1998) surveyed administrators and teachers about elementary reading and language arts instruction. The results were based on teachers' self-reports of their beliefs and practices. One of the major findings from their surveys was that a majority (89%) of the teachers surveyed preferred a balanced, eclectic approach to elementary reading instruction, which means the teachers prefer a program that involves both reading skill instruction and immersion in enriched literacy.

> We found that teachers design reading and language arts programs that provide a multifaceted, balanced instructional diet that includes an artful blend of direct instruction in phonics and other reading and writing strategies along with a rich assortment of literature, oral language, and written language experiences and activities. (Baumann et al., 1998, p. 646)

The research studies discussed in this section are indicative of best practices, what really helps students' literacy skills to improve.

TEACHER CHALLENGES

According to Hill (1989), teachers increasingly find themselves in multicultural/diverse classrooms, yet they have not been trained to be effective multicultural, ethnically diverse teachers. Educators in this country are overwhelmingly White middle-class females (Kuykendall, 1992). Foster (1997) explained that many programs are being developed to recruit more non-White teachers into the profession, but the predictions for increasing the number were not promising.

Underqualified teachers are disproportionately found in predominantly African-American, Hispanic, and Native American schools and classrooms (Dilworth, 1992). Many times the blame is placed on the student when it is really the teacher's inability to teach the student and not the student's inability to learn. Darling-Hammond (1996) shared that teacher education in the United States has been thin and uneven in quality:

> In addition to the tradition of emergency certification that continues in more than 40 states, some newly launched alternative certification programs provide only a few weeks of training for entering teachers, unskilled in such fundamentals as learning theory, child development, and subject matter pedagogy and placing recruits in classrooms without previous supervised experience. Each year about 20,000 individuals enter teaching without a license, while another 30,000 enter with substandard credentials. (p. 7)

Dilworth (1992) explained that there are specialized skills that teachers need to be most effective with African-American students. There is a growing body of research that suggests better, meaningful, and more comprehensive methods to enhance the literacy of African-American students (Strickland, 1994). Teachers need better training if they are to experience success in the classroom; they need training in how to instruct reading, spelling, and writing. Teachers need the knowledge, skills, and supported practice (continuous coaching) that will enable their teaching to be successful (American Federation of Teachers, 1999). According to Huber-Bowen (1993), as educators become more culturally responsible, they possess a multitude of methods, and whether students make rapid or slow progress in becoming skilled readers depends on the methods the educators utilize.

TEACHER ATTITUDE

Hopson and Hopson (1990) noted teachers of African-American students should examine their own attitudes about race. Collins (1992) and Ladson-Billings (1994) believed teachers' attitude toward a certain group of people alters the way they treat those students. Teachers should assess their own feelings concerning students of various ethnic groups (Kuykendall, 1992). If a teacher believes a student will fail, that student will most likely fail. Wyman (1993) and Kuykendall (1992) noted that a student's attitude toward school, confidence, and behavior are influenced by the teacher's attitude and expectation. The teacher's expectations are essential in encouraging a student's pursuit of knowledge; positive expectations should be shared with the student on a daily basis. Bryant and Jones (1993) offered that positive praise from the teacher would result in the student's positive self-concept; therefore, the student learns more efficiently. The student should feel a sense of caring and acceptance from the teacher and not the feeling the teacher is just going through the motions or pretending (Kuykendall). She also explained that a student's self-image would not be enhanced if a teacher provides an academic experience that is defeating and discouraging. Teachers must abandon the negative opinions about African-American students to enhance the student's self-image by building on his or her positive strengths.

It is noted that good teachers are the most important element in successful learning (National Commission on Teaching and America's Future, 1996). Darling-Hammond (1996) argued that major changes in the productivity of American schools depend on the ability to develop and sustain a highly prepared teaching force for all, not just some, of our children. Kuykendall (1992) described some educators as exemplary because they are successfully educating African-American students and these educators are committed, but many are frustrated and overwhelmed because they do not feel their African-American students are reaching their full academic potential. Educators are genuinely interested in exploring ways to meet all their students' educational needs.

The studies discussed in the previous section and this author's observations/experience and research conclude that the following methods/practices are beneficial (effective) with African-American students: balanced literacy approach, which includes instruction in reading and writing, independent reading and writing, phonics and vocabulary, and guided reading. Also included in daily practices are teacher modeling; multicultural education; parental involvement; prior knowledge/schema; cooperative learning; teachers with positive attitudes toward students; and teachers who are well trained with expert assistance available. As we continue to research and seek the advice of effective teachers, we continue to improve our teaching of all students.

Reflections/Observations as a Lead Reading Teacher

While serving as a Lead Reading Teacher (LRT) for a large urban school district, my responsibilities were many. I had seven predominately African-American elementary schools for which I was responsible, which meant visiting those schools at least once a week to assist the kindergarten through third-grade teachers with enhancing their students' literacy. As the teachers were learning theories, concepts, and various methods and strategies, my job was to support them through the implementation process. I would model/demonstrate strategies such as structural analysis lessons or how to effectively use the Word Wall, and then a teacher would allow me to observe her while she taught that same lesson. We would then debrief or discuss the lesson. We discussed what he or she did that was correct (effective) and what he or she could do better the next time. I would also offer suggestions on how to make the lesson more effective.

Once the kindergarten teachers observed me with their groups of students (approximately five in each group) during a guided reading lesson, they were convinced that this method would work in their classrooms. We selected the appropriate texts and examined them for skills that could be worked on with the students. With the Hispanic kindergarten students in this district, we wanted to enhance their vocabularies so we chose low-level books that had pictures with the text to match. Once these students had a lesson and experienced success, they were on their way to becoming readers with life-long useful strategies. Also these positive experiences for the teachers confirmed that they were making the right choices for their students by delivering balanced, comprehensive reading instruction. I continued to visit their classrooms and support them as they taught their students.

Teachers need this type of support as they implement the best literacy methods in their classrooms. Researchers have spent many hours and millions of dollars on researching the best methods to teach reading, and they have discovered that there are many best practices. Now we need to support teachers as they endeavor to teach their students. These teachers desire to be effective teachers; they do not want their students to fail, but they need the support of reading specialist/experts such as LRTs or master reading teachers. These experts must be available to assist classroom teachers as much as possible. With this type of plan in place, we can ensure our students that they are getting the best possible reading lessons available. These teachers must also have the materials needed to implement effective methods, such as multicultural books for small-group instruction and magnetic letters to develop vocabulary.

Teachers who were most effective diversified their methods and utilized the balanced literacy approach, which involved guided reading, comprehension strategies, vocabulary development, oral language enhancement, phonics, writing, daily independent reading and writing, and multicultural education books/materials. These teachers involved the students in cooperative learning so that the students could work together on various projects/assignments. Prior knowledge/schema of the students was always a consideration during lessons. I observed teachers modeling via read-alouds and shared reading as to how good readers read and what strategies they used. Effective teachers in this urban district wrote in front of their students to model good writing. Demonstrations for the students helped them understand particular literacy strategies. These teachers also constantly monitored their students' progress and adjusted instruction according to the students' needs.

The administrators I observed who were the most effective leaders were those who understood what effective literacy methods and strategies looked liked. They were instructional leaders and understood the reading process. When the principal walked into a classroom, he or she knew what should be taking place in that room with those students that would enhance the students' literacy. If the principal was observing a guided reading lesson, he or she knew what to expect.

Several of the schools I worked with were most successful; their students learned to read and performed well on the state assessment. These schools and I collaborated to accomplish the goals. We all cared about the students and wanted them to succeed. The teachers were receptive and worked diligently to meet the challenges they faced on a daily basis. The results were rewarding because we saw our students moving forward on the literacy path.

CHALLENGES AS A LEAD READING TEACHER

My biggest challenge as an LRT was convincing teachers to change their old ways of teaching. Several veteran teachers were reluctant to discontinue the whole-group instruction and stop using so many worksheets, although these things were not enhancing the students' literacy. These teachers required several demonstrations and constant motivation to change. I must admit that some did not change. Another challenge I experienced was students who were not on grade level and many who were several levels lower than their appropriate grade level. The teacher and I knew these students could learn, but they needed time-consuming assistance that a regular classroom teacher could not provide. We attempted to meet their needs, but we were not always successful.

On many occasions, I had to convince the teachers to practice *tough love*. Yes, this child's parent is in prison and he just visited his mom over the weekend, but he still has to learn. Some teachers did not want to complicate the child's life by asking him or her to complete class assignments when the child was in such an emotional state. The teacher felt sorry for the child and allowed the child to feel sorry for her or himself. My job was to convince the teacher that she still had to teach this child although he or she was not motivated. This was challenging, and a few White teachers resigned in the middle of the year because they could not deal with these types of complications.

CONCLUSION

African-American students' acquisition of basic literacy skills serves as the foundation for ongoing education and success in their adult lives. Therefore, they must be effectively taught to read. Literacy serves as a cornerstone throughout their life. Through education, African-American students should gain knowledge and strategies to enable them to function productively within their culture, the dominant culture, and across other ethnic cultures. These methods need to be identified to assist teachers in their endeavors to successfully educate their African-American students.

Through successful acquisition of literacy, many of these students can overcome the economic and educational barriers that limited their parents and grandparents' success in school (Hill, 1989). It is necessary for educators to develop and implement methods to assist African-American students in enhancing their literacy acquisition. It is incumbent on teachers to develop and implement methods in working with these students (Dilworth, 1992). Educators must assess means for providing delivery systems or student-specific pedagogy (Dilworth) that would best improve the learning of African-American students. It is important that the instruction is aligned with student characteristics.

RECOMMENDATIONS

1. Intensive staff development programs for teachers are a must.
2. Staff development is needed on diversity concerning the contributions of minorities and multicultural education.
3. Staff development is needed on various literacy strategies such as structural analysis and comprehension.
4. Practitioners (teachers) should begin and continue to document effective methods that can enhance the literacy of African-American students (all students); this documentation is useful in identifying responsive pedagogy (Dilworth, 1992).
5. Preservice teachers need field experience in working with diverse students.
6. Preservice teachers should be encouraged to look more carefully at the communication and behaviors of African-American students.
7. Preservice teachers should also examine their own behaviors and beliefs concerning African-American students.
8. Preservice teachers should be taught to examine culturally relevant pedagogy. This pedagogy involves students in the knowledge-construction process; they must have a sense of ownership of their knowledge, empowering, and liberating. This pedagogy uses the students' culture to transcend the negative effects of the dominant culture (Ladson-Billings, 1994).
9. Teachers need expert assistance and continuous coaching.

10. Reading experts need training on how to work with teachers (coaching) and need to be available for teachers.

11. Education programs must reexamine their programs and make the necessary changes to address our urban students' needs.

12. Education programs that prepare preservice teachers should include books in their courses that would address many of the issues discussed in this chapter. Several of the books listed in this reference would benefit teachers (books written by Crystal Kuykendall and Gloria Ladson-Billings).

REFERENCES

Allington, R. L., & McGill-Franzen, A. (1991). Every child's right: Literacy. *The Reading Teacher, 48*, 15–27.

American Federation of Teachers. (1999, June). *Teaching reading is rocket science: What expert teachers of reading should know and be able to do.* Washington, DC: Author.

Banks, J. A. (1991). *Teaching strategies for ethnic studies* (5th ed.). Needham Heights, MA: Allyn & Bacon.

Banks, J. A. (1994). *An introduction to multicultural education.* Needham Heights, MA: Allyn & Bacon.

Baumann, J., Hoffman, J., Moon, J., & Duffy-Hester, A. (1998). Where are teachers' voices in the phonics/whole language debate/results from a survey of U.S. elementary classroom teachers. *The Reading Teacher, 51*, 636–650.

Billingsley, A. (1992). *Climbing Jacob's ladder.* New York: Simon & Schuster.

Bryant, B., & Jones, A. (1993). *Seeking effective schools for African American children.* San Francisco, CA: Caddo Gap Press.

Collins, M. (1992). *Ordinary children, extraordinary teachers.* Norfolk, VA: Hampton Roads Publishing Company.

Comer, J. P., & Poussaint, A. F. (1992). *Raising black children.* New York: Penguin Group.

Cunningham, P. M., & Allington, R. L. (1994). *Classrooms that work: They can all read and write.* New York: HarperCollins.

Darling-Hammond, L. (1996). The quiet revolution rethinking teacher development. *Educational Leadership, 53*, 4–10.

Dilworth, M. E. (Ed.). (1992). *Diversity in teacher education: New expectations.* San Francisco, CA: Jossey-Bass.

Dougherty, P. S. (1997). *Reading informational trade books aloud to inner city intermediate fourth- and sixth-grade students: A comparison of two styles* (Doctoral dissertation, North Texas University). Ann Arbor, MI: UMI Dissertation Services.

Foster, M. (1997). *Black teachers on teaching.* New York: The New Press.

Hill, H. D. (1989). *Effective strategies for teaching minority students.* Bloomington, IN: National Educational Service.

Hopson, D. P., & Hopson, D. S. (1990). *Different and wonderful: Raising black children in a race-conscious society.* New York: Simon & Schuster.

Huber-Bowen, T. (1993). *Teaching in the diverse classroom.* Bloomington, IN: National Education Service.

Irvine, J. J. (1989, March). *Black students and school achievement: A process model of relationships among significant variable.* Paper presented at the annual meeting of the American Educational Research Association, San Francisco, CA.

Kuykendall, C. (1992). *From rage to hope: Strategies for reclaiming Black & Hispanic students*. Bloomington, IN: National Educational Service.

Ladson-Billings, G. (1994). *The dreamkeepers: Successful teachers of African American children*. San Francisco, CA. Jossey-Bass.

National Commission on Teaching and America's Future. (1996). *What matters most: Teaching for America's future*. Woodbridge, VA.

Obiakor, F. E. (1992, November). *The myth of socioeconomic dissonance: Implications for African American exceptional students*. Paper presented at the Council for Exceptional Children (CEC), Minneapolis, MN.

Person, W. A., Amos, N. G., & Jenkins, R. L. (1995, November). *Reassessment of program focusing on instructional strategies for culturally diverse students*. Paper presented at the 24th annual meeting of the Mid-South Educational Research Association, Biloxi, MI.

Perkins, J. H. (2001). Listen to their teachers' voices: Effective reading instruction for fourth grade African American students. *Reading Horizons, 41*(4), 239–255.

Stanovich, K. E. (1986). Matthew effects in reading: Some consequences of individual differences in the acquisition of literacy. *Reading Research Quarterly, 21*, 360–407.

Strickland, D. S. (1994). Educating African American learners at risk: Finding a better way. *Language Arts, 71*, 320–333.

Wyman, S. L. (1993). *How to respond to your culturally diverse student population*. Alexandria, VA: Association for Supervision and Curriculum Development.

PART FOUR

SUMMARY AND CONCLUSIONS

CHAPTER EIGHTEEN

Reflections of a Reading Czar

Robert B. Cooter, Jr.
University of Texas at Arlington

THE 900-YEAR-OLD SHEEP

Several years ago, I used to serve as a faculty sponsor for a college study abroad course in Great Britain for students interested in literacy education. We began by first making our way through London schools, then on to Edinburgh for a look at Scottish education practices. Our final destination was Oxford University, where we discussed international literacy policies and their effects on Western learning with one of the dons.

One year we were given a tour of Oxford's famous Bodleian Library by its distinguished head, Mr. David Vaisey. It was with great anticipation that I led my the students into a conference room to meet our host, especially because Bodley's Librarian (his formal title) was well known for his compelling stories about this celebrated edifice. He began by explaining that we were seated in the Bodleian Board Room where many staff meetings were held.

"Notice that the table at which you now sit," said Mr. Vaisey, "is indeed a long board, several hundred years old, mind you, that has had legs attached to create the table. Hence the term 'board-room,' or the room in which the board is found. This is, in fact, was the first *boardroom* in the world, and the one from which all other boardrooms got their name." I could see that this raised a few young eyebrows and caused several students (and one instructor) to run fingers slowly across the table's texture as if stroking a piece of history. In retrospect, I suppose we were.

As the tour progressed, we visited several chambers in the Bodleian not normally seen by the hordes of summer tourists. We made our way through the catacombs that are the Bodleian stacks, and Mr. Vaisey explained that the term *stacks* is another Oxford invention. It described the way in which the many bookshelves are hung from the ceiling on casters so that they can be rolled together or *stacked* to save space.

Mr. Vaisey eased a book of olden vintage from one of the shelves and explained that we were standing where many medieval and other ancient volumes were housed. As he gingerly opened the treasure, he said, "The book I am now holding was written in the 11th century by a monk. There were no printing presses then, of course, so the only way one could reproduce a book was by hand, one of several reasons why books were so precious. Note that the pages of this book are not really paper as we know it," he continued, "but parchment—which is to say, animal skin. In this instance, the skins used were from sheep, a very common practice. If you have ever wondered why college diplomas are sometimes referred to as 'sheepskins' it is because of this ancient practice." I could see that most of the students were now entranced by this scholar's narrative, as was I.

"What you may not know," he continued, "is that it was only possible to get a single sheet of parchment from *one* sheep. I see from an early notation that this particular book has some 186 separate pages of parchment, so it quite literally took a flock of sheep to make this one book." There was an audible gasp from one of the students as she considered the great cost of these organic links with history.

Mr. Vaisey concluded this part of the tour by drawing our attention to the solid covers of the book. He gently knocked on one of the covers and we heard the magnified effects echoing around the stacks. "The covers on ancient books needed to be heavy, and were generally made of wood covered by cloth or leather. Our modern tradition of 'hard cover' books dates back to these early times."

One student asked why the books needed to be wooden and heavy. Was it not mainly to protect the pages? His answer was intriguing. Although the heavy wooden covers certainly provided some protection for the manuscript, their main purpose was to keep gentle pressure on the pages.

"One of the characteristics of parchment," Mr. Vaisey explained, "is that the skin has a kind of *memory*. Even after 900 years it wants to go back to being a sheep! Without steady pressure from the heavy covers, the pages would soon begin to curl back into their original sheep-form and ruin the book. Conversely, with the aid of steady pressure from the hard cover, these 900-year-old sheepskins continue to be imbued with the ability to transport the author's message into the future . . . for what has now been nearly a millennium."

The transformation of common pelts into organic time machines of thought is a notion that has stayed with me over the years as a parable for many truisms in education. As with most parables, it is in the implicit details of the account that one may discover points of meditation or even wisdom. The point I hope to draw from this story of 900-year-old sheepskins is the need for *steady pressure* on our educational systems to produce effective urban schools. If we are to move the needle in the right direction for urban students, we must find effective, long-term solutions to our nation's literacy crisis.

QUESTIONS FOR FUTURE RESEARCH

In *Perspectives on Rescuing Urban Literacy Education: Spies, Saboteurs, and Saints*, the contributors illuminated a number of important issues. As with all research, these issues have only been partially explored and, certainly, were at times subject to the interpretations of the witnesses. Yet because these same events in DISD were recounted from multiple viewpoints, a degree of triangulation was achieved, thus enhancing the reliability of common findings. A unique and informative aspect of *Perspectives*, indeed its strength, is that most viewpoints expressed here were by those so often (and inexplicably) excluded from scholarly conversations elsewhere—practitioners in the field. The writing styles and observations of these professionals in the field bring a kind of refreshing authenticity to our exploration of urban literacy education. Although in some cases chapters may have lacked the usual format and style one finds in the scholarly journals, the content is of undeniable validity and timeliness.

I believe all of the contributors came away with many more questions than answers—questions that may be worthy of further examination by others. In this final section, I offer some important questions for further study, some of which were medially addressed in *Perspectives on Rescuing Urban Literacy Education: Spies, Saboteurs, and Saints,* and others that are critical issues, but went untouched. It is the exploration of these and other pertinent issues that can apply the kind of *gentle pressure* sorely needed in urban literacy education.

National, State, and Federal Policy Issues

- What has been the cost-effectiveness of the Title I program for reading, writing, and mathematics since its inception in the 1970s?
- Would a required national curriculum help highly mobile children have a less-fragmented school experience?

- What has been the cost–benefit of federally funded reading research for urban populations since 1970?
- Has middle-class flight to suburban areas effectively resegregated U.S. schools (i.e., middle/upper classes segregated from lower socioeconomic groups)?
- To what extent have federally funded reading initiatives (e.g., *Reading First*) been dominated by a small coterie of publishers and consultants? Is there public reporting of these expenditures? Is funding ultimately denied to states or school districts not using preferred vendors or consultants?
- Are there alternatives to the current high-stakes testing models that seem to unfairly penalize urban school districts having a majority of low socioeconomic students (in addition to the value-added model proposed by Webster in this text)?

School District/Systemic Research

- Do high-need/hard-to-staff schools tend to have experienced or inexperienced teachers? Principals?
- What are the most effective ways to counteract high student mobility?
- Which tactics seem to slow teacher attrition in urban schools?
- What is the relationship between low reading/literacy levels and student dropout rates?
- To what extent, according to independent research data, do urban school boards help or sabotage long-term literacy reform efforts?

Curriculum and Program Issues

- What does the research tell us about effective uses of technology in urban reading instruction?
- What are the common characteristics of effective schoolwide reading programs in urban settings for Grades 5 to 8?
- Should stronger vendor accountability measures be put in place? Specifically, how do public school districts, state agencies, and legislators ensure taxpayers that they are protected from spurious claims and corruption of school officials when major reading adoptions are in process? What happens when student performance improvement claims made by vendors are not achieved?
- Which commercial reading programs have been proved through scientific research to be effective with urban students in Grades 4 to 6? Grades 7 to 9? What are the drawbacks of K to 3 reading programs

that claim to be proved effective (i.e., poor comprehension or vocabulary development)?

Home and Preschool Issues

- What does the research tell us about effective parent involvement programs in urban communities?
- How can we improve the listening and speaking vocabularies of preschool children in urban environments?
- What are the long-term reading benefits of preschools offering structured language development programs? (For example, Texas Instruments has sponsored the Cone School in Dallas for about a decade and has an enormous database as yet unreported. Are there others, and what has been the result?)

Special Populations

- How can we best meet the literacy needs of English language learners (ELL) in urban settings?
- Which reading instruction methods have been shown to be effective for *slow learners* in urban classrooms (i.e., those having an IQ of 70–85)?
- How well are the reading needs of students having special needs being met (i.e., special education students, AD/HD, BD, dyslexic)?
- How well are the reading needs of gifted students being met in urban schools? Do school district resources go exclusively to meet the needs of low-achieving students?

Teacher Training

- Are there colleges of education specializing in urban teacher education? If so, what research evidence is there that their teacher education program is more effective (or substantially different) from traditional programs?
- Are there graduate schools of education specializing in educational administration programs for urban school leaders? If so, what research evidence is there that their program is more effective (or substantially different) from more traditional programs?
- How can we better prepare large numbers of qualified teachers who can succeed in urban classrooms?
- Do other Reading Academy models exist in urban school districts? What has been the result?

- In which ways do current models for preparing educational administrators (i.e., principals, superintendents, and curriculum directors)
  fall short in urban education? Does research show that administrators
  are more successful or less successful if they have attained an advanced degree or certificate in educational administration versus
  other training (e.g., MBA or CPA degrees, military leadership)?
- Are there cost-effective models for school districts wishing to provide
  lead reading teachers (LRTs) as coaches for teacher capacity building?

About the Authors

Lee Allen is the executive manager for Technology Services with the Dallas Independent School District. His responsibilities include business systems, technology infrastructure, and instructional technology. Allen is also an adjunct professor for the University of Maryland. He is currently completing the doctoral program at Pepperdine University, and is the project manager for a $30.3 million migration of the Dallas school district's financial and HR systems to an Oracle database and Internet-based applications.

E. F. Baskin, since 1996, has consulted in the area of human resources, including strategy, change management, executive development, and education and training. He has been a consultant to groups within Allstate Insurance, McDonald's, Motorola, and American Management Systems. Prior to 1996, Baskin was an executive at the Center for Professional Education, Andersen Worldwide, where he started such organizational units as Management Development Education, Research and Evaluation, and Educational Technology. He had overall responsibility for visioning, planning, and implementing the design, development, and delivery of worldwide curricula for consulting professionals. He led the program and project teams that developed Method E (educational methodology) and E/ Warp (online knowledge sharing tool). He redirected client seminar efforts to education consulting, which was the forerunner of the change management practice of the current consulting company, Accenture.

Baskin was responsible for the program design, development, and implementation of an executive development program, which was founded on customer satisfaction and introduced 450-degree evaluations. He interfaced with major international universities and consultants from Harvard, INSEAD, Stanford, University of Hong Kong, Center for Creative Leadership, and CED. Prior to his work at the Center for Professional Education, he taught at Michigan State University, University of North Carolina at Chapel Hill, and Oklahoma State University, where he was selected the Outstanding Teacher in 1978. Baskin has a BBA (Lamar University, Beaumont, Texas), MBA, and PhD (Michigan State University, East Lansing, Michigan).

Kathleen S. Cooter currently directs the two laboratory schools at Texas Christian University—Starpoint School and Rise School—both of which serve children with disabilities. She holds a PhD in Special Education and School Psychology and teaches graduate and undergraduate courses in the TCU School of Education. She has over 25 years of service to people with disabilities and has held a variety of teaching and administrative positions from early childhood to high school, including being an assistant principal, principal, assessment specialist, and director of special education. Her greatest honor is being named Teacher of the Year as a special education teacher in Grapevine Colleyville Texas schools. She has presented at hundreds of local, state, and national conferences about literacy development, exceptional children, and educational leadership.

Robert B. Cooter, Jr., serves as professor and director of the national Center for Urban Literacy at the University of Texas at Arlington. He is particularly interested in ways to offer comprehensive literacy programs to urban children in Grades K to 12 and to assess and correct reading difficulties. Cooter served as the first Reading Czar (Associate Superintendent for Reading/Language Arts) for the Dallas Independent School District. There his team engineered the district's highly acclaimed *Dallas Reading Plan*, a collaborative project supported by Dallas area business and community enterprises, which involved training approximately 3,000 teachers in scientifically based comprehensive reading instruction. In March 1998, Dr. Cooter was recognized as a Texas State Champion for Reading by then-Governor George W. Bush and Texas First Lady Laura Bush as a result of the many successes of the Dallas Reading Plan initiative. Cooter is co-author of *Teaching Children to Read, 3rd Edition* (Merrill/Prentice-Hall, 2000), which is currently used at over 200 universities to prepare elementary teachers. He has also authored or co-authored four other professional books. He has had over 50 articles on reading assessment and education published in journals such as *The Reading Teacher, Journal of Reading, Language Arts*, and the *Journal of Educational Research*.

Katy Denson taught all levels of special education for 18 years, including in the classroom and a work-study program. She has an MEd degree in Vocational Education and a PhD in Educational Research. She has been an evaluator in the Dallas Independent School District for 8 years and is currently the Director of Title I Evaluation. Dr. Denson has researched and evaluated the Dallas Reading Plan extensively, focusing on the *Dallas Reading Academy* and its influence on teaching behavior and student achievement, as well as the *Principals' Fellowship* leadership development program.

John Fullinwider teaches at Metropolitan Educational Center, an alternative public high school in Dallas, Texas. A long-time community organizer, Fullinwider is the co-founder of East Dallas Community School, an inner-city Montessori school for young children, and Common Ground, a grassroots nonprofit corporation that provides housing for homeless people. He serves on the board of the School of Community Organizing in Dallas and the Austin-based Texas Low-Income Housing Information Service.

Jerry L. Johns has been recognized as a distinguished professor, author, and outstanding teacher educator. He completed his BA at Oakland University and his MA and PhD at Michigan State University. Johns was a teacher in the public schools of Waterford and Pontiac, Michigan, and then taught for 30 years at Northern Illinois University in DeKalb. Johns has published over a dozen books (including his well-known *BasicReading Inventory*, now in its eighth edition) and several hundred articles and research studies. His more than 500 presentations and workshops involved travel throughout the world. Currently, Johns serves as a consultant and president of the International Reading Association.

Barbara Mathews is currently the director of K to 3 Reading in the Dallas Independent School District. She has spent her entire career working in urban education, teaching in both Dallas and New York City. She co-authored and provided training for the Priori Program, an intervention program for struggling readers, for 12 years. She also co-authored the summer enrichment program for over a decade. She has provided teacher and administrator training locally and statewide. She holds a PhD in reading from North Texas State University.

Jane Moore has worked in the field of literacy education for 26 years as a classroom teacher, consultant, reading specialist, and teacher educator.

She is currently a Lead Reading Teacher with the Dallas Independent School District. In addition to conducting literacy workshops for teachers, parents, and administrators, she works alongside fellow teachers in classrooms, acknowledging their expertise and supporting their efforts. She holds certifications in reading, administration, and special and elementary education, and she is a doctoral candidate at Texas A&M University-Commerce.

J. Helen Perkins presently serves as an assistant professor in the Center for Teacher Education at Southern Methodist University in Dallas, Texas. Prior to this position, she was a Lead Reading Teacher for Dallas Public Schools. With over 25 years of experience in the field of literacy, she now teaches emergent and conventional literacy courses to preservice students. She researches and presents on literacy-related topics from how to work with young children and encouraging literacy development to how to support the professional development of Master Reading Teachers. Currently, Dr. Perkins also serves as the Master Reading Teacher Coordinator for her campus.

William F. Tate is professor and chair of the Department of Education in the College of Arts and Sciences at Washington University in St. Louis. Dr. Tate is former scholar-in-residence and assistant superintendent—mathematics and science of Dallas Public Schools. He also served as the Project Director and Co-Principal Investigator of the Urban Systemic Program (USP) funded by the National Science Foundation. Dr. Tate had district-wide responsibility for mathematics and science education.

Georgia J. Thompson is the director of training in the Reading Department of the Dallas Independent School District. She has 25 years of classroom experience in K–6, is a trained reading recovery teacher and a Texas-certified Master Reading Teacher, holds principalship certification, teaches graduate courses in reading as an adjunct professor, and is currently working on her doctorate in Supervision, Curriculum, and Instruction.

Leigh Walker is a Texas-certified Master Reading Teacher. After completing the alternative certification program, she worked in the Dallas Independent School District as a third-grade teacher and reading specialist. She and her husband are currently working on their newest project, their son Jackson William.

William J. Webster has been head of the Dallas Independent School District's Department of Planning, Research, and Evaluation for 33 years. He currently serves as special assistant to the Superintendent–Evaluation and Accountability. Much of his work over the past 10 years has been in the de-

velopment and implementation of value-added assessment models. He
has authored over 150 journal articles and papers, many in the area of
value-added assessment. Dr. Webster holds a master's degree from the
University of Michigan and a PhD from Michigan State University.

Judith Zimny is the principal of L.L. Hotchkiss Elementary School in the
Dallas Independent School District. In 2002, the Texas Education Agency
named her school as an Exemplary School. Zimny is completing her doctoral dissertation at Texas A&M University–Commerce and serves as an adjunct professor for Southern Methodist University. Zimny has worked for
many years with the Texas Instruments Foundation on discovering ways
to improve inner-city children's literacy achievement. In 1998, Zimny received the prestigious Principal of the Year award in the Dallas Independent School District—a district with some 225 schools. Zimny is married
and has two sons.

Glossary of Selected Terms

Academic Excellence Indicator System (AEIS)—Part of the Texas academic assessment scheme and includes campus, district, and statewide performance data. AEIS matches demographic information with performance data in an attempt to measure academic progress among campuses and districts. AEIS includes *TAAS* (*TAKS* as of 2003) results from special education and limited English-proficient students (see Webster's chapter for more details).

Action-learning approach—Begins by focusing on a real-world issue that impacts both the supervisor (superintendent) and the supervised (principal). Objectives and goals are established between the supervisor and supervised and monitored for proper implementation. The supervisor is not just involved in the selection of the participants, but continues to be involved as he or she would be in a real situation. Needed content knowledge is brought to participants as the need comes to bear on the real problem the group is addressing. By focusing on a real-world issue, motivation is high and the reward structure stays in play. In most classroom settings, reward structure is more remote (see Zimny's chapter for more information on this topic).

Advocates—Key players in the change process because they have great need. They may have money or other vital resources, but do not have formal authority or power.

Awareness training—Introductory training that creates awareness of a topic, but not expertise. Teacher inservice programs are one example.

261

Backward Mapping—Using prioritized vision components, along with any district or state mandates, to create a plan of action. Educators often must discipline themselves to maintain a focus on measurable student achievement results versus means for achieving those results (see Zimny's chapter for more information on this topic).

Capacity building—The development of new expertise in professionals. Deep learning and expert coaching are potent and necessary tools for capacity building in teachers.

Central office—The administrative offices within a school district.

Change agent—A leader designated by sponsors who has responsibility for both strategic and tactical activities. Change agents have resources and authority as delegated by the sponsor or may assume authority not challenged by others. Change agents handle the day-to-day activities of the change effort.

Change management—Efforts by the change agent and his or her team to bring about desired innovations that will produce something better in terms of operations, products, or outcomes. Most change efforts fail because the emphasis is on the technical attributes and processes that will produce the intended result (see Baskin's chapter for more information on this topic).

Coaching model—The use of expert mentors to help professionals gain new expertise.

Comprehensive reading program—The leading research—or evidence-based alternative to traditional and so-called *whole-language approaches*. Comprehensive reading programs teach students skills in reading and writing based on their individual needs and within the context of appropriately leveled reading materials. Comprehensive reading programs often use commercial basal reader programs, decodable text, and other more traditional programmed reading materials, but they also include daily encounters with fiction and nonfiction trade books, guided oral reading, direct skill instruction, comprehension instruction, fluency drills, vocabulary development, and writing instruction. (For more information on comprehensive reading instruction, see *Teaching Children to Read, 4th edition* by D. R. Reutzel & R. B. Cooter published by Merrill Education/Prentice Hall, 2004, or contact the editor for this book via e-mail at cooter@uta.edu.)

Dallas Literacy Profile—A research-based reading assessment developed by Dallas teachers for the Dallas Reading Plan initiative in both English and Spanish. (Editor's Note: Due to state mandates and consequent political pressure, the *Dallas Literacy Profile* was replaced by the *Texas Primary Reading Inventory*—an adequate, but less comprehensive instrument.)

Dallas Reading Academy—The training arm of the Dallas Reading Plan initiative. It included some 90 hours of deep training on comprehensive reading instruction coupled with weekly in-classroom coaching by expert mentor teachers (i.e., Lead Reading Teachers).

Dallas Reading Plan—An ambitious literacy initiative in the Dallas Independent School District operating from 1996 through 2001. It involved teacher capacity building in comprehensive reading instruction methodologies as a means to improve student learning in kindergarten through third grade.

Disruption—Considered the major barrier to change. Disruption generally causes a loss of control (e.g., change of superintendents or principals, new state mandates, interference by school board members, etc.).

Early adopters—Those in the target audience who are willing to adopt reforms quickly (about 13.5%). They are considered leaders within their local networks and, thus, important to the adoption process. Because of this respectability, others tend to follow their lead, thus these are key persons in the change process.

Early majority—They are not leaders in the local system, but interact frequently with peers and, thus, are important to communication about the change and the process. The early majority (usually about 34% of the target audience) takes its time adopting a new idea, but is earlier to adopt than the remaining majority.

Evidence-based instruction—Teaching practices based on scientific evidence. For example, the National Reading Panel published an important summary of such evidence in reading instruction, which continues to influence federal policy and funding opportunities. (Note: The Report of the National Reading Panel is available free online at www.nationalreadingpanel.org.)

Executive development—Capacity-building efforts for key program administrators. In the Dallas Reading Plan, the *Principals' Fellowship* was designed to meet this need.

Expertise—The attainment of professional capacity such that consistent results are achieved relative to desired goals and objectives.

Failure analysis—A method for determining the most essential needs and outcomes of the organization (see R. Cooter's chapter for more information about failure analysis).

Force field analysis—Provides change agents with a listing of the most significant drivers to maintain momentum in the change process. It also helps staff identify problem-solving strategies addressing the most significant barriers to change.

Fragmented instruction—Inconsistent teaching and learning most often caused by high student mobility. Sometimes referred to as the *Swiss cheese effect* because of the holes in learning occurring due to the mobility issue.

High-stakes testing—Student performance assessment conducted at selected grade levels by state education agencies. They are considered *high stakes* because schools/students not attaining minimum scores can be placed under sanctions by the state as a punishment. High-stakes testing is under fire by many urban school leaders because they appear to have an inherent bias in favor of more affluent children and school districts. For example, school systems that employ unadjusted outcomes on testing programs as their basis for evaluation produce results that are too highly correlated with context factors such as ethnicity, socioeconomic status (SES), and language proficiency. These systems are biased against schools with larger proportions of minority, immigrant, and low SES students and are biased in favor of schools that contain larger proportions of White and higher SES students. The essence of these arguments is that with unadjusted outcomes schools are ranked primarily on the types of students they receive rather than on the education they provide (for more information on this subject and possible remedies, see Webster's chapter).

Highly qualified teachers—A rather ambiguous term coined during the administration of Secretary of Education Rod Paige and his staff. In essence, stiffer capacity-building guidelines for teacher colleges have been demanded while pressure has been exerted by the administration to flood urban schools with new teachers graduating from alternative certification (AC) programs having little pedagogy training and without an internship under the guidance of a competent mentor teacher. A government staffer recently told an audience of educators that highly qualified teachers for urban schools could be defined as *good-enough teachers*.

Innovators—About 2.5% of the target audience who are readily accepting of risk and new ideas. Their network of relationships tends to be outside the local environment in which they work, and they do not worry too much about whether the innovation is successful.

Late majority—About 34% of the target audience, these persons are not negative about change, just skeptical. They tend to want a lot of evidence about the need for and success of the change.

Lead Reading Teachers—A cohort of master reading teachers who taught in the Dallas Reading Academy by night and mentored teachers participating in the Academy during the day to ensure implementation of evidence-based teaching strategies.

Literacy—Competence in reading and writing.

Literacy Materials Center—A professional library of teaching materials held within a school. LMCs typically include such materials as multiple copies of leveled books in English and Spanish, commercial programs for supplemental instruction (e.g., phonics, phonemic awareness, vocabulary development), and big books for group instruction.

Maintenance mode—Supporting the status quo operationally after an innovation has been implemented.

Mobility—The frequent relocation of students or teachers. Student mobility has an extremely adverse effect on student achievement.

National Reading Panel—In 1997, the U.S. Congress asked the director of the National Institute of Child Health and Human Development (NICHD) and the Secretary of Education to convene a national panel to assess the status of research-based knowledge on reading instruction. This National Reading Panel, as it came to be known, issued its report in April 2000. The Report of the National Reading Panel is available free online at www.nationalreadingpanel.org.

No Child Left Behind Act (H.R. 1)—On January 23, 2001, President George W. Bush sent his *No Child Left Behind* plan for comprehensive education reform to Congress. The president emphasized his deep belief in the power of our public schools, but expressed concern that "too many of our neediest children are being left behind" despite nearly $200 billion being spent since the passage of the Elementary and Secondary Education Act of 1965 (ESEA). Following the events of September 11, 2001, President Bush and a bipartisan coalition in Congress succeeded in the passage of the *No Child Left Behind Act of 2001* (NCLB Act), also known as H.R. 1. Intended to close the achievement gap between disadvantaged and minority students and their peers, H.R. 1 has four key provisions: stronger accountability for positive results, expanded flexibility and local control, expanded options for parents, and an emphasis on teaching methods proven to work (i.e., evidence-based methods).

Phases of change—Defined by Baskin in this text as (a) preparation, (b) acceptance, (c) commitment, and (d) internalization.

Planned change—This is generally classified into minor or major change, with a major change given such labels as *transformation*. In many organizations, quality process improvement has been thought of as minor change, whereas many new strategic plans have been labeled *system transformations*.

Principals' Fellowship—A capacity-building model for principals developed as a companion to the Dallas Reading Academy. District research showed that the schools making the most rapid progress in student reading achievement were those having (a) teachers participating in the Dallas Reading Academy, and (b) principals participating the Principals' Fellowship.

Professional development—see Capacity building.

Quick dispersion approach—Tests the technical ideas of most change efforts, but does not test the infrastructure of the system or identify system barriers.

Reading Wars—The continuing debate among reading researchers, textbook publishers, and other stakeholders over the best ways to teach reading to children. The reading wars are fueled by the enormous profits to be made by publishers of reading programs totaling in the billions of dollars.

Resistors—In the infusion of innovation, resistors usually make up about 16% of the target audience. They tend to focus on how things were done in the past and have little tolerance for ambiguity. They do not like change. Their decision process for change is very slow. It is easy to think of resistors as negative, but this is generally not the case. Resistors just see more disruption to their normal activities—the status quo. Resistors are part of the group we refer to in this text as *saboteurs* (see Baskin's chapter for more information on this topic).

Safety Net Instruction—Instructional interventions particularly aimed at neutralizing the negative effects of high student and teacher mobility.

Sponsors—Persons who are the leaders of change efforts. They do not handle day-to-day change activities, but have money, authority, or formal power. Sponsors are motivated to identify and begin change. Further, sponsors see to it that change is implemented so that issues and problems are addressed (see Baskin's chapter for more information on this topic).

Student mobility—High student mobility fragments student acquisition of literacy skills and often leads to failure and concomitant problems (e.g., dropouts). Nationally, about 31% of students change schools two or more times after entering first grade. According to national data, White students are less likely to change schools than Asian, Hispanic, or African-American students. Students who live with their mother and father are less likely to change schools than students living in other types of families. Students in low-income families (under $10,000) are more likely to change schools two or more times after entering first grade than are students whose family income equals or exceeds $20,000 (see Denson's chapter for more information on this subject).

Target audience—The group at which the change efforts are aimed. This is the group whose behavior we are trying to modify (see Baskin's chapter for more information on this topic).

Technological literacy—The ability to use, manage, assess, and understand technology. A technologically literate person understands what technology is, how it is designed, how it influences social structures and interactions, and is in turn shaped by societal structures (see Tate's chapter for information).

Texas Assessment of Academic Skills (TAAS)—The now famous end-of-course examinations phased out in 2003 and replaced with a more difficult high-stakes state assessment test (the Texas Assessment of Knowledge and Skills [TAKS]). It holds schools accountable for student performance and dropout rates.

Texas Assessment of Knowledge and Skills (TAKS)—Replaced the *Texas Assessment of Academic Skills* (TAAS) in 2003.

Texas Primary Reading Inventory—A state informal reading assessment instrument.

Trainer-of-Trainers Model—A kind of trickle-down training model wherein selected teachers learn new modes of instruction and then return to their schools to train their peers on those same innovations. Also know as the *vertical team concept,* this model of capacity building was found to be quite anemic in the Dallas Reading initiative and unsuccessful in improving teacher capacity. However, trainer of trainers is sometimes used because of its political benefit—it presents an image of addressing important needs.

Unplanned change—Change created by a crisis generally from outside or *exogenous* to the system in which change is needed. If all perceive a crisis and, therefore, the necessity for change of some sort, there is inherent motivation within the system (see Baskin's chapter for more information on this topic).

Urban literacy education—An emerging field of research and teaching expertise focusing on the diverse needs of children living in metropolitan areas. Commonalities of these children include high student mobility, high levels of poverty, language development needs, and a high incidence of dropouts.

Value-added assessment—A component embedded in state-level high-stakes testing to lend fairness to the process by revealing schools and teachers making substantive improvements. It assesses the impact of a teacher or school staff on important student objectives or outcomes. Value-added assessments contrast sharply with the more absolute system used in Texas, which is viewed as being biased in favor of school districts serving more affluent populations (even when they show no real gains over time) and against urban school districts (even those showing significant gains in student performance, but not yet meeting the state absolute standard[s]; see Webster's chapter for a full explanation, examples, and a proposed value-added model).

Vendors—Commercial for-profit producers of reading and writing materials. (Editor's Note: There are *some* vendors who, for financial gain and/or to satisfy personal power needs, actively interfere with the administration of district-wide reading and writing initiatives, thus making these individuals charter members of the group we refer to as *saboteurs*.)

Author Index

Subject Index

Science, mathematics, engineering, and
    technology (SMET) teachers, 138,
    139
Scorpions (Myers), 107
Scripted reading program interventions,
    14–15
  combining teacher development inter-
    ventions and, 22–23
  cons, 16–18
  pros, 15–16
  as stand-alone programs, 17–18
  success, 16
Scripted reading programs to stabilize in-
    struction, 22–23
Self-awareness, 36–37
Social reconstruction, literacy and, 110
Special needs, learners with, 22
Special populations, 16, 253
Sponsors (S), 28
SRA/McGraw Hill's Open Court reading
    program, 18, 162, 176, 180, 195
Staff development, 165, 166, 168,
    178–179, *see also* Coaches
  different levels of, for different levels of
    staff, 220
Standards, 140–143, 221
  ISTE, 135, 136
  NCTM, 139–140
Student achievement, barriers to, 218
Student behavior, disrespectful, 218
Success, 88
Success for All (SFA) reading program, 17,
    18, 162
Success With a Team (SWAT), 175
Superintendency, turnover in the, 45
Superintendents, 44, 48, 52
System transformations, *see* Transforma-
    tion

T

Talent, 88
Target audiences (TA), 29, 30
Teacher capacity building, 17
  "moving the needle in the right direc-
    tion," 93–94
Teacher development, *see also* Profes-
    sional development
  capacity-building model for, 88–94
  inservice training, 89–90
  as intervention, 14, 18–22

in teachers colleges and school districts,
    improving, 91–93
  and turnover, 223
Teacher development program, imple-
    menting an aggressive, 23
Teacher education, 239, *see also* Higher
    education; Teachers colleges
Teacher mobility, 46, 121–122
Teacher preparation, entry-level, 46–47
Teacher research team, 230, 231, 233
Teacher technologists, 144–145, 149–150
Teacher training, 112, 198, 253–254
  making it first priority, 206
Teachers
  accountability, 206
  attitudes and expectations, 239–242
  characteristics of effective, 241
  effects of mobility on, 121–122
  improved incentives for urban, 52
  incompetent, 222–223
  must know best ways to teach reading
    skills, 20–21
  must know how to assess knowledge of
    reading skills, 20
  must know reading skills, 20
  remembering the affective needs of,
    206–207
  stabilization of instruction with under-
    trained, 15
  talent, 88
  time to collaborate and plan together,
    220
  underqualified, 238–239
  uneven knowledge and inconsistent
    practices, 167–168
Teachers colleges, *see also* Higher educa-
    tion
  why they fail urban children, 83–85
  lack of accountability, 86–87
  perilous homogeneity, 85–87
Teaching materials
  dearth of, 43–44
  providing adequate, 51–52, 172–173
Team monitoring of student performance,
    219–220
Teaming, 38, *see also* Teacher research
    team
Technological action, 136–137
Technological literacy, 109, 137, 143
  areas of, 135–136
  defined, 135–137